LIVING ALIGNED

MOSAICA PRESS

LIVING ALIGNED

RABBI BARUCH GARTNER

Writer/Editor: Y. Golshevsky

Mosaica Press, Inc.
© 2018 by Mosaica Press
Interior design and typeset: Brocha Mirel Strizower

ISBN-10: 1-946351-34-2
ISBN-13: 978-1-946351-34-0

Published and distributed by:
Mosaica Press, Inc.
www.mosaicapress.com
info@mosaicapress.com

I dedicate this work to my best friend, my life partner, and devoted wife

Yaffa

*W*ith very little help from anyone, you brought an amazing family to the world. You take care of all of our needs and ask for little in return. You have created an atmosphere of warmth and love that has enabled all of us to have peace of mind and grow happily.

*T*his book and these teachings are all yours.

In loving memory of my parents

לעילוי נשמות הורינו

Yaakov ben Tzvi Kalman

Frieda Yehudis bas Shabti

and my in-laws

Yeshaya ben Yitzchak

Shifra Gittel bas Tzvi Yehuda

תנצב״ה
Baruch Gartner

אשר זעליג וייס

כגן 8

פעיה"ק ירושלם ת"ו

בס"ד

תאריך _____

גם אמרתי בזה את דעתי לבקש חוות דעת רבני העולם ... אשר ... חכמה ... רבה
בחכמת ה' ... ... אשר ... ...
ולקיים ... ...

... ...
... ...
... ...
... ...

בברכה
... ...

אשר זעליג וייס
גאב"ד וראש ישיבת
"דרכי תורה"
פעיה"ק ירושלים ת"ו

Rabbi Y.M. Morgenstern Rosh hayeshiva of "Toras Chochom" Yerushalaim	יצחק מאיר מארגנשטערן רב ור"מ דק"ק "תורת חכם" לתורת הנגלה והנסתר פעיה"ק ירושלים תובב"א

בס"ד, יום ה' לסדר והייתם לי סגולה וגו' תשע"ח לפ"ק, פעיה"ק ירושת"ו

כבר נודע בשערים שבח תהלות מעלת ידידנו הרב הגאון החסיד הנעלה מזכה הרבים מרביץ תורה שנים רבות ומוציא יקר מזולל ה"ה כמ"ר מוה"ר ברוך גערמטנער שליט"א שכבר זכה להעמיד תלמידים הרבה בתורה וביראה ובחסידות, ורבים יאותו לאור שיעוריו הנפלאים, והן עתה מוסיף והולך מחיל אל חיל לזכות הרבים בתורתו שבכתב, וכאשר הראה לפני גליונות מספרו הנפלא "לייוונג עלייינד" בלע"ז שעינינו לבאר דברי רבינו הקדוש והנורא מברסלב זיע"א בעומק גדול בשפת העענגליש בשפה ברורה ונעימה השוה לכל נפש על יסוד דברי אדונינו חסידא קדישא הרמ"ק זיע"א בספרו תומר דבורה כי ראוי לאדם שיעשה עצמו מרכבה אליו ותמצאנה בו כל הי"ג מדות האמורות בחנינה - שזהו כללות ענין עבודת ה' ושורש כל רזי היחוד והאמונה, כנודע כמה הפליג רבינו האריז"ל ביחוד המרכבה (שער רוח הקודש דף ג' ע"ד) במעלת קדושת ענין זה עד שבתוך דבריו שם כתב כי "אין ספק כי אם יתמיד האדם להתג עצמו בכוונות אלו שיהיה כאחד מן המלאכים המשרתים ברקיע", וכן מבואר בדברי מרן הרש"ש זיע"א (נהר שלום דף ל"ג ע"ד) "כי האדם הוא מרכבה לאדם העליון ובו מתלבשים כל הבחינות שלמעלה ממנו וכו' והוא סולם מוצב ארצה וראשו מגיע השמימה וכמו שאמרו חז"ל האבות הם הם המרכבה". ובהמשך דבריו שם (דף ל"ד ע"ב) אתר שהאריך בסודות היחוד מסיק עלה "באופן כי ישים האדם שם ההוי"ה הנזכר לנגד עיניו במסד שויתי הוי"ה לנגדי תמיד ודי בזה למבין", יעויין שם, ועוד לו בהקדמת רחובות הנהר (דף מ' סוף ע"ב) ובנהר שלום (דף י"א ע"א, י"ג ע"ב) ובהקדמת ברכת מלביש ערומים (שם דף כ"ג ע"א ע"ב), ואכמ"ל. ועל כן גם ברו"ך יהיה ידידנו הגאון המחבר שליט"א כי טוב עשה בעמיו לזכות הרבים לבאר דברי רבה"ק על פי יסודות דברי רבותינו הקדושים, ובטוחני כי דבריו היוצאים מן הלב יכנסו ללבות מבקשי ה' ויעשו פירות לקרב הלבבות למלאכת שמים, יפרנו מעיינותיו חוצה ויזכה לזכות הרבים ולהרבות פעלים לתורה כנפשו הטהורה עדי נזכה כי מלאה הארץ דעה את ה' כמים לים מכסים בביאת גואל צדק במהרה דידן.

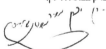

ניסן דוד קיוואק

ישיבת מאירת עינים

רח' הרב סורוצקין 33

פעיה"ק ירושלים תובב"א

בס"ד

לפנות יום חמשה עשר בשבט תשע"ח

הנה ראיתי את הספר הנפלא שחיבר ידידי היקר פה מפיק מרגליות כבוד הרה"ח ר' ברוך גרטנר שליט"א, וביודעי ובמכירי קאמינא, כי הנני מכירו רבות בשנים עוד מאז שבא מצפת להשתקע בירושלים עיה"ק לפני שלשים שנה, דיברנו הרבה שיחות עמוקות בענייני חסידות ועבודה, וגם זכיתי לבוא לישיבת דרך המלך שייסד אז למבקשים ומתמידים לדבר בפניהם דברי חיזוק, והתרשמתי אז מאד מרמת הלימוד של התלמידים והצלחתם בתורה ויראת שמים, וכוחו להבהיר דברים עמוקים באופן ישר ופשוט, שמביא לידי מעשה, ומתוך שפירותיו מתוקים והעמיד תלמידים הרבה לתורה ויראת שמים בישוב הדעת, ניכר כוחו וגודל עמלו במסירת נפש להבין לנפש המבקשים להביאם לקנות דעת בדרך ישרה.

הן חזיתי ספרו החשוב באנגלית הנקרא LIVING ALIGNED שמאיר לנבכי הנפש בדרך פשוט את האמת הפשוטה, בהו ימצא הקורא קנין יקר מזהב וכל סחורה, כי ימצא אור תורה, הספר אשר מבאר ומפרש דברי חסידות העומדים ברומו של עולם בואפן ברור ושוה לכל נפש, עד שהדברים נכנסים ללב ובזה ימצא כל הרוצה ללכת בדרכי העבודה את הבנה ביסידות מוכרחים אשר נפשו ביקשה לטעום זה רבות בשנים, כארש נתרבו מבקשי השם אשר אור תורמצ יקבל בשפה האנגלית, אינני יודע אם כבר היה זה ספר שיתלבש בשפה זו, שהקריאה בה ניעמה מוך הסדר והנושים אשר מוצגים בטוב טעם ודעת בהירים ונוחים להבנה, זה אילן נאה וחדש אשר בודאי פירותיו יהיו מתוקים ובצלו ימצאו הצלחה והבנה.

אסיים בברכה שהספר יהיה לתועלת גדולה וישפיע על ליבם של המוני מבקשי האמת ויקבלו הדרכה נכונה ואמיתית בדרך עבודת ה' למלא חדרי דעתם בדעות ישרות לעלות בדרך העולה לעבודת השם דרגא לדרגא, שיזכה המחבר החשוב להרבות פעלים לתואה עוד רבות בשנים להפיץ מעיינותיו חוצה מוך ביאות ונהורא מעליא.

באתי על החתום

ב"ה, חודש שבט תשע"ח

כולל הוראה

כולל ללימוד תורת החן והנסתר

בית התבשיל ועזר ליולדות "נעימות החיים"

חלוקת מצרכים ועזרה לנזקקים

קמחא דפסחא

גמ"ח הלוואות וקרן חתנים

שיעורים והפצת יהדות

מכון והוצאה לאור "אור מתתיהו"

בא לפני הרב הגאון הנודע בשערים עמנו הקדושה, אחד המחנכים הגדולים שבדורינו הגה"ח ר' ברוך גרטנר שליט"א, שזכה ללמד מאות תלמידים, ובפרט מהציבור האמריקאי מודרני שיצאו תחת ידו כעובדי השם וחסידים ות"ח מופלגים אחרי כמה שנים של השקעה והדרכה כאב על בנים ממש.

הרב הנ"ל ידוע ומפורסם גם כן בדעתו הרחבה ובהבנת הנפש באופן מופלא ביותר, והכל על פי דברי רבותינו המסורה לנו מדור דור ובפרט דברי הבעש"ט ותלמידיו הקדושים והנוראים.

והנה אחרי כמה שנים של שיעורים לתלמידיו עמד הרב הנ"ל וקיבץ חלק קטן מהדברים שנאמרו לחברים המקשיבים דברים נוקבים אמיתיים וברורים מאד בהאיך לחיות באמת בעולם הזה שלנו בדור של העדר הסתר מצד אחד, וגילוי אלוקות וכיסופים עצומים מצד נשמות ישראל להשם מצד שני, איך לחיות בדביקות ומקושר להשם יתברך בחיי היום יום ולעלות מעלה מעלה בדרכי העלייה של עבודת השם, על ידי יציאה מהיישות להוויה של נתינה והשפעה.

אני בטוח שהספר Living Aligned יעשה רושם עצום על כלל ישראל ויתקבל על שולחן מלכים, ואני מרגיש זכות עצום שזכיתי להכיר מחברו היקר, ואברך אותו בזה שיזכה להמשיך לשבת כל ימיו באהלה של תורה ולהפיץ ספר זו בישראל וירחיב גבוליו בתלמידים ולהאיר העולם באור תורתינו הקדושה מתוך אהבה ויראה אמיתית, ולזכות לשתי שלחנות עם בני וחתני רבנן.

בזה באתי על החתום בכבוד ובהערכה עצומה

[חתימה]

[חותמת]
פינחס דוד ישראל בונקר
נשיא מוסדות "אור מתתיהו"

רחוב המגיד ממעזריטש 62 ביתר עילית 90500 ארץ ישראל, טל. 02-5807319 פקס. 02-5804026

Hamagid M'mezritzh 62 Fax. 972-2-5804026 Beitar Illit 90500 Israel, Tel. 972-2-5807319

SHMUEL MOSHE KREMER

Author Of Mayanim B'Nechalim

President, Talmud Tora BRESLOV

Rosh Kollel OR HANELAM

8 Yochanan Mizrachi St. Tel: 972-2-5829514

JERUSALEN

שמואל משה קרמר

מח"ס מעיינים בנחלים

נשיא מוסדות התורה והחינוך

ברסלב

ירושלים-בית שמש

ורו"ק אור הנעלם ברסלב

עיה"ק ירושלים תובב"א

בס"ד ע י ב בהיכנכה מ"ש

הנה יו"ט התמוב עיקרי חייני חסודו קדושים יבו דרך התסוד
רבי הכוק בנר ערסיני אביסא... הוה וזו. ולקוטיו היו הלו אוז סערי יקר
לחיבר ברצא של יוסא ערוכ רבינן הק הלקוטי... ד" ...רוני ,ואל
הע"ורב"פ"

לאוזי יוסא מלחות... לאא איק נול הס... להאלות ערוינא ני...ת...
תורה ולהבוק מאתי... ובצבויות ויה... ולצאת כהן ...
פל התודם.

...בדו ... .ן ...ד נ ... ...ם האתי... על נון
הבי"ת תהווני... ... .

של ביתר ערוי בק...ות ער... הסן ....ני... ... .

...ם ...רי"ם.

והנה היין ...ר ...דוך ... ...בי האתמי... ... ...ר...ד פ...ינ... בה
....ן ... רבי... ...ני ... ...ני... ... ...וק ...וכ... ...ל ...
לסברים ... ...נ...ם ,וס... א...אי דכ ל...י... דצא רבין הק ....ק...ם ,ו...
...ך ...ו ...רבת ...קים לאר ... ...וק ... ...ה.

...ק...ת לפ ...ול בה ...ב... ...ה...ת ...ות נו. וי... ...ב... ...

...ד ...ז ... ...ק האתת ...א ...א... ...א... ...ו ... ...א ...

...וך ...א ...ת ...ך חיי... ...ק ... ...אנת ... ...א...

שמואל משה קרמר

CONTENTS

Section Three

THE TORAH MASTERS

Section Four

YOU AND ME

ACKNOWLEDGMENTS

NO WORDS CAN DESCRIBE my gratitude to the Creator for the abundant kindness that He has shown me! From the dust He has elevated me and graced me with the opportunity to toil in His holy Torah in the Land of Israel. He has given me the privilege of drinking the wine of the holy masters of the past and allowed me to be touched by the greatest of the righteous of our generation. Thank you, Hashem! My heart is filled with joy that You have chosen me to be Your faithful servant.

There have been many great *rabbanim* who have contributed to my life, and I am grateful to them all. There simply aren't enough pages in this humble book to recount all the teachers in the chapters of my life. That being said, I feel it important to focus on the four major influences in my life until today.

Almost immediately after marriage, my wife and I moved to Tzfat, where I met HaRav Elazer Mordechai Kenig. He invested in me countless hours and gave me the solid foundations of the teaching of Rebbe Nachman of Breslev. He attached me to the flowing brook of wisdom that I drink from until today. The sweet memories of those seven years will always remain in my mind, and I sincerely thank him.

When we returned to Jerusalem, I began my long-lasting relationship with the *tzaddik* whom I call my *rav* until today, Rav Shmuel Moshe Kremer (the brother-in-law of Rav Kenig from Tzfat). He serves as a role model for our entire family. He is a pillar of wisdom, humility, joy, and simplicity all in one being. It's been a great privilege to be close to him.

Once again Hashem blessed me and brought me to my next teacher the great *tzaddik* Reb Tzvi Meir Zilberberg. Everyday, I am grateful to him for teaching me the excitement of Yiddishkeit. Each and every moment is *gevaldik*.

Finally, the holy Reb Mottel, Mordechai Menashe Zilber, the Stuchiner Rav. It's impossible for me to describe what this holy person did for me, for his holiness is not from this world. I will forever be thankful for all of the time and effort he put into me.

I am greatly appreciative to Rav Moshe Weinberger for all of his efforts to help create Yeshivas Derech Hamelech. I recently attended the wedding of the daughter of the *mashgiach* Rav Doniel Faber and saw many of the students with their children, and it brought such joy to my heart. To all of the amazing staff, the *rabbeim*, and students, I say thank you for having that opportunity to learn together.

There is nothing like family! Thanks to my brother, Shabsey Gartner, and my sister-in-law, Chava, for all the love and support. May Hashem continue to bless you with *nachas* from all your children and grandchildren.

As mentioned in the introduction, this book came into the world through sessions of a small group of friends. My sincere appreciation goes to all my friends and students. For the past several years, you have given me this amazing opportunity both spiritually and physically to perceive and share these teachings. Without you these ideas would not have been conceived, and without you they could not have gone out to the world: Avi Weisfogel, Adam Green, Etan Butler, Oscar Seidel, Adam Simon, Jonathan Glaubach, Avraham Goodfriend, Dr. Harry Zemon, Yechiel Labunskiy, Morris Sarway, Doug Deitel, Chaim Dov Cohen, Sam Septimus, and Tuvia Sablosky. Each and every one of you has made an invaluable contribution, each in his own way. No words can adequately express my personal gratitude!

This book took a considerable amount of time and a lot of effort. I would also like to acknowledge everyone who had a part in that process.

Avi Noam Taub from TFE, whose team transcribed thousands of pages of classes in an amazingly professional way.

Rebbetzin Yehudis Golshevsky, who took transcripts, notes, and conversations and miraculously turned them into a flowing book. Thank you for your good-spirited patience.

Cindy Scarr, who very quickly and efficiently smoothed out all the corners, making the book an easy read.

Dr. Rabbi Eliezer Shore, for all his advice and encouragement. You are a true friend!

Ari and Sari Webber, for all their help and encouragement—especially with the concept for the cover.

Matt Dieterich, for his amazing picture used for the cover, "Fire in the Sky."

The entire staff at Mosaica Press, headed by Rabbi Yaacov Haber and Rabbi Doron Kornbluth. My sincerest appreciation for giving this project top priority. You have prepared everything so quickly and not sacrificed quality.

Finally, and really most importantly, I want to thank "Sam."

It was you who pushed me to grow. You helped me to find parts of myself that I didn't know existed. May you continue to blossom and spread your light throughout the world!

INTRODUCTION

A Beginning

According to the Kabbalistic tradition, the master keys to unlocking the secrets of Creation are connection and compassion. And this book is my way of sharing these keys with you.

I was inspired to put these ideas into writing after a moment born out of connection and compassion.

During the autumn, every year right after the Jewish high holidays, we begin the Torah-reading cycle over again, starting with the account of Creation and the story of Adam and Eve. No matter how many times I learn it through (and I've learned it countless times), that narrative always makes me think about life at a deeper level. Every year — *every* year! — my curiosity about certain basic questions wakes up all over again.

So I went back to the beginning, and as the weeks went by I was filled with questions that weren't new, but I was experiencing them in a new way.

What is man's role in Creation? Why did there have to be a flood? What was unique about Noah? And then, one day, I got stuck on the image of the raven.

Yes, the raven. The biblical bird in Noah's ark. The first bird sent out to seek dry land, but which went "to and fro" until another bird, a dove, was chosen for the mission in its place. That image of the raven, flapping its wings and vacillating, instead of flying off to carry out its task — stuck in a useless cycle — struck me.

I thought about all the ways that people get caught up in negative cycles, caught up in rigid thinking and self-defeating behaviors. I realized that if I looked deeper, the raven would provide important lessons.

I delved into the words of the sages — you'd be surprised how much the ancient texts have to say about one bird! I explored mystical texts that were already familiar, but that now opened up for me in a new way.

And I found my way back to a teaching of Rebbe Nachman of Breslov, one of the great Chassidic masters.

It was a teaching about the raven — about *raven-states of mind*. It was a teaching I'd shared countless times with students over the years, but now somehow it was different. It was deeper. I was *feeling* it, not just learning it. Something had changed.

At the same time that my thoughts were in motion about the raven, I met Sam — the son of a friend of mine — while I was vising the States. He was in terrible shape — depressed, apathetic, and tortured by thoughts about traumatic events in his past. I literally pulled him out of bed and brought him back to Israel with me, holding his hand on the plane.

Sam was so grateful I'd connected with him, that I felt compassion for him. Finally, someone cared enough to step into his suffering to help him out of it.

For years, Sam had spent the better part of his day in bed; now, freshly arrived in Israel, he was getting up early to meet me where I go to pray in the mornings. We'd sit down afterward and have a cup of coffee together, and he started to share his feelings with me. He'd really despaired of ever being free of his negative thoughts. He was convinced he had no hope of real and lasting change.

Sam was such a prisoner of his past, so locked into his negative thinking that he would repeat his story over and over again to anyone who would listen.

I wanted so badly to help him.

Now, it's not as though I'd never worked with students before, trying to help them find their way emotionally and spiritually. Years ago, I opened a center for Torah study — a yeshiva — to help young men just like Sam. The center's uniqueness lay in it being not only a space for serious Torah study, but an accelerator for personal growth.

At a certain point, however, sustaining and maintaining the center started to outweigh my focus on the students. *The cause had become more important than those it was designed to serve.* My intentions were right, but in meeting the daily demands of running an institution, I'd stopped being present in the moment with the students. Eventually, the center closed.

Now, my reconnection with Sam was operating on a different level.

I wasn't the director of any institution; I was just listening and paying close attention to the way his mind worked.

It was an education for me. It made me an expert in what I like to call "constricted consciousness" — tight and unproductive modes of thinking. By just being present and observing without judgment the trend of his thoughts, I learned a lot about how certain mental habits sabotage life and health.

And then I got an education about myself, as well. Was I really so different from Sam? Sure, I was healthier and fully functional, but didn't I also succumb to his way of thinking and feeling, even if to a lesser degree?

Weren't we both sometimes like that raven in the ark, batting back and forth, unable to let go and set out on his mission?

Stuck...
Isolated...
Afraid...
Suspicious...

Again, I was flooded with compassion for Sam. I started to search within and without, through every teaching I found, for tools to help him.

And then things finally began to change.

I'm sure the channels opened up because I wanted so badly to help Sam. A fresh, very relevant Torah awoke within me, and I started to share it with him and then with others. I began to live it myself. The more I spoke about it with students and friends, the deeper it took root within me. More powerful insights revealed themselves all the time, and they shed new light on so much I'd already learned, clarifying it in an absolutely new way; it seemed that all the understanding I'd acquired before just paled in comparison.

That is the essence of this book. It's where it began, and this is its purpose. We only achieve true growth and change by letting go of the self. We do it by connecting with others, by opening up our wellsprings of compassion and reaching out.

> *The desire to connect with another arouses compassion.*
> *Together, they bring growth, unity, and inner peace.*

So in a way I owe everything to my dear friend, Sam. I've told him many times just how his eyes called out to me for love and connection when I was on that trip to the States. I'm so grateful to him for waking me up to a new life. And as I've continued this journey of discovery and change, I've been blessed with many teachers, students, and friends, who have opened new gateways of perception and insight.

> *My dear friends…*
> *May you discover inspiration within these pages, and may these ideas free you from your locked places. My hope and prayer is that these words will shine a new light on the cosmic path of truth and unity. This book is an ark that can lift us out of the flood of disconnection that rises around us. Together, we can build a new world of clarity, unity, and compassion.*

A Vision: Back to the Garden

Let's begin our journey.

Close your eyes and envision your perfect world. This ideal world of yours is probably free of suffering, free of disease and hunger; it's a place where everyone has everything they need. Human beings no longer exploit one another, peace reigns, and people devote their energies to building rather than destroying.

When everyone works together in harmony, new worlds open up. When people aren't scrambling for survival, they have the space to grow and develop into their highest selves.

Sounds like paradise, doesn't it?

Let's consider...*What would it take to make this world the paradise it was meant to be?*

We live in a world where all of the elements necessary for fulfillment are available to us, but it's hard to find genuinely fulfilled people. If our world already contains all we need to make it that paradise, why does it seem like we're further than ever from getting back to the Garden of Eden?

> What would it take to make this world the paradise it was meant to be?

The devices that promise to make our lives so much better — our technologies, our smartphones, our ever-more complex appliances — just end up ramping up our stress and anxiety. Once upon a time, people watched the six o'clock news; today, there's no escaping the 24/7 barrage of mind- and heart-numbing information. So many of us are depressed, but what do we have to be so down about? Isn't life so much better than it used to be?

Many people spend their whole lives just trying to get by, but life can be so much more than that. And in a world addicted to "more, more, more," and "bigger is better," I don't mean that the goal of spiritual development is to get more stuff.

It's not about the quantity of our possessions; it's about the quality of our existence.

Over the years, many students and clients have asked me for help with their financial lives. They're working hard, but not seeing the results they seek. When we find that all our time is taken up just trying to make the next mortgage payment or pay the next bill, we also find it's hard to devote time to the things that are really important to us: family, community, and our spiritual and creative selves.

I work with them on incorporating more of a soul-dimension into their life plan. The teachings I share with them, and will share with you here, can help *anyone* find his way out of the stressful and confining maze that characterizes modern life for so many of us.

Most of us are so busy reliving the resentments of the past and obsessing over our fears about the future that we lose the only thing we do have: today. One of the basic teachings we'll explore is how to realize the infinite possibilities of our now, our today, without being dragged down by the past or overwhelmed by the future. Instead of living a limited number of days of twenty-four finite hours, you have the potential to live a truly amplified life. Each day can be so saturated with spiritual vitality that it has more life in it than most people experience in eighty years.

The goal of this book is to teach you — in a straightforward and practical way — the key to unlocking a spiritual flow of abundance so that physical abundance can also enter into our lives.

I can't guarantee that these teachings will make you wealthy, but they can help you earn your living more easily and efficiently so you'll be free to pursue the ultimate purpose of your existence and discover true wealth. And this isn't only going to change you — it also has the power to change the world.

SECTION ONE

THE
BASICS

IN THIS SECTION, WE
GET FAMILIAR WITH THE
KABBALISTIC CONCEPTS WE
NEED TO UNDERSTAND THE
DYNAMICS AND PURPOSE
OF EXISTENCE.
THIS IS THE BEGINNING OF
ALL BEGINNINGS…

THE ROOTS
OF WISDOM

BEFORE WE GO ANY FURTHER, I want to clarify a term I used earlier that might be unfamiliar. I said most of the ideas found here are rooted in Kabbalah, the Jewish mystical tradition. The word Kabbalah is from the Hebrew root, *kabel*, which has two basic meanings: to receive and to correspond (to be similar or analogous).

The first thing to realize is that Kabbalah is a *received* tradition. Although many books have been written *about* it, you can't really learn Kabbalah from books. It's meant to be received from a teacher, who in turn received it from another teacher, and so on, going back to the earliest roots of this tradition, laid down well over three thousand years ago.

The definition of *kabel* as "corresponding" has its own nuance. We can say that Kabbalah teaches us the dynamics of how physical reality *corresponds* to spiritual reality. We can also say that Kabbalah teaches us how to correspond with the Divine Will and vibrate on His wavelength.

Similarity with God brings us closer to God. We'll return to that idea again and again throughout this book, because it's the core of a genuinely great life.

So — what does it mean to correspond with the Divine Will?

It means that if I want to be on God's wavelength, I first need to know what it is.

> Similarity with God brings us closer to God.

I need to learn about God's relationship with the universe (what the mystics call the Divine attributes, which we'll discuss later on) and mirror that relationship within the small universe of my own life.

If you asked people, "What is Godliness?" they'd probably say: kindness, mercy, generosity, humility, patience...Those are all Divine attributes. To live in alignment means taking those life-affirming and positive characteristics and making them my own.

If I want to be on God's wavelength, I first need to know what it is.

Mystics who have *received* the genuine Kabbalistic tradition haven't just received a body of information; it's not about the data. They've fine-tuned themselves into vessels so clean and clear that they're able to achieve contact with the Divine by making themselves *similar* to the Divine, by *corresponding*. Although they have received a certain wealth of knowledge from human teachers, true Kabbalists receive their wisdom from a higher Source — a more direct form of communication. Sometimes their experiences are described as communicating with angels; sometimes with the souls of great spiritual teachers who lived long ago.

The spiritual light that can be accessed through this tradition is extremely powerful. Because of that potential, its light has always been carefully guarded and protected. Those layers of protection — the tradition was always revealed only to very few students, and its language is very code-like — are necessary for two reasons:

- Powerful information is for people who have the discretion to use it wisely.
- Powerful light needs very strong filters so that it can be grasped without causing damage.

These layers, or filters — the words and metaphors that cloak Divine knowledge — do two things at once: they conceal and they reveal.

They conceal because they are not the light itself — *talking about* the Creator is not the same as *experiencing* the Creator. *Reading about* mystical unity isn't the same as *experiencing* it.

These filters also reveal, because if you don't talk and learn about the Infinite One, you won't have the knowledge you need to also experience the Divine.

Every stage of the transmission of this mystical tradition introduces new sets of filters and garments. These garments conceal by hiding their information in parables and codes that can only be penetrated by students who already hold the key to unlock them. They reveal, because when you do have the key, you can access this Divine light at your own level.

I'm not promising anyone a revelatory mystical experience — that's the product of a lifetime of work and a gift from above. It's not *secrets* of Kabbalah I'm sharing with you, but the basic outline of the Kabbalistic worldview — universal, cosmic truths that apply on some level to all of us.

After learning about these ideas, it's important to seek further guidance from someone well versed in the authentic tradition. I don't mean someone who's read a lot of books; I mean someone living a genuinely elevated and connected Torah life. And even with all those factors in place, it's possible that the concepts I'm presenting might seem beyond your present reach. If that's the case, more time in the great academy of life can be helpful, and you can always approach these ideas again further down the road.

The world is evolving constantly on the spiritual plane. Ideas considered esoteric for most of history are now much more widely known.

When we think of an evolving situation, we tend to visualize a gradual crawl from below to above, from a lower state to a higher one. When it comes to the soul, however, the paradigm is one of downward descent. God's infinite light is absolute, and where it shines without filters, it can obliterate everything else. Knowledge of the Divine enters the world from above to below, gradually, with more filters and garments at every stage.

Two thousand years ago, the greatest mystical teachers in this tradition spoke about kings and queens and princes and princesses; their parables made use of the concepts of their time.

Two hundred years ago, the bearers of this tradition spoke about peasants and shepherds, wagon drivers and water carriers.

Today, we use the parables of smartphones, lattes, and technology.

At every stage, the parables have to suit the mindset of the generation, because the point of the garment is not just to conceal, but also to reveal. The dance of concealing and revealing lies at the root of Creation. And every age needs a new language of revelation.

When I first came to Israel thirty-five years ago, I was twenty years old. Young and idealistic, I wanted to discover what I could about myself and about God, and I was blessed to be sent the right teachers at the right time. I remember traveling up north to the holy city of Safed with my mentor, and how he took me under his wing to give me a taste of the deeper aspect of the prayers found in our prayer book.

Every age needs a new language of revelation.

At that time, there weren't any good interlinear translations of the Hebrew into English; all you could find was a clumsy facing-page translation that was a little stiff. It was hard to find yourself in it and really enter into the prayers, but my teacher knew exactly how to speak to me, he knew just which words to say.

The first prayer of the morning begins, "*Modeh ani l'fanecha...*" — usually translated as, "I give thanks before You..." We start our day, every day, with a statement of gratitude for life and its opportunities. The Hebrew word *modeh* has a lot of nuance in it, though. It's about acknowledgement, about admitting the truth of something, about coming into alignment with another.

My teacher made a motion as if to erase the English translation on the facing page. Instead, he told me to write over it (and, yes, it was the tail end of the '70s): "*I groove with You.*"

My teacher was telling me, in language that spoke directly to me, to start my day by getting into alignment with the Creator. I've gone with that ever since.

IN THE HOUSE
OF THE BLIND

DUTIES OF THE HEART, ONE of the great classics of Torah philosophy and inner work, offers a parable to help us understand our misaligned relationship with the gifts of this world:

Once upon a time, a truly generous man commissioned the greatest medical experts to help him design a clinic to heal the blind. He hired technical experts and contractors to build the center to the medical experts' exact specifications, to ensure that the blind patients would have everything they needed to regain their sight. Their benefactor filled it with every device that could help the patients navigate their new environment as independently as possible. He also employed the best doctors and nurses to teach them how to take full advantage of these gifts as their vision gradually returned.

The patients were admitted to the new facility, but despite the staff's best efforts, the blind would not listen to their instructions about safe and proper use of the equipment. The doctors' attempts to treat their patients also failed; the patients refused to follow the guidance of the experts entrusted with their care.

Instead of thriving in their perfect environment, it became a stumbling block for them; they literally tripped and fell over the very equipment designed to help them. Now not only blind, but filled with fear, the patients tore through the clinic, bruising and injuring themselves on the very devices meant to help them.

In the end, the hurt and furious patients complained to the generous man who'd set the entire plan into motion. They accused

> him: "Why did you bring us here? To torture us? To punish us? And what was the point of all of these pieces of junk — they only brought us pain!"
>
> The blind patients never realized that he'd only intended to help them, and had provided exactly what they needed.
>
> As if physical blindness hadn't been enough, their mental blindness kept them from realizing that they were at the root of their own suffering.

The parable illustrates that this world already contains everything we need for our healing. This rehab center — our universe — is filled with every mechanism we need to become whole. Nothing is lacking. Wise teachers and guides have always been here, waiting for us to accept their instruction. The Torah — a mystical and practical blueprint for living — is available to us. We weren't born blind; we became this way over time. But if we weren't always blind — if we started out whole — that means we *can* regain our original vision. What was lost can be restored, but not when we're tripping over the very tools designed to help us.

> This world already contains everything we need for our healing.

We've been given such great gifts — material abundance, the capacity to experience physical pleasure, and a need and potential for the joys of intimacy. Embedded within the fabric of our being is the drive to form relationships; to bring children into the world and raise them; to contribute our energy and talents to build businesses, provide services, create new works of art, and devise technologies.

We feel naturally drawn to ownership, and we work to earn money so that we can fill our lives with more, newer, better. We're showered with an array of delicious and sustaining foods to keep us healthy and strong, but we don't know when to stop. So the devices — perfect tools to help us heal and become whole — start tripping us up.

We want and really need loving companionship, only to discover that the first rush of love and desire doesn't last very long. What happened?

We thought our relationships, so good at the start, would just keep getting better forever. But somehow, we find ourselves sprawling over the fallout from failed partnerships that have lost their vitality, and disappointment in ourselves and the people closest to us.

So how can we find the healing and wholeness we need so badly? The means are all available, but how do we take hold of them so they work for us instead of against us?

When it comes to our bodies, we usually know when we're on the right track and what derails us.

When we're eating what works for us, we don't need someone to tell us we're doing it right. We know we're doing it right, because we feel alive, strong, and vibrant.

There are endless options for exercise, but when we're getting our body moving in the way best for us, no one has to tell us we're doing it right. We don't need that outside confirmation because our body doesn't lie. We just feel *good*.

But that's not as far as we can go, because we're more than our body, more than our mind, even more than the energy that animates us. At the core of our being lies a piece of Infinity, a spark of Godliness itself. There are ways to be in touch with that core so that every other part of us and our life flows with Divine energy and the joy that lies at the heart of the universe.

Electricity only moves through a system when its circuit is complete. In the same way, Divine energy waits for us to complete our circuit so that it can flow down to us and through us. When we're doing it right, we'll know it and feel it, just like we know when our body is in alignment. When all of the parts of our self are aligned, they'll work together in harmony to serve our purpose in the most effective way possible.

THE
TREASURE

THE GREAT CHASSIDIC MASTER REBBE Simcha Bunim was known to share this true story with every new disciple that came to study with him:

There was once a poor man named Reb Isaac of Krakow who lived in dire poverty for many years, barely eking out a meager living. One night he dreamed of a beautiful bridge in Prague, a city he had certainly never visited in his life.

In his dream, he saw that a treasure was buried under that very bridge. At first, he ignored the dream; wouldn't anyone in his sorry situation dream of buried treasure? But when the dream returned night after night, he started having second thoughts. Perhaps his vision held some grain of truth?

So Reb Isaac sold, borrowed, and begged whatever he could, until he had enough money to travel to Prague. He set off on a long and exhausting quest, and when he finally reached the beautiful city, he was thrilled to find that it looked just as he had seen it in his dream. But although the bridge was exactly as it had appeared to him, night after night — in the light of day, soldiers walked up and down its length, guarding the span.

Reb Isaac settled down to wait for the soldiers to go off duty so that he could explore beneath the bridge. To his dismay, however, he discovered that it was watched around the clock. Had God brought him so far only to deny him the chance to dig for the riches his dream had promised?

But Reb Isaac was not easily deterred. He returned to his post near the bridge day after day, until the guards became used to his presence. Eventually one of them became curious and summoned him. "Why do you come to the bridge every day?" the soldier asked. "Are you waiting for someone?"

Reb Isaac decided to speak truthfully, hoping the soldier would allow him to search the area in exchange for a share of the treasure. He revealed his dream, but after hearing him out, the soldier threw back his head and exploded in laughter.

"You came all this way because of some foolish dream?! What dreamers you Jews are! I also had a dream, that a certain Jew named Reb Isaac who lives on the outskirts of Krakow has a treasure buried beneath the stove in his house, but do you see me going all the way there to check? Of course not!" And he walked away, braying with laughter.

Upon hearing those words, Reb Isaac ran to catch the first wagon back to Krakow — straight to his own home. When he arrived he immediately shoved the heavy iron stove out of the way and began to dig at the hard dirt floor. Soon enough, his spade hit something...a chest filled with gold! In his joy he cried, "Now I know that the treasure was here all along! But I had to go all the way to Prague to discover that it was with me the entire time."

The "treasure" is within every single one of us, but we might need to travel "far and wide" — through teachers and books and experiences — until we discover it. Ultimately, all of the teachings turn us back home, to the wealth of Godliness that lies within us.

THE DIVINE DANCE

THE INFINITE ONE CREATED THE universe so that the Presence would be revealed. But He left a space to discover the Presence, which means it has to be concealed.

Because you can only reveal something if it's hidden.

In Hebrew, the word for universe is *olam*, which shares the same root as the word for concealment. The universe is the theater of the revelation of Godliness, but God remains behind the curtains, waiting for us to draw them aside and discover Him. We're provided an arena of revelation, the space we need to "learn the steps and do this dance."

> God remains behind the curtains, waiting for us to draw them aside and discover Him.

To dance with God, you need to know the moves. They aren't complicated, but when it flows there's nothing that can compare. When we're dancing, we're in a state of unity — we're one. That oneness is the source of all good and vitality and pleasure. This is what it means to get back to the Garden. Everything began from this state of oneness.

The teachings I'm sharing are really part of a system, an interlocking group of ideas that, together, help us navigate the territory. As I introduce new concepts, keep in mind that these ideas work synergistically with the rest of the system.

The principles we're working with are rooted in the Kabbalistic tradition, an ancient school of wisdom transmitted faithfully among the Jewish people, both orally and in written form, for thousands of years. Nevertheless, the basic principles that underlie the Kabbalistic tradition apply equally to everyone. They're cosmic truths that predate the Jewish people; in fact, they predate Creation itself.

They are the most fundamental truths of the Infinite One and yet the most simple and straightforward ideas that exist.

18

This is not fad Kabbalah — no little red strings or "Kabbalah water." I won't be offering your astrological forecast for the coming month. I want to share with you a new way to see yourself and your place in the universe, a path of discovering your Godly nature and potential so your life can change for the better, and you can be a part of helping the world become the paradise it was designed to be.

When I first began my journey into Judaism's deeper teachings, I wasn't really ready for it. Too much was new to me, and I was suffering from information overload. I'd learn these beautiful concepts and then ask myself, *Is this really relevant to me?* It was just too much to process and integrate all at once. But then I was blessed to meet a person who suggested that I act like an anthropologist. He told me to read, and reread, and see Judaism as the ancient system it is — with its own logic, its own vast history. And to remember that I was just a visitor in venerable territory.

I took his advice. I studied and gave myself time to absorb the information, and it began to take form as a comprehensive whole. I was able to see it not only as ancient, but as time-tested, and I began to feel it working within me and changing me.

And now, with these teachings, I can speak directly to that Godly core within you, because your innermost self is going to resonate with them — the knowledge (the "treasure") is already inside you, within your soul.

Kabbalah is the study of the blueprint of existence; much of it deals with dynamics that preceded Creation, and to most people they might seem irrelevant. But when we start to see that these dynamics are cosmic patterns that repeat throughout every level of existence, down to the most intimate areas of our lives, they become essential for navigating through life.

These are the steps of the Divine dance. These steps repeat over and over again, as part of a continuing historical process unfolding all around us and within us.

ALIGNMENT ESSENTIALS

BEFORE WE GO ANY FURTHER, I want to lay out a set of fundamental principles rooted in the mystical tradition of the Torah, which serve as guidelines to alignment. They're so essential, we're going to return to them again and again in this book in a number of forms. These are the basic "Divine dance steps":

1. The Infinite One is the Source of all of the vitality that fills the world; when you're connected with the Source, that energy flows to you.
2. God is infinite; as finite beings we get on the Divine wavelength through consciously corresponding with His way of being.
3. All of the multiplicity that exists in the world around us and inside of us emerged from the unity of the Creator. Multiplicity is what allows us to work to discover God's unity.
4. Ego is another way of saying, "Edge God Out" — it is the way of disunity.
5. Existence as a whole is constantly evolving physically and spiritually, and we also need to progress and grow.
6. The Creator left pockets of imperfection in the universe to provide us with space to express our Divine nature — to freely choose to do good.
7. Conscious awareness leads to connection with all that exists, and this fosters true compassion.
8. The Infinite One is accessible to everyone equally; at every moment, we are only a motion away from alignment. It does not require radical change, just the activation of will through making a single choice in the moment.

9. The more important a concept is, the more prone it is to distortion. But distortion allows you space to choose, and that is the highest expression of your Divine self.

INFINITELY SIMPLE

SO, WE'VE OUTLINED THE BASIC "dance steps," learned a little bit about the nature of this mystical tradition, and talked about how important a pathway to alignment is. Without alignment, life can be so hollow; with it, our outer actions and inner purpose and Source of spiritual vitality are brought into harmony.

But what is this Source of vitality, what is this Infinite One — this God we're talking about? What understanding of God is the beginning of all beginnings?

I work with people from every imaginable background — Jewish and non-Jewish, religious and non-observant. A client once said to me before our first session, "Rabbi, I want you to know something important about me; it might affect your ability to work with me. But I really need to tell you...I'm not sure I believe in God."

I could see he thought he'd thrown me the curveball that might end our relationship before it even began. I'm sure he was expecting some kind of an argument from me.

I asked him, instead, to share his definition of God. Just because we're using the same term doesn't mean we're talking about the same thing. He described a pretty immature take on Zeus — an imposing old man with a long beard up in the sky, tossing down lightning bolts at puny, unsuspecting humans. He couldn't believe in that kind of God. Who could blame him?

I said, "My friend...I don't believe in that God either!"

A lot of people are holding on to serious

> A lot of people are holding on to serious misconceptions about God.

misconceptions about God, and these false underlying beliefs and images generate questions and doubts about the Creator.

Questions and doubts aren't the problem; it's through our questions and doubts that we uncover just where our false impressions are causing us trouble. That we can question, that we have the space here to doubt and seek, is beautiful — it's the essence of our humanity.

The truth is we never really stop questioning and seeking, because God is infinite. And infinite means without end, without limit. Therefore, our questions can never be fully answered, because the infinite truth of God is beyond what our minds can grasp. But we keep expanding our awareness to whatever extent we can.

Most people make the mistake of thinking, "God is just a little bit smarter than me," or "God is just a little bit more merciful than me." Because I'm smart and I'm compassionate, and I believe that God

> We never really stop questioning and seeking, because God is infinite.

is bigger than me...So that must mean that God is like me, only the next level up. Me, just supersized.

Of course, that's a false belief. There's a big difference between *my* wisdom and mercy, and *infinite* wisdom and mercy. Infinite is so different in quantity that it's completely different in quality, too.

The Creator is infinite, and our minds and words are limited. That means whenever we think and talk about God, we're always standing with our feet on the ground trying to reach up into the expanse of infinity. And that's impossible; there's only so much we can grasp.

This is where the beauty of the Kabbalistic tradition and its practical teachings within the Chassidic works really shines. Through its lens, the impenetrable questions about life — the very questions that used to perplex us and give us no rest — stop being obstacles and start to be gateways and wondrous doorways to new directions.

That which always seemed so complicated turns out to be so simple. Yes, simple.

You might ask how it's possible that the biggest questions of all can be reduced to simple answers.

And the answer is it's because the Creator is simple.

> *Simple means being of a single nature, not a complex of multiple parts.*

That's God. Infinite Oneness is infinitely simple.

That is the foundation upon which we build our worldview. It's also the basis I use with my clients, because they generally come to me after having snarled up their own lives, inside and out. They've taken something so simple and made it impossibly complicated.

And I introduce them to the KISS principle: Keep It Simple, Sweetheart.

I can assure you from experience that your success in understanding this material — and, really, your success in life — depends on keeping it simple. Throughout this book we'll discuss many ideas, but you'll soon realize it's all a single stream of simple ideas in a variety of contexts.

So...KISS — Keep It Simple, Sweetheart.

BOUNDLESS GOODNESS

AS WE MENTIONED, QUESTIONS ARE the gateways through which new awareness comes. So let's now go back to one of the original questions asked — and answered — by the great Kabbalists: Why did God create the universe?

In other words, what does an infinite and perfect being want with insignificant creatures like us? Why bring this world — with all its pain and suffering and darkness — into existence? What's it all for?

Whenever I speak to friends and students about this subject, I use this example to make it more approachable.

Imagine a fabulously wealthy man — someone with unlimited resources. He owns homes, cars, planes, helicopters — even his own islands.

He can go anywhere, he can do anything. Any time he wants to. He literally has it all.

There's only one small problem...

He's completely alone. He can't share any of this with anyone. He's got the most delicious foods...but he eats them alone. He looks out from the deck of his luxurious yacht and watches a sunset so glorious it brings tears to his eyes...but he watches it alone.

That's the Creator, all alone with His infinite goodness, before the universe began.

So the initial impulse of Creation was simple:

The Creator wanted to connect.
The Creator wanted to share His goodness.
For that, there needed to be an other.
We are that other.

25

This first principle is the foundation upon which everything else rests. When this concept becomes the bedrock of your worldview, it has the power to change your life.

What went wrong in the Garden of Eden? The root of the problem was that Adam drifted away from this foundation. The seed of doubt about the Creator's good intentions was planted in Adam's heart — and this seed grew into a terrible, destructive force. That's what happens when we detach from solid trust in the Infinite One's love and goodness. It complicates our life. It causes gridlock where there needs to be flow.

Mistrust of God's essential goodness is the main obstacle to living a connected and joyous life.

Let's think about what life could be like when we have *complete trust* in the absolute goodness of the Creator, when we know that everything that happens is orchestrated for our eternal benefit by a loving God.

> Mistrust of God's essential goodness is the main obstacle to living a connected and joyous life.

When we have complete trust in the absolute goodness of our Creator, the good we experience isn't just pleasant — it feels like a magical gift, a token of the Creator's love and care. The beauty and the wonder of existence isn't a random collision of matter and energy — it's a communication, an opportunity for communion.

If my wife left me a beautiful dinner but went out to visit a friend, the dinner might be delicious, but it would be missing something. Sure, I could appreciate it as a loving gesture...but wouldn't it be so much better if we were sitting at the same table, enjoying it together? Certainty in God's goodness is the main way for me to live my life sitting together at the table with Him, so to speak. We're living the marvel of life — together. And that makes it all the more wondrous.

This might sound abstract or mystical or difficult. It's not. Developing this foundation does require an investment of energy and attention, but it's within the easy grasp of anyone who really wants it. That's because it's already woven into the fabric of our being.

God is good, and the nature of good is to share goodness.

Our nature is rooted in God, and we share this quality naturally with the Creator. So not only do we have an inherent need and desire to connect and give, we also have the capacity for turning our good nature into action. What's great is that it's not too difficult because, in our deepest self, we're already there.

This gift of experiencing closeness and contact with God — this great goodness that the Creator wants to share — is only fully possible when we become *like* the One we want to experience. We need to achieve a kind of similarity, or there won't be anything to join us together.

> God is good, and the nature of good is to share goodness.

When it comes to our personal relationships, we know we have a certain affinity with the people we're close to. To develop a relationship with God, I align with His nature by bringing my own Divine nature to light. And even though I'm finite and God is infinite, I can create affinity between us by choosing to be *like God*. To be a sharer, a giver, a reservoir of goodness.

To truly connect with God, we emulate God. We align.

And *that is why this universe exists* — to provide us with the opportunity to do this...to *be* this...to *become* this.

MAKING SPACE

CONNECTION AND ALIGNMENT IS THE goal...but to do this work, you need space to do it. A good relationship also requires that each party makes room for the other. The Creator's relationship with the universe, and with each of us, is no different.

Before Creation there was nothing but the Infinite One, unmanifest. There was no space or time, no Names, no attributes; there was just the essence of God. For lack of a better term, we call that essence "endless light," but of course it's not physical light. We just use the word light because it's the closest term we have to express the concept of vital and illuminating energy.

To make a space in which reality could exist, in which *we* can exist, God retracted the light of His Infinite and unmanifest Self so that the full extent of His mercy and compassion could be revealed. This Kabbalistic concept of the *tzimtzum* — the Primal Contraction — is a concept we'll be returning to in different ways, because it's an archetypal act that has application in many spheres of our lives.

Here's one look at the way the concept of *tzimtzum* comes down to earth. What does it mean to us when we talk about making space for someone? The most elevated way to view anyone standing opposite us is to say, "I have space for you inside of me, and I acknowledge that you're free to be who you are, and who you will become."

That's called emulating God.

Most of us have a hard time doing this in our relationships, though. We're often afraid and find ourselves trying to manage other people's lives even when we know it doesn't work well.

When I make space for someone else — knowing full well that the other person might make mistakes — it provides them with the gift of my trust. By leaving them room, they're empowered to *become*. I can allow them the freedom to act because I have faith in them. I trust they can do whatever it takes to be their best self.

In our relationships with other people, we tend to be results-driven; we want to see change and growth. But when we emulate God, we find the patience to give people space to just become, at their own pace. Providing others with space gives them the peace that allows them to become more elevated — just like God waits patiently for each of us to evolve.

The making of space for another is the original act of Divine compassion and love. When the Divine makes space for us, we have potential to grow in that space. We also have the potential to fail there. If we don't have the ability to make a mistake, we can't really succeed either. If we don't have room to doubt, there's no room for faith and trust. You can't have one without the other.

> When we emulate God, we find the patience to give people space to just become, at their own pace.

Our freedom to choose — to pursue a relationship with our Source, to fulfill our potential or throw it away — is our space. It appears empty of the Presence because otherwise we'd have no choice but to develop a relationship with God. We'd be angelic automatons, praising God all day. But is a universe filled with spiritual robots what the Creator really wants? No. Not even close.

Since the essence of God is absolutely free in its giving, in its goodness, the creation with the greatest potential to emulate God must also be free. If we were automatically good, reflexively righteous, we'd be effectively useless to the Creator.

So we were given the very great gift of a universe where the Presence doesn't overwhelm us, where we *appear* to be on our own. The space leaves room for free will, room to reach out as seekers. It leaves us freedom to develop faith. This making of space is an act of Divine self-restraint, and like all acts of withholding, it can — at first glance — look like the opposite of kindness.

Because if giving is kindness, isn't withholding naturally unkind?

But when we look deeper we find that the primal act of withholding is really the highest form of mercy. Without it, there's no space for reality to unfold. There's no room for revealed love and kindness to evolve. No room for *us* to evolve.

So that first *tzimtzum,* contraction, is really just the first step in the Divine dance of love and giving.

THE LIFELINE

MAKING SPACE IS ONLY THE beginning. Now that the universe has been created within this apparent vacuum — the place where the Divine Presence is in eclipse — it's time for the next dance step.

Within the space, there's also a lifeline of potential for connection that extends into the very heart of the place that seems void of God's presence. Because even as God withdrew to leave this space in which all the worlds could come into being, He dropped a line, an "umbilical cord," into this womb of Creation.

It's through this line that Divine vitality constantly flows, maintaining and sustaining all of existence.

The First Two Divine Dance Steps

1. *The primal contraction (tzimtzum) to create an illusion of space.*
2. *The dropping down of a line through which God's infinite light descends into the space in a hidden way*

If you want a relationship, it really comes down to those original dance steps of Creation — to align with God's giving nature by providing space and extending a beam of loving-kindness into that space. That means we really have to transform ourselves.

We enter life as receivers. But although we're all born takers, to fulfill the purpose of our existence we need to remake ourselves into Godly givers who act freely, willingly, and consciously.

Now we can look back at one of our hard questions and see it in a

31

new way. If the apparent dead spaces in Creation pain us — poverty, sickness, suffering — what we're really looking at is a manifestation of the primal *tzimtzum*. That's the as-yet-unfilled empty space.

The only response to those apparently empty spaces is to shine the light of compassion and kindness into them. There, in the apparent absence of God, *we send our own Divine nature in to fill the void with acts of mercy.*

The First Two Human Relationship Dance Steps

1. *To relate to the empty space as my area of free will, and to make that space for others, to allow them room to become.*

2. *To actively draw my Godly capacity to give into that empty space and fill it with kindness in a way that the other can receive.*

SEEKING ONE IN A WORLD OF MANY

SO HERE WE ARE IN the universe generated in that primordial empty space. It's a place that appears empty of God, but it also has a lifeline of Divine vitality we can grasp onto if we seek it out.

Our world is colorful, filled with smells and sights and sensations that just knock us out. This is exactly the way it's supposed to be. The Creator doesn't bowl us over; He waits for us to discover Him. All the beautiful sensations available to us are garments behind which the Creator hides.

In the created universe, our task is to gather everything — every experience and sensation and object that we encounter — and draw it toward our conscious awareness of the Infinite One.

When we're able to hold on to the lifeline, to connect with that cord of Godly awareness, the darkness and limitation of the physical universe is no longer the constricted space it was. It's now a portal to the infinite.

We don't have to withdraw from material reality — eating, working, loving — to do this. Quite the contrary. All of existence is sustained by hidden Divine light and energy via that lifeline. We encounter those sparks of Godliness every day of our lives, all day long.

> We encounter those sparks of Godliness every day of our lives, all day long.

Some of these sparks are really nourishing to the soul; some only provide an illusion of light. Some things we uplift by consciously making use of them. Some things will draw us further away from the Creator, no matter how good our intentions may be.

We're always making choices about where we go to derive energy. When it comes to food, I can choose the fast-food burger or the brown basmati rice with tofu and vegetables — or anything in between. When it comes to my need for intimacy, I can invest in a relationship that calls for my physical and emotional presence, or choose to scatter my energy on adventures that leave me unfulfilled. The possibilities are endless.

The same goes for where I seek entertainment, information, and pleasure. I can seek out a source closer to the center, to the real core of Divine vitality that fills the universe, or I can pick up energy from the fragments that don't really sustain me. It's a choice.

The search for a feeling of connection and vitality can sometimes pull us into acting in ways that violate our own convictions. We can get our life force from the Source or from the fragments — but the fragments can never satisfy us for long because fragments aren't strong enough to sustain the soul.

A lot of us will say we know that running after food, money, or sex isn't going to bring us to the highest joy, but if we *really* knew that we'd be living vastly different lives. When we choose to live off the fragments while our real yearning for connection remains unfulfilled, we wind up suffering for it.

When our bodies begin to protest — too much or the wrong kind of food makes us sick; overwork and stress over money make us miserable; sex that's empty of true intimacy just makes us feel more alone — it's a blessing in disguise. Because if the fragments could ever really satisfy us, we'd never feel driven to seek the Source.

> If the fragments could ever really satisfy us, we'd never feel driven to seek the Source.

All physical pleasures sooner or later lose their appeal; fragments can only take you so far. But true and unadulterated good never gets old. That's because, unlike the body, the soul has endless capacity for vitality and pleasure.

When you're plugged into the Source, you feel good and you don't burn out.

Ego-based and fractured navigation through the material world is like walking through a beautiful garden, plucking the loveliest blossoms you come across. What's wrong with picking the flowers? After you pick them, they look good for a few hours, a few days if you're lucky. But no matter how much you enjoy their vibrant colors and heady fragrance, they're actually dead. They were dead from the moment they were cut off from their roots.

A person could get really angry about those wilting, drooping flowers. He spent a lot of time and energy hiking through that garden looking for perfection; it seems like every time he thinks he's finally found the most beautiful one it just dies on him. He cannot figure out what the problem is, and that's frustrating.

But the solution is actually quite simple and straightforward. The only way to enjoy the flower for more than an hour is to leave it attached to its root. When we focus on using the gifts of the material world only as a means of staying connected to God, those gifts never lose their beauty and delight.

And now that we have a more comprehensive understanding of Creation based on the mystical tradition, we can better appreciate the nature of the world into which Adam was introduced. The Garden of Eden was a place with only one essential choice to make: for Adam to bind his consciousness with the Oneness of his Creator, or to turn away and seek the multiplicity of his own will.

This was Adam's primary challenge and, guess what? It's ours now, too.

THE EARLY MASTERS

IN THIS SECTION, WE TRAVEL THROUGH EARLY HISTORY AND LEARN ABOUT THE GREAT SPIRITUAL MASTERS WHO ACTIVATED GOD-CONSCIOUSNESS IN THE WORLD. WE BEGIN WITH ADAM AND FOLLOW AN ARC THAT TAKES US THROUGH NOAH AND DOWN THE FAMILY TREE OF ABRAHAM, ISAAC, AND JACOB…UNTIL WE ARRIVE AT THE QUANTUM SHIFT IN GOD-CONSCIOUSNESS THAT TOOK PLACE AT SINAI.

ADAM'S MISSION STATEMENT

PEOPLE SOMETIMES SHARE WITH ME how they feel their lives lack purpose, how they don't feel there's real meaning to what they're doing.

I tell them, "That's only because you're not in touch with the Creator's purpose. If you know what inspired God to create, you'll also know what will infuse your own actions with meaning."

Adam's (read: humanity's) Divine essence mirrors that of the Infinite One. What sparked the great act of Creation is the same force that fills us with a feeling of purpose and meaning. When we're consciously attuned to that purpose, we're naturally filled with vitality and energy.

It's about connection, compassion, and filling the empty space with revealed goodness and mercy. That apparently empty space that was the beginning of Creation isn't only the source of our free will, it's our room to work. The space allows us to live with the same purpose that animates all of Creation.

The main way to fill the space is through God-consciousness: when our thoughts, words, and actions are filled with awareness of God and His purpose for Creation. But it's not enough to develop this consciousness within ourselves. The greatest act of mercy and compassion is to share the light of this awareness with others, *so that the empty space of Creation becomes filled with illuminated minds.*

God didn't set up this beautiful universe as a pretty toy. He certainly didn't set it up to be a place of pain and lack. The space here is meant to be *completely and absolutely filled* with activated human minds and spirits, joyous and alive in a state of connection with their Source. The Creator blessed Adam, "Be fruitful and multiply and *fill the earth*" — I don't need My world filled with animalistic human beings. I want you to populate My Creation with fully actualized human hearts and minds.

The human being is a composite of the heavenly and the earthly — a fusion of soul and body. We have the potential — really, the mission — of joining the physicality of existence with its spiritual source. We weren't designed to be like other creatures; we were made to be partners with our Creator.

That's what we can give, *because only we can give it.* It's our unique human nature — a material body fully of the earth, joined together with the absolutely spiritual "bit of God" that animates us — that makes it possible for us to partner with the Creator to carry into reality the original purpose of Creation. Only we are able to reveal Divine mercy to the fullest extent possible by expressing our soul's needs and purpose by way of material experience.

> Adam isn't a creature like other creatures. He's meant to be a partner with his Creator.

If we go back to the account of the Garden, we find that "there was no rain...because there was no man." (Genesis 2:5–6) What does rain have to do with Adam not yet being on the scene? Our tradition teaches that there was no rain because *there wasn't yet a partner in the world to pray and arouse Divine mercy,* which is the trigger for the descent of rain. The world was sustained until then by a "mist" — a steady and pervasive lifeline of minimal Divine loving-kindness. But the greater revelation of Divine mercy — rain — had to wait until a human being was there to draw it down.

We learn from this that God created the universe with built-in lacks — empty spaces — to provide us with purpose and to allow us to partner with its Creator.

That's Adam's mission statement...and if it was Adam's, it's ours, too.

THE RIGHT
FOUNDATION

FOR YEARS, I'VE BEEN WORKING with people who seek deeper meaning and purpose in their lives. And one thing I've discovered is that the most basic element of the work is often the most neglected: the nature of their relationship with God.

One of the most basic mitzvot is to love God. And a common question is: "Some people love more easily, and others have a harder time with it. Is it really fair to require us to come up with a *feeling* for the Creator?"

But — and this is a key point — if God instructs us to do something, that means we can do it.

We *do* have a natural reservoir of love for our Creator within us, and it's up to us to tap into it. The feelings are there because we have an innate bond with God, and we're constantly receiving a flow of goodness — life itself and everything we need — from the Creator. Gratitude and love go together, and both are natural to us when we're in a healthy spiritual state. That means paying attention to the good and allowing it to affect us emotionally.

> If God instructs us to do something, that means we can do it.

It's hard to feel grateful when you think that, no matter how much good the giver has shared, it was for ulterior motives, without genuine love and goodness directed toward you personally. That's the difference between emotionally healthy and happy people, and those who have a hard time getting out of bed in the morning. How do they feel about the circumstances of their lives, and about the One Who orchestrated them? Is the good (and there's *always* good) just something they take for granted, or do they feel the love and care invested in them by the Creator?

The sages compared this to the difference between a good guest and a bad one. The good guest says, "Everything my host has done, he did for my sake." The house is clean, there's food to eat, the people are pleasant...and not because the host would do these things anyway to make his life more pleasant. He did it *for me*. My host cares about me, and I naturally want to express that love right back.

The bad guest says, "Everything my host has done, he did for himself." He needed to eat anyway — what's an extra portion to him? He *wants* to live in an orderly space. Nobody did anything special to make *me* feel more at ease. I can't feel personal and genuine gratitude unless I feel deep down that I personally have something to be grateful for.

We've all probably gotten a taste of both kinds of guests in our lives. The question is — which one would *we* rather be?

I mentioned earlier that the first words in the prayer book — the first thing we say even before washing our hands in the morning — is a simple prayer: "*Modeh ani l'fanecha...*" It's usually translated as, "I give thanks before You..."

Every new day opens with a reflection on gratitude. This is the foundation of my day; it's the basis of my relationship with my Creator and it's how I stay in harmony with God.

Now, if we go back to Adam in the Garden, we can look at what unfolded there with fresh eyes. In the third chapter of Genesis, we're introduced to the serpent. If we cut down the primordial serpent's argument to its most basic elements, it's that the Infinite One commanded you not to eat this fruit because *He doesn't love you.*

The serpent hisses, "Isn't it beautiful? And it's going to make you so smart. Why would God keep you away from something so good? It must be because...God doesn't really love you."

Of course, this wasn't only bad advice; it was also a lie. If you've been told not to eat from a particular tree, *and the basis of your relationship is trust in God's benevolence and gratitude*, then it must be that staying away from that fruit is crucial for you.

Listening to the serpent's voice changed Adam's understanding of his relationship with God. Instead of trust, there was now suspicion. Instead of love — competition. With his new serpent-view, Adam lost sight of the fact that the Divine rules are just good advice offered by a loving Creator. By acting on his now twisted perception, Adam created his own reality.

> *Adam lost touch with the basis of his relationship with God: that the Infinite One is good and only seeks our good.*

This is really the point on which everything rests. How do we see the Creator? Do we see the Creator as kind, generous, loving, and merciful or — the exact opposite — out to get us? When we're confident of God's love — an inherent love, like the natural love a parent has for a child — then our whole world is built on the right foundation. Then, you wake up in the morning, open your eyes, and say, "What a wonderful world the Creator has made *for me — Modeh ani!*"

IN THE GARDEN

OKAY, LET'S KEEP THIS SIMPLE.

There is only you and God. You are Adam on the first day of your creation and God says to you: "Adam, here are some basic ground rules. I created you, I love you, I'll do everything so that you can reach your highest potential. You're free to follow these instructions or not — *it's your choice*. But I just want you to know...*if you use your free will to carry out My Will, it's going to be really great for you.*"

Why does Adam have to be free to choose? Because that's the essence of his Divine nature. Just as the Creator is free, so too must man be free. Just as the Creator is a giver and not a taker, man needs to be provided with opportunities to give rather than just receive. *Adam can only really develop a relationship with the Creator by emulating God's essential qualities.*

The Torah teaches that after Adam's creation, "God took the man and placed him in the Garden of Eden." But in that second chapter of Genesis, we see that Adam was already in Eden. So from where was Adam taken so that he could be re-placed in the Garden?

> Why does Adam have to be free to choose? Because that's the essence of his Divine nature. Just as the Creator is a giver and not a taker, man needs to be provided with opportunities to give rather than just receive.

The *Zohar* — the classic work of Jewish mysticism — teaches us that Adam was "taken from...the four elements." Each of the four basic modes — grounded like the earth; expansive like water; transcendent like air; and fiery hot with fervor — have positive and negative potential.

44

Adam is *removed* from the negative manifestations of his material nature, and then *settled* into Eden to align with the Divine Will. But he needed to remain in sync with this perfect world. During the first phase of existence, the Creator *did the act of alignment for Adam*, so he would be suited to the nature of Eden.

No one just *lands* in Eden — you have to actively synchronize yourself with it to be there.

But Adam wasn't created to be passively acted upon. He was placed here to actualize his Divine potential, and work to repair and perfect the world in which he'd been planted.

But what if, like Adam, you choose not to stay aligned?

God doesn't need to punish anyone for that — Creation itself, all of its four elements, rises up against the person who introduces division into the Garden. When a person chooses to leave the world of unity and seek out separation, the natural result is bitterness. As we saw in the story of the House of the Blind, all the things created to help us carry out our highest purpose — marriage, children, wealth, our own bodies — instead become the instruments of our unhappiness.

Adam could only live in Eden if he was aligned with its perfection. So when Adam damaged his refined nature, he was naturally ejected from the Garden. He didn't really need to be exiled. He was out of sync with the place and no longer fit.

Anyone can make "working and guarding the Garden" the center of his life.
Working means acting as a partner with God's Will.
Guarding means refraining from anything that would interrupt that connection.

When what's essential is at the center, everything good naturally flows out from that source. For each of us, life has the potential to be like a taste of Eden — abundant, joyous, and flowing with blessing. But, just like Adam, to achieve that, we're going to have to work for it.

TWO
TREES

IN THE GARDEN, THERE WERE all kinds of beautiful and wondrous trees, but in the very center of the garden there were two that were unique: the Tree of Life and the Tree of Knowledge of Good and Evil. Although both trees sprang from the same root, they didn't bear the same kind of fruit. According to Kabbalistic tradition, those two trees represent many different concepts. One of these concepts sheds light on our everyday experience, and I want to share it with you.

Everyone has two essential parts to his life.

We have our "Tree of Life" — our inner purpose, our center, our connection to the Divine, a connection nourished through prayer, meditation, and study.

> We all have something to accomplish in the wider world of action. That external purpose is our "Tree of Knowledge."

And then we all have something to accomplish in the wider world of action. That external purpose is our "Tree of Knowledge."

When we look at the verses in Genesis, we tend to zero in on the Divine directive to avoiding eating the "forbidden fruit." Most of us fail to see that Adam was first told: "You shall surely eat freely of all the trees of the Garden" (Genesis 2:16). That's a recommendation, a piece of important advice from God: "Go ahead and partake of your Tree of Life — of the sources of nourishment that feed your bond with your Creator. Enjoy!"

Had Adam *eaten first from the Tree of Life* — had he first nourished his spiritual essence — he could have eaten from the Tree of Knowledge of Good and Evil afterward without suffering. It's only when we go out into the world of action in a state of disconnection from our Source that we find ourselves in a state of spiritual confusion. It's only when we're not conscious of the Infinite One at the root of our varied experience that the fruit of the Tree of Knowledge of Good and Evil is spiritual poison.

A centered and aligned person — a *unified* person — can go out into the physical world of multiplicity without suffering. So start your day by centering yourself with Divine wisdom and meditative prayer; then you can go out into the world of the Knowledge of Good and Evil and stay connected to the Source. When you're connected *inside*, everything you do *outside* becomes bound up with that lifeline and unified. And if you feel yourself losing your unified focus during the day, just stop and reorient yourself. Study something that feeds your soul; take five minutes to focus on conscious contact with God.

> "You may eat freely of all the trees of the Garden" — The fruit of knowledge isn't the problem...the problem is disconnection.

Do whatever you need to do to get back in touch with the Tree of Life.

It's the fruit that makes Adam leave his paradise and go out into the world of multiplicity — *a fractured universe he created with his own perceptions*. But it's also by getting out there that Adam has the chance to undo the damage. By discovering unity and alignment in the place of multiplicity and concealment, Adam has a chance at getting back to the Garden.

The Torah teaches that after Adam's departure, God placed a particular obstacle at the gates of Eden to prevent exactly that return: an angel grasping a "flashing, revolving sword." These images from the Torah aren't just colorful, descriptive parts of an ancient story; they're symbols that describe our reality *right now*.

The "flash of the revolving sword" is a part of my everyday life — it's a state of confusion that keeps me from getting back to the Garden. Again, the revolving sword isn't some kind of punishment; it's simply the consequence of Adam's choice. This sword that turns every which way represents a state of internal conflict and confusion. It's like you're standing at the fork in the road and not only do the signposts point in different directions that all seem equally attractive, but the signs themselves flash like neon lights that just stupefy you.

Most of us live in doubt about what our next move should be, what direction we should take. I call this the "functional dysfunctional mind." Our thoughts race, and we're deafened by the internal chatter and static. We're so used to this chaos that we think it's totally normal, but if this noise was amplified we'd be mortified at how crazy it sounds. Our thoughts ricochet back and forth constantly, sapping our vital energy.

This isn't our natural state; it's not how we ought to be living. It's just a result of Adam eating from the Tree of Knowledge of Good and Evil. This is the work of the revolving sword in our lives.

So we go right back to the beginning and repair the situation by doing for ourselves what Adam failed to do — connect with our Tree of Life *first*, and only then go out into the world of multiplicity and confusion. Starting our day spiritually connected helps us stay centered so we can function sanely in a crazy world.

The world is full of choices whose lights flash in our eyes, dazzle us, and make it even harder to make decisions. The goal is to be able to interact with the vast world of options without losing our way; to find clarity in the midst of confusion, unity in the place of multiplicity, and peace and quiet in place of internal chaos.

That's how we can walk the path back to Eden.

STARTING
FRESH

IF WE WANT TO BE able to take the road back to the Garden, it's important to take a look at two forces within us that keep us from taking those first steps in the right direction: guilt and shame.

The first recorded moment of guilt and shame was immediately after Adam and Eve ate from the fruit of the Tree of Knowledge of Good and Evil. Adam chose to pursue the ego-agenda rather than the Divine directive — and he fell out of alignment with the Divine Will. His connection with the vitality and soul of the universe was disrupted; it needed immediate repair.

Directly following Adam's error, the Creator made an opening for him, issuing an invitation to come forward and reestablish contact. "The voice of God was traveling through the garden... And God called out to him, 'Where are you?'" (Genesis 3:8–9).

But Adam's instinctive response — driven by a sense of guilt and shame — was to avoid the voice of the Infinite One (as if that were really possible). And so, initially, Adam chose to hide rather than face his Creator.

> *God wants us to stay connected and aligned,*
> *but guilt keeps us separate.*
> *Shame over the past keeps us from reconnecting with our Source.*

Adam's sin had long-lasting repercussions; in fact, we're still feeling them today.

Try to put yourself in his position. You've just made an error that's going to impact the rest of human history. We have a hard enough time picking ourselves up off the floor after making a *minor* mistake — imagine how devastated Adam must have felt! Adam very much wanted to correct his error. But we see that the obstacles of guilt and shame didn't bring him closer to correcting his mistake.

Our tradition teaches us that after leaving Eden, Adam spent 130 years in a state of deep repentance. He changed his life and changed himself, investing all of his energy in trying to repair the damage he'd caused. The great lesson we learn from Adam is that although it seemed like it was too late, *he did not give up.* He did not give in to the natural human tendency to allow guilt and shame to keep him from trying to repair whatever he could.

By the way, there's a big difference between guilt and repentance.

> The roots of redemption lie in refusing to despair, and believing in ourselves and in the possibility of repair.

Guilt — because the offense seems so great, so unfixable — leads to paralysis. It's how our past can swallow up our future.

But repentance, *teshuvah* — which really means to *return and restore* — is all about taking responsibility in the present for mistakes made in the past, so the future opens clearly before us. *Teshuvah* is a way of clearing out all the chaotic "revolving sword" thinking, so we can start fresh.

Clearing out that space is a reflection of that initial space-making of Creation. Again, we're doing the basic steps of the Divine dance.

Adam spent a whole lifetime in this process of return, and for this he's called a *chassid* by the ancient sages — a pious man. Not because he managed to completely clean up his mess, but because he didn't give up, and devoted his life to doing what he could to repair the damage he'd caused.

And what about us? Sometimes we're so overwhelmed by all the damage we see in our lives, we can hardly think where to begin.

Look at the mess we've made of our own private worlds — our marriages, our children, our communities.

Look into your own heart — at the pain that lies within each and every one of us.

And then, paralyzed, we give up.

Now wait just a minute!

That sense of accountability you feel? That deep regret? That yearning for something better?

What you're feeling is the essence of returning, the essence of *teshuvah.*

The difference is that we feel all of that — *and also refuse to despair.* When we realize how unequal we are to the task of restoring everything that was lost, it's exactly then that we can open up the channels of assistance from Above. The great masters taught, "It is not incumbent upon you to complete the work, but you are not free to leave off from it either!" (*Avot* 2:16). Like Adam, we begin by doing whatever we can — and we trust that the Creator will complete the work, even if it takes generations.

Even if it takes the rest of human history.

After those 130 years of *teshuvah,* Adam had a son, Seth, who eventually had a son named Shem, the forefather of Abraham, Isaac, and Jacob. Shem is the source of the entire future of the Jewish people and of the Messiah, who will eventually come to repair the world.

Let's stop for a moment and think about that.

Repairing the world.

Redemption.

Our ultimate future is rooted in Adam's refusal to fall into despair, and his persistence in starting again. And that's true for us no less than it was for Adam — we need to believe in ourselves, in our ability to repair the world if we'll only begin the process.

Rebbe Nachman of Breslov taught:

"If you believe that you can ruin something... believe that you can fix it!"

On the surface, this simple-seeming quote sounds nice and easy, but try to visualize what it really means. Imagine a very expensive vase on the dining room table and my ten-year-old — after being told endless times not to play ball in the house — breaks the vase. Will I then turn to him and say, "Don't worry, sweetheart, if you can break it you can also fix it"?

No. Because in an instant of carelessness,

> "If you believe that you can ruin something... believe that you can fix it!"

my son broke a valuable object, and all the superglue in the world won't help.

So what does Rebbe Nachman really mean? I suggest that, instead of emphasizing the "ruin" and "fix" lines, the focus should really be on the word *believe*.

If you *believe* your actions have spiritual ramifications, that things count, and after having made your mistake you're really out of alignment with your Creator, *you can also activate that power of belief to empower your repair*. Belief in fixing is what gets you back out there, looking for opportunities to make any amends you can. It's the belief in the process of repair that catalyzes it.

Our very first tzaddik is Adam — yes, Adam! He might have made a mistake, a huge mistake, but he also laid the groundwork for all the repair that would happen throughout the generations. Like all the great souls that came after him, he moved the progression of the revelation of God's mercy forward until the next tzaddik came along to take up the work.

That tzaddik was Noah.

MERCY
UNFOLDS

ACTUALLY, BEFORE WE MOVE ON to Noah, we need to talk a bit about mercy. As in Divine mercy.

With the Bible as our guide, we can see the Divine Will unfolding in stages, in a progression that spans the entire course of history, and features figures who serve as focal-points in the revelation of the Infinite One's Will and mercy. Each of these figures has practical guidance to share with us as we navigate our personal journeys.

Because these "personal" journeys aren't only about us. We're all bound up together, across time and space, working toward a single, universal goal.

The desire of the Infinite One is to reveal the full extent of His mercy.

Mercy is the balanced expression of kindness and restraint,

with love at its root.

The Infinite One's quality of mercy is infinite. As finite beings, we can't grasp just what that means, but every time we seek out and are conscious of the expression of Divine mercy in our lives, we help to fulfill the purpose of Creation. Everywhere we look, we're face to face with Divine mercy. And that's true even when we see things that don't appear to be so positive on the surface.

> The desire of the Infinite One is to reveal the full extent of His mercy.

With love and mercy, the Infinite One made space for Creation — and that space created an apparent vacuum of that Infinite Light. And so love and mercy became the agents of generating a place that *can also be dark*, that *can also include evil*, and that *allows for the choice between light and dark, and good and evil.*

And *that* is called Divine mercy. Because making space is that first Divine dance step that allows Creation with all of its goodness to unfold.

Divine mercy isn't manifest where everything is always smooth and nothing goes wrong — quite the contrary. But it's specifically down here, where every mistake can (and will) be made, that we witness the full unfolding of Divine mercy. And there will always be individuals who share with the world the eyes they've cultivated to see Divine mercy within everything. These individuals have a clearer vision, and they don't just keep it for themselves, but make it their task to share that vision with others. They work to spread their awareness of Godliness with others.

We call this type of person a tzaddik — a "righteous one." Really, a tzaddik is someone who always sees — or, even without clearly understanding, accepts — the rightness of the Divine plan as it unfolds, and who helps others reach that clarity and acceptance.

If we break it down to essentials, Adam's task was to bind himself to the Infinite One, and then to turn around to the rest of Creation — mineral, vegetable, and animal — and say, "Let's all devote ourselves to serving the Creator." If Adam had done that, he would have fulfilled the role of tzaddik, a bridge to the Divine. Instead, he lost sight of the foundation idea — the Creator's mercy and goodness — and fell into disunity. And dragged the rest of the world down with him.

> A tzaddik is someone who always sees — or, even without clearly understanding, accepts — the rightness of the Divine plan as it unfolds.

The tzaddik knows that the universe rests on two pillars: justice and loving-kindness. These are just another way to talk about those two primary Divine dance steps we've already learned about — concealing and revealing.

But the tzaddik also knows one thing more, one thing that makes all the difference. He knows that:

God loves justice...but He loves mercy even more.

If you lose sight of this, you've lost the most important piece of the picture. If you lose touch with this, you're in danger of thinking that the Infinite One has placed burdens *on* you, instead of opportunities *before* you!

And this is how humanity's relationship with the Creator began to deteriorate. After Adam and Eve, generation after generation wandered further away from the consciousness of Divine unity and love. They tore a hole in the unified fabric of Creation. And with weaker awareness of loving-kindness, there was less and less willingness to hold onto the structure of justice and righteous action, causing mankind to lose its inborn moral stature. For ten generations, humanity descended into ever-deeper pits of immorality, blocking the Divine flow of mercy and abundance more and more — until Noah.

THE BALANCED MAN

TEN GENERATIONS AFTER ADAM, A new soul descended to the world — Noah. His name teaches us about the role he played in the progression of history. Noah, really *Noach*, stems from the Hebrew root *nach* (the letters *nun-chet*), meaning rest, ease, and comfort. And when the letters of his name are reversed (to become *chet-nun*) they spell *chein* — grace that is the outward expression of inner balance.

The Torah tells us, "Noah found *chein* — grace — in the eyes of God." And why did Noah find favor in the Creator's eyes? Because Noah unified the two qualities represented by the letters *chet* and *nun* of *chein*. *Chet* symbolizes the expansive force of wisdom or *chochmah*; *nun* symbolizes the "kingly" or "controlling" point of restraint. His generation desperately lacked the capacity for self-restraint, and the counterpoint force of receptivity to Divine wisdom.

Noah found mercy in God's eyes and reflected the Creator's own mercy right back into the Divine Eye. By doing so, he opened a channel for God's endless mercy to begin to flow again to the world — in a revealed way.

God's endless mercy is always flowing in a hidden way, though. It has to, otherwise nothing could exist; there would be no energy to keep the universe running. Divine mercy is always there, behind the scenes. But it's not supposed to be hidden; it was meant to be brought into our awareness, developed and expanded. And that requires our participation.

The people of Noah's time were steeped in theft and sexual immorality, and Noah was the only person who stood up as an example of the very opposite — charity and justice. Again, we return to our basic dance steps of Creation — making space through self-restraint (justice) and righteous giving (charity).

In a time when corruption was woven into the fabric of society, when no one could trust anyone else and no one was safe from being exploited by anyone else, Noah was a giver. In a time when the untamed sexual impulse was destroying the world around him — even the animals had begun to defy their natures and mate outside their species — Noah lived a life of purity and simplicity with his wife. And each of their three sons followed in their parents' way and held to their spouses in an increasingly unstable world.

During their year inside the ark, all four couples refrained from intimacy; while the world is in the process of being destroyed, you can't be focused on your own pleasure. That's just confirmation of the righteousness of that family. When it was time to act with self-restraint, they did. They spent that year, instead, devoted to the care of the creatures in their traveling biosphere — a year of selfless attention to the needs of every form of life, from tending the deer to cultivating the kind of grass on which it feeds best. Again, those two dance steps, justice and mercy,

The flood teaches us that human immorality can corrupt all of Creation; Noah teaches us that a single individual can realign Creation with its purpose. Righteous individuals who perfect and live with a balance of these two qualities act as eternal bridges to the Divine. God's pact with Noah will *never* be broken; in the merit of one man, no flood like that will ever return.

> Your actions can uplift the world or destroy it — that is your Divine potential.

A tzaddik is like a laser beam; he cuts through the externals of every situation to its inner, Divine workings. He connects with the unified truth at the heart of everything he encounters. This is the grace Noah found in God's eyes. Noah saved the world and he saved himself, but he couldn't save the people of his time. At Noah's stage of the progression, not enough work had been done to get all of humanity back into alignment. That would require the efforts of other spiritual masters over the course of history...

THE ARK

NOAH'S UPRIGHTNESS, HIS BEING TUNED in to the Divine Will, and his desire to serve as a conduit for the revelation of the Divine Will, transformed him into a kind of receiver. Noah made himself "available" to the Creator, Who shared with Noah His vision to ensure the future: *the ark.*

The ark would transport Noah, his family, and their Divine gene-bank out of a world of destruction and limitation into a pristine, new world so that humanity could have another chance to realign itself.

The ark was meant to be a traveling biosphere that ran on loving-kindness, so the reborn world could begin from this ideal starting point. It was going to be really hard work. It demanded constant selfless attention to the needs of other creatures, for the sake of a future hanging by a thread. The ark isn't really a boat; it's a bridge, a conduit for channeling Divine mercy into the world. The person willing to serve as that channel cannot allow self-interest to get in the way.

When we look at God's instructions for building the ark, we immediately notice how detailed they are. *These* materials, *these* specifications, this exact size, this exact form.

The Creator of the universe hasn't got anything more important to do than planning a construction project?

> *Light needs a vessel to contain it.*
> *A vessel without light is an empty shell,*
> *but light without a vessel has nowhere to dwell.*

The command to build the ark came with detailed specs — the constrictions and measurements that give it form so it can serve as a vessel for the Divine light. The ark is actually the prototype of every mitzvah, Torah commandment. That's because every Torah commandment is a "connection-bridge." And just like the ark, every mitzvah has its definition, its materials, its time and place in which it applies. Each mitzvah is a fully formed vessel with its own structural integrity.

> Just like the ark, every mitzvah has its definition, its materials, its time and place in which it applies.

We learned earlier that contraction had to come before Creation. The Infinite One's first act of Creation was making a space in which reality could come to be. To make that space, God contracted Himself and withdrew, and then drew a channel of Divine light into it to provide it with vitality. This paradigm is at the root of the structure of all mitzvot. Mitzvot are light-containers, and like all well-engineered vessels, they're extremely precise in their construction.

Let's bring this down to earth by looking at a very detail-grounded mitzvah like tefillin. These are the black boxes I bind onto my head and left arm every day, which contain parchments from the Torah. In the mitzvah of tefillin, we see this perfect joining of vessel and light.

For years I worked as a scribe, inking the ancient scripts the exact same way Jews have done for thousands of years. The particulars are super-specific: boxes are made of leather, not of gold; text written on parchment, not paper; four specific paragraphs from the Torah belong in them, and no others; every letter precisely formed, every space just this size. And to properly carry out the mitzvah of writing the texts for tefillin, you must give it your complete focus. That includes restraining yourself from doing anything else at the time.

All these strictures and structures are only to ensure the integrity of the vessel so it can fulfill its purpose. The vessel is a conduit — like the ark — designed to carry the flow of Divine light and mercy.

And the flow isn't only meant for you; it's meant for the whole world.

You dance with the Divine — you follow particular steps to stay aligned — and the Divine energy just flows. It flows into you and through you, and reveals Godliness throughout the world.

THE
RAVEN

DO YOU REMEMBER OUR FRIEND from the introduction, the raven? Who gets stuck in his unproductive patterns and can't get himself loose? As we learn more about Noah's role in catalyzing a shift in the history of spiritual consciousness, we need to get better acquainted with that raven. He has a lot to teach us about ourselves...and we're grateful to him for it.

The first time we meet the raven in the Bible, it's just as the floodwaters begin to subside. Remember, every animal that made it onto the ark got there because it felt a natural pull toward the aligned path of the tzaddik, Noah. So the raven is far from a villain, and it's important to remember that as the story unfolds.

Noah sent out the raven to look for a sign of life; he tapped the bird on the shoulder, so to speak, and said, "Have I got a mission for you!" The sages taught, though, that the raven was — unfortunately — suspicious of Noah's offer. It fluttered around the ark instead, refusing to set out on the search for dry land.

Again, we find that seed of doubt that goes back to Adam and the serpent: *"You don't really mean that this mission is for* ***me***, *Noah. You're really out for yourself and just loading your burdens onto my feathered shoulders. Well, who says I'm interested? What's in it for me? And who's going to keep an eye on my mate while I'm gone?"*

Noah was giving the raven — the bird of self and ego — an opportunity to be a player, to be a participant and a giver, for the benefit of everyone. But the raven didn't want to take up the challenge, so all we see in the Bible is that Noah sends the raven away and then hands the mission over to the dove, who was willing.

We said the raven has a lot to teach us about ourselves. Here's one of those teachings: Every day, we get the same chance the raven did. Every day, my Creator taps me on the shoulder and says, "Have I got a mission for you!" And I have to believe that the mission, which might appear to be a narrow channel, will actually help me transcend my limitations and access all the infinite goodness within that mission.

The raven only sees the limitation — he can't see the opportunity.

We can learn from the raven's mistakes. Learn to look beyond the limitation, and see the opportunity. To recognize what it feels like when the Creator is tapping us on the shoulder. To trust the Creator's missions.

> *Opportunities to bond with the Infinite One arrive in packages that are defined and limited.*

The universe is filled with billions of people, endless objects and forces, and my day is only a microcosm of that. Just as all of that multiplicity is only a mask for the Creator's unity, so is my day with all of the forces that drive right through it. Each day has many portals to infinity hiding within it, if our minds and hearts are focused. If we can leave our raven-minds behind.

By the way, I don't want to sound negatively disposed to ravens; they're beautiful, majestic birds, but ancient tradition depicts them as having a cruel nature. Maybe it's the blackness of their plumage, or the fact that they're uncannily clever scavengers, but they remain the symbol of selfishness.

The Talmud states that ravens withhold food from their young, leaving them to fend for themselves. And poor Edgar Allan Poe, getting tortured by that big bird croaking, "Nevermore." Even that has something to teach us:

> *The raven is the symbol of "never more" — absolute limit, end of story, don't look for mercy or another chance here.*
> *We all have a raven inside of us.*

During the reign of Ahab and Jezebel, the prophet Elijah was sent to the royal couple with a message of Divine displeasure. After delivering it, the Infinite One sent Elijah into hiding to escape the king and queen's fury, to a desolate place far from civilization where he would have access to water but not food. God promised Elijah, "And I will send the ravens to feed you," and they arrived right on schedule. But they didn't just bring him bits and crumbs scavenged from the fields and towns. They brought him bread and meat straight from the king's table — feasts delivered to the prophet, morning and evening.

But why would the Creator send the food through ravens? Why not peaceful birds like doves? Or powerful and lordly birds like eagles? Why would God send Elijah his sustenance — for several years — through birds that are the mascots of cruel self-interest?

The Infinite One made it clear that when you align with the Divine Will — like Elijah the Prophet did — even the least likely agent can be the emissary of boundless kindness.

The great Chassidic master, Rebbe Nachman of Breslov, used this image of the raven — and how even the raven's nature can change — to express the ways in which it's possible for us to break out of our ingrained habits and tendencies. We're all ravens, stuck in various "nevermore" modes — tight, ungenerous, cruel, self-focused. But we don't have to stay stuck there. We can break out of the "raven haven" — the mindset of limitation and lack. To do that, however, we need to understand the raven-mind really well.

Here's a great example of someone who really understood the raven-mind:

> *Rabbi Usher Freund, a tzaddik who lived in Jerusalem until not long ago, devoted his life to helping the poor and disenfranchised. His home was open to all.*
>
> *During the late afternoon meal of Shabbos, the spiritual pinnacle of the holy day, it's customary for tzaddikim to share words of Torah at their gatherings. Yet Reb Usher, as he was known, would instead sit at the head of the table and ask each guest (and there were often dozens of them) exactly what he*

wanted to eat. He would spoon out spreads and salads onto each person's plate, just as they ordered, and by the time he was finished there was never any time for him to teach.

Once, a prominent rabbi came to join him for the meal, and when it was over he asked Reb Usher why he had spent such precious time doling out food instead of Torah.

Reb Usher answered, "By nature, I'm not a giver. Every spoonful of tahini is deep spiritual work for me — I must overcome my tendency to withhold. So my highest moments are best spent giving out food to the hungry."

THE RAVEN HAVEN

MOST PEOPLE LIVE IN FEAR whether they realize it or not. They fear sickness. They fear poverty. They fear rejection and loss, and, more than anything, they fear death. That primary fear of our own mortality affects us all. But we only begin to really live after we accept the reality of death. People afraid of dying are in a state of conscious or unconscious fear every moment of every day of their lives. But the Infinite One didn't create us to exist in chronic fear. That's not the way we're meant to live.

Mortality isn't a punishment — it's a gift that prods us into remembering that our lives need to have purpose.

Imagine a group of children sitting and playing on the floor. There are all kinds of kids there, but one of them is really uptight because he knows that Mommy said, "At 3 p.m., the game is over." So even though it's only 1 p.m. right now, all this child can think of is that soon the game will be over. So even though he sits and plays along with the rest for those two hours, he's not really enjoying himself. Knowing it'll be over soon ruins all his pleasure.

All of our fears are grounded in the seeming hard limits of physical reality — there's only so much time, only so many resources, only so much space. But physical reality isn't all there is. There's a spiritual plane of existence, unbounded by time and space, and we align with the spiritual plane every time we transcend the natural boundaries of our own natures and fears.

We don't really talk about Heaven too much; the Torah tradition speaks instead of "The World to Come." But even that's a pretty poor translation for the original Hebrew, *olam haba*, better translated as "The World That Is Constantly Coming." *Olam haba* is a spiritual future of absolute vitality and revealed Godliness, and it is the innermost soul of our physical universe.

There aren't really two worlds — This One and The Next One — anymore than there are two of you, a physical you and a spiritual you. There's only one world, but just like the body asserts its presence far more than the soul does in the physical world, this world's physical nature is far more apparent than its inner, spiritual nature.

Nonetheless, the innermost essence is in a state of constant and increasing manifestation. Our highest purpose is to help that process unfold. How can we help that process? Through activating our own hidden spiritual nature. We'll be learning a lot more about this idea later on, in the section called, "Beyond Time." But we've already seen that the key to that activation is through giving.

When the Torah speaks of the natural human tendency to be tight, to remain in the realm of physical limitations, we find that it warns against the "selfish thought in your heart" — that's your raven-voice telling you to withhold your assistance from your brother who needs it.

But: "You shall give to him and *don't feel badly about it when you do*; God will bless you in all that you do *because* of your giving." Through the transformative act of radical giving, you'll bring yourself into alignment — and experience Divine blessing.

Don't be afraid. Just keep giving.

But we also learn that, "The poor will never cease from the land..." Does a kind and omnipotent God really tell the world to expect poverty to remain forever? Shouldn't we look forward to the end of poverty? I, for one, would really love to live in a world where everyone has exactly what they need. So, why did God create pockets of darkness in the world?

> Don't be afraid. Just keep giving.

"...Therefore, I command you, to open your hand to your brother, your poor, to the destitute among you."

When we participate in drawing abundance into those dark spaces, we reveal an even higher degree of Divine mercy. It isn't only the Infinite One Who is merciful; the Godly spark in every one of us is capable of mercy and compassion. Sure, the Creator could eliminate poverty all by Himself; He could have kept it from existing in the first place. But it's when the sparks of the Infinite within us are mobilized to alleviate suffering that the infinite nature of His mercy is revealed.

TRANSFORM YOUR RAVEN

WHEN WE TALK ABOUT GIVING, there are layers and levels. Opportunities for giving are infinite, and the general guideline is to follow your heart's desire. The form of compassionate action that resonates with you — with your nature, your resources, and your circumstances — is the best place to begin. But when we talk about the heart's desire, we're leaving out another important element of giving — *transformative giving*. They're not always the same thing.

If a stranger stops you on the street and asks for money for food and you pull five dollars out of your pocket, you've fulfilled the obligation of giving charity. But although you've given, you haven't necessarily done the spiritual work, the transformative work that makes you *a giver*.

You've given, but you haven't yet received the gift of transformation.

What's the difference between handing out money, and the kind of giving that alters you as a human being?

> We're here to stretch our natural boundaries...to transcend the limitations of our natures.

Everyone has his own unique nature, and our task is to stretch the boundaries — gently, intelligently, and in a healthy way — so that we participate in *becoming* our ideal self.

So for example, when you're a kind person by nature — and the word *nature* here is very significant — then giving comes...naturally. That's great — it means that helping other people comes more easily and you can accomplish beautiful things in the world. But the act of giving, when it's coming naturally, isn't a transformative act *for the giver*. It's not the spiritual work of giving charity, even though it's a generous act of kindness.

Good people — and thankfully, that's a lot of us — have giving natures and that's great. But there's nothing spiritually dynamic in that kind of giving. When we get static in our giving — when there's no real internal movement there — it's a bigger missed opportunity than most of us realize.

I'm not talking about giving until it hurts, so far above and beyond your comfort zone that it's unnatural and painful. It doesn't have to be that way. But stretching our limits and breaking out of our raven-nature (even when we're pretty generous naturally) is the key that opens all doors of spiritual growth and change. It is *the* transformative act. It is the beginning of all beginnings.

No matter how much of a natural giver you are, you still have the raven inside of you. You have your lines of demarcation, your usual limits of to whom you want to give, what to give, how much to give, when to give, and in what way you're most comfortable giving. "I'm willing to go so far for another person, but not an inch further." It's healthy to have boundaries, but if we really want to change and grow, those boundaries need to expand. And they don't expand on their own. Going past our usual limits in giving in any of these ways is our gateway to a new, higher self, but the first act of transformative giving — the stretch — will always be a challenge.

In the basic dance-move of existence, first there's a contraction, then there's creation. First is the darkness, then the light. "And it was evening, and it was morning...one day." To grow into the possible you, you're going to go through contractions — but as laboring women know, those contractions are really expansions.

When we really *know* that the feeling of pressure and constriction is actually the gateway to life, it no longer fills us with fear. Rather, it gives us energy to dance through the darkness.

THE CHANNEL
OF BLESSING

WE'VE SEEN SO FAR THAT the goal is to trigger the flow of Divine abundance by breaking through our fears. Nothing is lacking — nothing is even scarce — because the One is Infinite and has more than enough for everyone. The only place we find lack is where there's an obstruction in the flow. How do we remove that obstruction? The main way to open the pathways of blessing is through openhearted giving.

We are created in the image of God, and we have free will rooted in the absolute freedom of the Divine Will. Everything we do, say, think, believe, and want powerfully impacts the degree of vitality flowing through the system. Our channels, our spiritual mechanisms, are patterned after the Divine model; that's what it means to be created in God's image. And when we change ourselves, we change the entire system.

If you want to experience the flow of Godly vitality through you, you have to make yourself into a channel that can carry it. If you want to experience Divine blessing...you have to **be** a Divine blessing.

Think about the difference between a pipeline and a vessel. If you take a cylinder of wood, you can drill all the way through and make it into a conduit. If you only drill most of the way through, it becomes a vessel.

> If you want to experience Divine blessing...you have to *be* a Divine blessing.

The vessel can receive, but it's just a cup — it keeps the flow for itself, and once it's full no more can get in.

The conduit, on the other hand, is open-ended. It isn't concerned with holding on to what comes into it; that's how the flow keeps moving.

Now imagine we're talking about a conduit that's alive, like your intestines. Their energy comes to them by way of the nourishment that flows through them; if they get blocked, however, not only would the whole system suffer, but the vessels wouldn't survive either. *When that which was designed to be a pipeline chooses instead to be a vessel, an end-user, it suffers along with those whose nourishment was dependent on it.*

So how do we transform our "end-user" selves into pipelines? If we want to flow with Divine blessing we need to overcome our natural fear of scarcity — our raven, remember him? — and share, share, share. We have to become less grasping, and stop holding on so tightly because we're scared that if we let go, we'll lose out. *We need to realize that in giving, we're exactly in tune with the flow of goodness...and we'll never suffer for letting go of that frightened, tightened grip.*

This world isn't naturally the place of abundance — *it's the place where our natural tendency to restriction has to be transformed into abundance.*

It's not naturally the place of goodness — *it's the place where our natural tendency to evil must be transformed into good.*

It's not the place of light — *it's where we can transform the pervasive darkness within ourselves into light.*

NOAH'S UNFINISHED BUSINESS

NOW THAT WE BETTER UNDERSTAND the nature of mercy and the ways of the raven-mind, it's time to return to Noah.

We all know Noah was a righteous man who saved the planet and a sampling of all its life, but Noah didn't draw down enough mercy to save the rest of the world. Not even close. *Noah's ark of connection was enough to save him...but it wasn't nearly broad enough to save the rest of the world.*

> Noah's ark of connection was enough to save him...but it wasn't nearly broad enough to save the rest of the world.

The mystical text of the *Zohar* lets us peek behind the scenes to learn a little more about what happened when Noah emerged with his family from the ark. When he saw a glorious world reduced to mud, Noah cried out, "God of mercy, where was Your mercy?" How could You, a loving God, have destroyed Your world and everything in it? *Where was Your quality of mercy when the world really needed it?*

The Infinite One answered, "Noah, where was *your* mercy?" I warned you that the world was in danger, but you only saved yourself and your family. You might have been right that the people of your time were beyond your reach...*but why didn't you pray that I would forgive them and let them live?*

Yes, Noah saved the world. He built an ark, a bridge, an eternal connection with the Divine that lives on even now...but it's a narrow bridge. It was a self-contained vessel. Noah's ark was wondrous, and in building it and entering into it with his small world, he is our model of a person who chooses to align with the *inner purpose* of life. But Noah didn't manage to translate his inner connection into a pathway *out in the world* that others could follow. His ark was a Tree of Life, a connected and thriving space, but it wasn't big enough to encompass the entire world. He drew down Divine mercy, but not enough to save the undeserving. It was a thin stream of Divine mercy, just enough for himself and those upright and deserving few...like him.

There was still a long way to go.

The next stop on the progression would be the individual the Infinite One called "Little Sister" — Abraham. In Hebrew, the word for sister is *achot*, from the same root as the word for mending and repair.

Abraham would begin to mend the original tear in Creation that Adam had caused. And although Noah's business was left unfinished, without Noah there could never have been an Abraham. Yes, Noah's bridge needed broadening, but without that narrow bridge, Abraham wouldn't have had a foundation on which to work.

You see? It's a progression.

THE BRIDGE

TEN GENERATIONS AFTER NOAH, A soul descended into the world —
"like a star rising in the east" — in Mesopotamia, the ancient cradle of civilization. This was Abraham. Despite being born into a home and a culture
of idolatrous polytheism, Abraham's shining soul was destined to expand
on Noah's work. He would widen Noah's ark-pathway over the floodwaters
into a bridge anyone could use to reach God. He would share a revolutionary concept with the world, in a radically new way.

Abraham was an independent thinker from a young age. As soon
as he was old enough to reason through his impressions of the world
around him, he came to the conclusion that there could only be a single
primal cause and active force within existence. And that's with a father
who sold idols for a living.

Abraham saw right through the false concepts of his own time and
culture. As he got older, he became more and more attuned to an inner
directive, while his dependence on the approval of people around him
got ever weaker.

Abraham journeyed through life paying attention to the implications
of phenomena and events. He didn't only *see*; he also contemplated
the significance of everything he saw. Abraham was seventy-five years
old when the Creator finally spoke with him. But Abraham didn't just
happen to stumble across God; he *tuned in*. His "receivers" to hear the
Divine voice were the result of decades of inner work.

What's fascinating is that this dynamic is as true now as it ever was:
if we want to experience contact with the Creator, we have to invest
energy in refining our receivers. To allow the Divine into our lives, we
align our own ways with the Creator's way — we straighten out what's
bent, and expand the good. It's the work of a lifetime.

Abraham was a truth-seeker, and he reached his most important
truth — that there is only one God — through paying careful attention

to the world around him. The Talmud describes his process by way of a parable:

> *Rabbi Yitzchak said: "Abraham's discovery can be compared to a traveler who passed a castle that blazed with light. He said, 'Can it be that the castle has no ruler?' The owner peeked out at him and said, 'I am the master of the castle.' Because Abraham would say, 'Can it be that this world has no ruler?' The Holy One peeked out at him and declared, 'I am the Master of the world.'"*

The world appeared to Abraham as a beautiful edifice, far too well designed to have just arisen by itself. And although it seemed empty and unclaimed, Abraham could see the inner Divinity illuminating the structure of the world from the inside, even though the actual owner was nowhere to be seen.

The world had already been subject to a flood, to social and physical breakdowns during early human history; Abraham was certain that an Infinite Intelligence was behind the illusion that these were just random events. And then the Creator revealed Himself to Abraham; the Infinite One *responded* to Abraham's search for truth. The master of the castle peeked out and showed Himself.

Abraham was on his own in his quest. In fact, he had to overcome fierce opposition as he developed and shared the monotheistic idea. The verse says that "Abraham was *one*" — he was the only person in his time with the strength to break away from a false way of living. And like Abraham, we all have to be willing to sometimes walk the path alone to stay in conscious contact with God.

> Like Abraham, we all have to be willing to sometimes walk the path alone to stay in conscious contact with God.

Walking an individual path doesn't mean being self-focused, however. It means staying aware that *you* have to do whatever spiritual work needs to be done. You can't do anyone else's, and no one else can do yours.

Just like Abraham.

GO TO
YOURSELF

AS WE MENTIONED EARLIER, WE find that the first words God said to Adam after he ate from the Tree of Knowledge of Good and Evil were, "Where are you?" Is it possible that the Infinite One was truly unaware of Adam's location? No, it's not. And that's because God's question is so much deeper. The Chassidic masters teach that those words reverberate to all of us through all time; they are relevant to everyone, everywhere. The Creator calls out to us, *"Where are you?"* Where is *the real you* hiding?

When the Creator first spoke to Abraham, in Genesis 12:1, it was with a simple phrase directing him to leave his place of birth. *"Lech Lecha —* go *for* yourself"; it's for your own good, you'll see blessing in it. But the mystics read this direction as "Go *to* yourself." Leave behind all of the false definitions and external selves you've built up over seventy-five years of living in this world. Go and discover who you really are.

This is the essential mission that every soul is sent out to accomplish, not just Abraham.

When we look back at the model of Abraham, we see that God told him to go to himself by getting away from "...your *land*, your *birthplace*, and from your *father's house.*" To uncover your true self, you have to be willing to shed the *assumptions of your society*, your *natural inclinations*, and the habits you formed in your *family of origin*.

Until we consciously "go forth from them," we're tethered to so many beliefs — both conscious and beneath the surface — that can keep us spinning our wheels for a lifetime.

Most of the thoughts we truly believe are the products of our own minds (*our* thoughts, not what we read online or saw on television) are really just projections of the ego, the external self that wants to Edge

God Out. But how am I supposed to get beyond these projections if the most internal I can get are my own thoughts?

The first step is to be aware that there's a soul.

The second step is to know that I *am* — not that I *have* — a soul.

When a soul descends from a purely spiritual existence into the physical world, its outermost garment is the body. So our primary approach to the body is that you aren't a body; you *have* a body. There is a *you* — a true internal you — that possesses or wears this body as its most external and material garment. The body, just like the world in its relationship to God, conceals and reveals the soul that inhabits it.

> The first step is to be aware that there's a soul.

The second step is to know that I *am* — not that I *have* — a soul.

The outermost soul-garment, the body, is the easiest to see — it's on the surface. So the body is a concealer. When a person is hyperfocused on the externalities of life, it really can hide the soul. On the other hand, when that outer garment acts as a real partner to the inner soul, it helps to reveal the soul — its existence, its goodness, its purpose.

A more subtle garment is one's external identity, what we call the ego. Just like the body, the ego can also hide the true self. But when the external self unites with one's essence, and expresses that soul at the core, the external self becomes our partner in helping us achieve our higher mission in life. Again, we're talking about uniting those two trees — that inner soul with the outer garments of our selves — so we can live in a whole and aligned way.

Even though we're carrying all of these different layers and acting through them, there's still only a single, true "I" that exists within, just as there's only one God within all of the layers and garments of nature and Divine attributes, instilling all reality with vitality and wisdom.

The external ego is naturally self-seeking — it does a lot of Edging God Out. The soul, however, is one with its source.

The ego is judgmental and negative — it has trouble connecting. The soul, on the other hand, is merciful and compassionate and yearns for unity.

The ego is embodied within the layers of false identity that have to be sheared away from the core.

The soul controls the balance-point of alignment with the Divine at all times.

God understands well the power of the body-soul-ego divide; He created us, after all. He also knows we're capable of living in a whole and aligned way — and uniting those two trees. The Creator invited Abraham — invites all of us — to leave false identities behind us and take a journey to the true self.

PIERCING
THE VEILS

ABRAHAM WAS TAUGHT OVER A long period of time that the state of nature is only meant to be a starting point; it's not the final destination. At nearly one hundred years of age, and after more than two decades of devotion to the way of mercy and unified God-consciousness, Abraham received another Divine communication.

The Creator was giving Abraham a new opportunity to further perfect himself and bond with Him. Just as God first provided Abraham with a family of origin and a primary nature and environment to strip away, God also formed him with a foreskin and only afterward commanded him to remove it.

Abraham spent a lifetime refining his nature and his receptivity to the Divine Will, and at a certain point the Creator made clear to him that to really carry forward that first instruction to discover his true self, Abraham would have to alter his relationship with his body in an essential way.

> *Circumcision provides us with a vision of an ideal...but we're supposed to be participants in reaching that ideal.*

If ego is Edge God Out, circumcision is the ultimate Let God In — let the Divine light of the soul into your body so it becomes a transformed garment. Circumcision, then, is a model of all of the places in our existence where God leaves gaps of imperfection and lack so that we can partner with our Creator to bring completion to reality. The word for circumcision is *brit*, which really means a pact or covenant. The relationship between God and Noah after the flood was also called a *brit*, but through Abraham's act, the *brit* was made personal and much more powerful.

The essential pact we make with God is to take the raw material of our lives — the circumstances of our birth, our natural inclinations, our assumptions — and pierce them to let God in. We don't rely on our default settings; we change them as needed, to get into increasing alignment with the Divine.

The foundation of the first mitzvah is this willingness to break away from the past, from the state of nature, to run after God.

This is Ground Zero of Judaism.

Breaking out of the state of nature to run after God is the foundation of Judaism

Since Abraham's time, Jews circumcise on the eighth day of a baby boy's life, when his parents do the work for him, in a way. This parallels God's taking the initiative to propel Abraham out of his land, his birthplace, and his father's house. "Go to yourself..." — it had the tone of command. Yes, it's "for yourself" — for your benefit — but there is a push inside that word, "Go!"

Abraham first *went*, and the journey brought him to the *brit*. As the children of Abraham, that first Divine push out of the state of nature is a gift. It's then up to us to continue our quest to discover our inner, truest selves.

THE HUMAN...
BEING

THE TRADITION TEACHES US THAT even though Abraham filled his life with mitzvot and devoted himself to the revelation of Divine loving-kindness in the world, he wasn't called "whole" until he circumcised himself.

What we would consider diminishment — the physical cutting away of a part of the body — the Torah calls wholeness or perfection. Really, it means oneness. Circumcision made Abraham *one*. "Walk before Me, and be whole," the Divine voice told him. By doing this small act — which isn't small at all — you will become whole.

Why *do* we circumcise our sons at the tender age of eight days? Why not wait until the child is old enough to assume the responsibility to bring *himself* into the state of *brit* — this covenantal relationship with the Creator? It's because we understand that, although the state of nature may be beautiful, it's only a starting point. We were placed here to participate in the *achievement* of wholeness and perfection. The child is given the gift of a unified beginning, without having to struggle through the preliminary stripping-away Abraham had to do for himself. Even though that child is still going to need to "go to himself," just like Abraham, he's given the opportunity to begin from a place of holiness and move forward from there.

The unity of body and soul, this wholeness, is called *being*, not *doing*. We gift the child with *human being* — the opportunity to start from the point of integration and unity.

> The unity of body and soul created by circumcision is the starting point for a life of being, not just a life of doing.

79

What the child does with this gift is up to him; it's up to all of us.

We're so busy *doing*; we're so busy performing our endless lists of tasks that we lose touch with ourselves. We can be in the middle of a business deal or a conversation with a client or a coworker, and our minds are somewhere else entirely. That's the human *doing*, not the human *being*. That's fractured; it's not whole.

We were created for greater things than that.

When that primary connection is made, when the light of the soul has a gateway through which it can permeate the body, that connection transforms the rest of the mitzvot we do.

The Kabbalistic tradition teaches us that every mitzvah is a specific packet of Divine light in a small, accessible form. Of these Divine directives there are 248 "dos" and 365 "don'ts" — paralleling the 248 "limbs" and 365 "sinews" of the soul-form called "Supernal Man." Mitzvot nourish and sustain the spiritual self, allowing the full flow of Divine vitality to reach every part of us. And the spiritual self is reflected in the physical structure of our bodies.

The *brit* allows the light of every mitzvah we do to spread throughout our bodies, to vitalize each limb and organ that corresponds to that *mitzvah*. This is the gateway to wholeness. That integration has a ripple effect on the way our minds operate so that we can live consciously. We can become *human beings* — body, emotions, mind, and soul all working together as a single, organic whole, toward a single purpose, with everything that we do.

SPIRITUAL EVOLUTION

ABRAHAM'S JOURNEY OF SELF-DISCOVERY DIDN'T end with leaving his father's land and setting out for a new one. His life was an evolution, where the new insight and action of each stage brought him forward into the next.

Abraham began by focusing a lens of faith on the world outside — and he found God. His discovery made him receptive to the Divine communication to leave his comfortable point of origin and step out into the unknown, to follow his higher destiny. This so refined him that his physicality came to reflect his transcendent spiritual nature — he circumcised himself.

Abraham then took his wife and household and began the next phase of his life — sharing his vision of Divine loving-kindness with a world badly in need of mercy and compassion. Everywhere he traveled, his tent became a haven for the hungry, the weary, the needy. The four sides of his tent were open to all passersby in a harsh desert climate — Abraham only wanted an opportunity to share God's bounty with his visitors.

Abraham's giving — he provided food, drink, and shelter to wayfarers in the deserts of Mesopotamia — changed him. It also changed his guests. His giving wasn't just the giving of an individual named Abraham. He was a living manifestation of the Divine attribute of loving-kindness, and people felt this. When they ate Abraham's food, drank his wine and water, and slept under the shelter of his tent, they felt the love of the Infinite One operating through him. He spread his message of monotheism throughout the ancient world by mirroring the Divine attribute of loving-kindness.

There is a joy to be discovered in the process of transformation, and that's the joy this universe was designed to deliver. Not that God's mercy and kindness should just shower down upon us (although we really do get a lot of freebies here), but that we should get to experience the higher joy that comes from changing this world from a tight, self-interested place into a fountain of Divine generosity.

The way we trigger the flow is by breaking through our own natural barriers and letting free those first streams of true loving-kindness that exist inside of us in potential.

Mercy isn't really kindness. Mercy is what you activate when you do kindness for the other *when you don't naturally want to*. It's when you give to the person *you think is undeserving*. Mercy is what happens when the channel of cruelty is forced to serve as the conduit of kindness.

Breaking out of our "stuckness" requires massive action, like getting the car whose back wheels are in a snowbank out and moving. You, your friends, your neighbors, are going to have to get behind that heavy vehicle and push; otherwise you're just spinning your wheels. Massive action is what gets the stuck mass moving.

> Mercy isn't really kindness. Mercy is what you activate when you do kindness for the other *when you don't naturally want to*. It's when you give to the person *you think is undeserving*.

That unmoving mass is us. Charity — the *stretching* kind of giving — is the massive action that can get us out of our stuck places. And there are many stuck places for all of us.

According to the Kabbalistic tradition, there is a custom to give charity before we undertake an endeavor or set out to fulfill certain mitzvot. Before we try to open a new door, we go back to the beginning of all beginnings. When the Torah speaks of giving charity generously, it says, "You shall surely open your hand to your brother" (Deuteronomy 15:8). In the original Hebrew, though, the words can be read, "You will open an opening..." Charity is what first opens the door to all new beginnings, and Abraham's opening of his tent to give so generously to everyone is the beginning of *our* process of spiritual evolution.

To get your foot in the door of a new opening in your spiritual life, you first need to get it open a crack. Charity gets the door open a bit, and once it's open, charity helps it open even more. But for that act of giving to serve as a transformative door-opener, it's going to take energy. The giving of self, the boundary-stretching kind of giving, is what does it. And giving money is not the only way to do an act of charity. It can be money or time, energy or skill. Give what's needed. Give what you've got.

This is the beginning of all beginnings. It is the opening of all doorways.

THE WAY OF CHARITY AND JUSTICE

AS ABRAHAM ESCORTED HIS ANGELIC guests in the direction of Sodom to carry out their mission, the Torah provides us with what seems to be a private Divine insight:

> *Can I hide from Abraham that which I am about to do, when he is going to become a great and mighty nation...? For I know that he will command his children and his household after him, that they will keep the way of God, to do charity and justice..."*
>
> *(Genesis 18:17)*

The Creator asks Himself what appears to be a rhetorical question, "Can I hide?"

Of course, He can hide the knowledge of what will happen to Sodom and Gomorrah! We're talking about God; He can do whatever He wants. Not only that, but the Infinite One is the master of hiding — His Presence is so well hidden in Creation that it's possible for a person to live a whole lifetime without seeing it. Concealment is necessary if free will is to exist. Hiding is second nature for God, so to speak.

The Infinite One is the master of hiding — His Presence is so well hidden in Creation that it's possible for a person to live a whole lifetime without seeing it.

But Abraham spent his whole life seeking out the Hidden One... aligning himself with the Divine way, especially through devoting himself to a life of loving-kindness. This made him receptive to the Divine Will to such an extent that God Himself asks, "*Can I* hide this from Abraham?" Can I keep knowledge of what's to be from

84

Abraham, who has dedicated every bit of himself to seeking out My Will? Knowledge of My Will has become an inseparable part of him, so much so that I *know* that his children will be suffused with this path he has paved.

One of my students once said, "If God wants me to keep Shabbat, why doesn't He just let me know? If He would just tell me what He wants, I'd do it. Until then..."

I answered, "And if you weren't so preoccupied with your own needs and desires, deaf and blind to the Divine voice in the cosmos, you just might hear the words!" Too often our bandwidth is already taken up by other transmissions. But Abraham *was* listening.

Can I keep this knowledge from him, when he has spent his life devoted to demonstrating My loving-kindness in the world? After all, "I know that Abraham will teach his children after him My path — the way of *charity* and *justice*." Abraham is attuned to My dual path of charity and justice — he is fully aligned with Me.

We've already learned about these two basic dance-steps of creation. *Justice* means the establishment of necessary limits; *charity* indicates giving. First there was constriction of the Divine presence, but it was only to make space for Divine mercy — *charity* — to unfold. That's the Divine way, and it's the path that Abraham follows and will teach his children to follow, too. It's the path of balance and alignment with the Creator's essential attributes.

Charity was Abraham's defining attribute — he brought that Divine quality into its highest expression in the world of action. Justice was also a force within him; how could it not be, when he had turned away at such great cost from the immorality of his time? But it wasn't expressed to its fullness within him. Abraham's foretold future — Isaac — would take up the mission of bringing the quality of justice to its fullest expression.

This is the point of origin of the first Jewish child, Isaac. And it would be Isaac's task to carry on with his father's work and expand upon it, so that the revolutionary concept of One loving God could be unified to the absolute demands of Divine justice. Isaac is the one who ensures that Abraham's mission has a future.

FATHER AND SON

ISAAC, THE FIRST JEWISH CHILD, was a miracle.

Born to elderly parents whose childless fate was "written in the stars," Isaac's soul had to fight its way into the world.

Isaac — Yitzchak, in Hebrew — is the model of overcoming impossible challenges to carry out the Divine directive *no matter what*. His parents devoted a lifetime to prayer, his father underwent the transformation of circumcision at an advanced age, and at long last the Divine promise was realized.

When angels came to deliver the news of Sarah's imminent conception, she laughed, saying that everyone who hears of her bearing a child will be in stitches. Who wouldn't be, if they heard about a hundred-year-old man having a child with a ninety-year-old woman? And so the child's name will be Yitzchak — "He Will Laugh" — but Yitzchak is the one who laughs last. Aside from the fact that there's something laughable in a couple that old having a child, what's the connection between Isaac's essential nature and his name?

According to the Kabbalistic tradition, Isaac represents the attribute of justice and self-restraint, and we see it manifest in his capacity to act with force for a higher purpose. It's about overcoming the expected... overcoming the natural boundary for the supernatural goal. If there's something funny about that, it's not so obvious. So let's go deeper.

What makes a joke really funny? It starts with an ambiguity (a space the Kabbalists would call a *tzimtzum* — a kind of primordial vacuum of the unknown), which is then broken by the unexpected punch line. When our assumptions are overtaken unexpectedly, we laugh. Isaac is that punch line. Isaac is what happens when a human being, through

86

activating his will and changing his life, alters the course of the heavens and changes his fate. It's all about overcoming the locked and bound expectations of the natural.

And Abraham and Isaac are so very, very different. Abraham was a channel for revealing the Divine attribute of loving-kindness, which is endlessly generous and infinitely giving. Isaac appeared to be the opposite: a master of self-discipline, overcoming his natural desires so as to align with the quality of Divine justice. Yet the Torah confirms, *twice*, that no matter how different they appear to be, Abraham and Isaac are from the same root: "These are the offspring of Abraham...Abraham gave birth to Isaac" (Genesis 25:19).

The whole world laughed and thought that Sarah's child must be someone else's because she conceived soon after being taken captive by a foreign ruler after a lifetime of infertility with Abraham. But the Creator made Abraham's and Isaac's faces identical so no one could make a mistake. The outward form expresses the internal essence. Even though it appears as though they can't possibly be related, they spring from the same source.

There are different pathways to achieving unity with the Creator; different attributes we cultivate to mirror the Divine attributes. But just as all of those qualities are only reflections of the Unique One, so too are all these different pathways unified at their source.

Abraham's path is so different from Isaac's, but both are involved in the same basic work. They just go about it differently. And each master that came to the world expanded on the path laid down before him; he just did it in his own, unique way. It's not only true of the tzaddikim throughout the ages, but also of every one of us. Every person has his own particular attribute to cultivate that is his individual contribution to the revelation of Godliness.

Isaac's gift is different from his father's, but we shouldn't think that just because he's a master of self-command that his channel isn't a wide-open conduit of blessing. That would be a mistake; there's abundance in the attribute of loving-kindness, and there's bounty to be discovered in *din*, holy judgment and restraint.

After the death of Abraham, we learn that Isaac settled down and planted measures of seed, and reaped one hundredfold of what he sowed. The verse ends, "And God blessed him." It was a time of famine, and Isaac's yield was one hundred times the expected amount. This was a degree of blessing even Abraham didn't see. Joining the work of father and son bore fruits that everyone could touch and appreciate.

The work of Isaac evolves from the completion of the work of Abraham. But why should "Abraham give birth to Isaac?" *Why* does perfection of the quality of loving-kindness pave the way for the completion of the attribute of Divine justice?

One of the main messages of this book is that the Divine directives flow from love and not from harsh restriction. To joyfully take up a life that includes holy boundaries, you have to really and profoundly feel and know that every limit is inscribed with the deepest love.

> To joyfully take up a life that includes holy boundaries, you have to really and profoundly feel and know that every limit is inscribed with the deepest love.

Over the years, countless people have joined us for Shabbos meals; our home has been open to guests and visitors from every conceivable background. Many students have asked me how my wife and I have managed to raise a family — children who are now raising families of their own — devoted to traditional observance in a world so often opposed to those ideals and practices.

"How do you do it?" they want to know. "We live in turbulent times, temptation is everywhere, and all of your kids are on such a good path. And your home was so open! Your children were exposed to so many different possible lifestyles; why were you confident that the exposure wouldn't draw them away from you?"

But that's exactly what we're talking about here. When love abounds, when kindness and understanding and trust are the foundation of our relationships with our children, what seem to be "restrictions" on their lives don't feel like that to them. They just feel like part of that love.

A child can accept the limits set by a parent *as long as the child is secure in that parent's boundless love.* And that will be true even if the limit that's been set isn't so comprehensible to the child. As we'll see in the next section, Isaac is the greatest model we have of a child acting with the highest degree of self-restraint. He could do the unthinkable — be willing to offer himself in total self-sacrifice — because he had total trust in his loving father, and in his beloved Creator.

As we learned earlier, Adam's interaction with the serpent in the Garden of Eden broke that relationship of loving trust with the Creator. Adam lost his connection. But Abraham and Isaac, with their loving-kindness and uprightness, restored it. Together, they did more than revive the old connection — they opened up a fresh path.

THE
BINDING

BOTH ABRAHAM AND ISAAC REACHED the apex of their lives at the same moment — on the top of Mount Moriah, at the binding of Isaac. It was the most challenging of Abraham's ten trials, and demanded of Isaac the seemingly impossible.

As we've already learned, there was no force within Abraham as powerful as his loving-kindness and compassion. He spent a lifetime cultivating that quality until it was perfect. And then he was commanded by God to offer up his own child, in whom the Divine promise of a future people rested! Abraham had to set aside everything he thought he knew about his Creator and accept a Divine decree that made no sense.

But what about Isaac? We have this image of Isaac being just a boy at the time of the binding, but in truth he was by then a fully grown man — thirty-seven years old — in full possession of his adult strength and mind. He wasn't a child being carried passively; he *chose* to overcome the strongest natural force within a living creature — the will to live — and submit to his own destruction.

The entire incident is filled with the darkest and hardest questions. Why would a kind and loving God test them in this way? And why reverse the command at the very last moment, sparing Isaac just as the knife was on his throat? If Isaac was never really meant to be sacrificed as an offering, why put them through that trauma?

And why does the binding of Isaac play such a central role in Judaism — the foundation of every day's morning prayers, the bedrock of our Rosh Hashanah service, and even the guarantee of our future redemption from exile?

Here we are again, back with our dragons — those concepts we find so threatening at first. These kinds of questions are challenging, but they also give us wings that help us soar. The dragons are the guardians of treasures. The binding of Isaac must have deep relevance to us on a personal level, but what exactly are we meant to take away from the story? What's the message we're supposed to live and work with?

If we examine the essence of the binding, it's about the reality that sometimes we have to overcome ourselves — even our most essential self-definition — to stay attuned to the Divine Will. Sometimes God's directives will clash

> "Dragon" concepts — the ones that we find challenging — are the guardians of the deepest treasures.

with our nature, our way of understanding reality, and our convictions. What do we do then? *We follow Isaac's example and accept the directive anyway.* And, for us, that's like getting up on the altar; it's a sacrifice of self-will.

But Isaac's setting aside of self didn't only have to do with his literal act of self-sacrifice. The Kabbalistic tradition reveals a surprising facet of Isaac's nature to us.

Isaac didn't possess what's called a "masculine soul." Physically he was a man, but he possessed a feminine soul. And this mismatch meant he wouldn't be able to father children. It would mean that God's promise to Abraham would be null and void — no future nation would come from Isaac.

On the soul-level, Isaac actually had no future until the binding. The mystics teach us that at that critical moment when Isaac was fully ready to give his life to carry out the Divine Will, Isaac's "feminine" soul flew out of him and immediately incarnated within his future wife, Rebecca. At that instant, his masculine soul entered him. The Isaac that descended from the altar wasn't the same man who had laid himself down upon it. This Isaac would be able to father a nation.

Even though these concepts are very mystical and abstract, there are lessons for us to learn from them that have relevance to us in very practical ways.

Everyone's nature — *without exception* — is also misaligned in some ways. It doesn't have to be something like Isaac's story; it could be a gender or orientation issue, or any inner quality of ours that we find is out of harmony with the Divine directive.

We all come into the world wired in some way that demands self-mastery, and then our tendencies get solidified in our families of origin and our home communities and societies. We're angry people, jealous people, acquisitive people, fearful people, inconsiderate people — no one is born perfect and we all have a story. We all have a place where we're going to struggle. We learn why in the story of the binding — that submission and acceptance of the Divine Will is the gateway to transformation.

The greatest revelation of the Divine Will is found in the Torah, but not all of those guidelines are necessarily to our liking! Some of them tell us to curb our natural human appetites. Others instruct us to overcome our character defects, even when it feels like it's going to take superhuman effort. Does God have unreasonable expectations of us?

No, because He knows we have it within us to tap into Isaac's quality — the Kabbalistic attribute of *gevurah*, restraint. It's our inheritance, the legacy that Isaac left inside of each of us. That means that we also have it within us to move forward decisively, with energy and force and self-mastery, and we become further empowered by the vitality that comes from carrying out the Divine directive.

> We have it within us to overcome nature — our *own* nature — and that's the biggest miracle that exists.

We have it within us to overcome nature — our *own* nature — and that's the biggest miracle that exists.

ISAAC'S DEFENSE

IN THE END, GOD DIDN'T demand the sacrifice of Isaac — the command was recalled. Just like Isaac's birth was a cosmic joke, the binding was the culmination of the story of "He Will Laugh" — the ending isn't what we expected. It started off so dark and ended with so much light... we're still accessing that light now, and will until the end of time. The Talmud shares a narrative about Isaac's powers of heavenly negotiation:

> In the future, God will tell Abraham, "Your children have sinned."
>
> Abraham will say, "They should be wiped out to sanctify Your Name." He meant that the sins should be erased, but since his words were ambiguous, God sought another answer.
>
> "I will ask Jacob who suffered so much from his own children. Perhaps he will pray for them!" But Jacob's answer echoed Abraham's.
>
> The Creator said, "The elder lacks reasoning, and the younger lacks good counsel... I will ask Isaac."
>
> Isaac answered, "Did my children sin? Aren't they also Your children? And how much have they actually sinned? Most people live only seventy years. Deduct the first twenty, for which You do not punish; half of the remaining fifty are night, so only twenty-five years remain. Half of the daytime is occupied with prayer, eating, and using the bathroom, so only twelve-and-a-half years remain.
>
> Isaac concluded, "If You will bear their sin alone, good! But if You prefer, each of us will bear half. And if You don't agree to

this, I will bear all of it. I already offered my soul for You when I was bound on the altar!"

In this Talmudic scenario, we get to see just how Isaac's attribute of justice — *din* — allows him to act like a kind of cosmic defense attorney, presenting a precise accounting of liability and his ability to compensate for it. And, as a last resort, Isaac presents *himself* as the final exhibit, because he has already made the ultimate sacrifice, not only on his own behalf, but on behalf of all of his children-to-be. It's specifically Isaac's quality of justice that has the potential to mitigate the harsh heavenly judgments that will arise before the coming of the final redemption.

WELLS OF
LIVING WATER

NOW ALL THE WELLS THAT *Abraham's servants had dug...*
the Philistines had stopped them and filled them with earth...
And Isaac dug again the wells of water that they had dug in the
days of Abraham his father, for the Philistines had stopped them
after the death of Abraham. And he called their names after the
names by which his father had called them...And Isaac's servants
dug in the valley, and found there a [new] well of living water.

(Genesis 26:15–19)

What are these wells of living water? Clearly, we're talking about
something beyond physical reservoirs of water, because who stops up
functioning wells in the desert?! You might want to steal the resources
or set your own guards over them, but close them up completely? Fill
them with earth so even you can't use them?

The *Zohar* explains that we're talking about the life-giving waters of
faith and God-consciousness. To access those subterranean currents —
because they are always available, giving life to material reality — we
need to dig.

Everything that exists — every object, person, and situation — has
its own innermost point of vitality that defines, animates, and sustains
it. Within human beings, it's the soul. Within objects, it's the spark of
Divine wisdom. Within situations, it's what we call Providence — the
active Will of the Infinite One. Just like water sits below the surface of
the earth waiting to be tapped, so too does this innermost point pulse
with life underneath the facade of dense physicality of everything that
exists, just waiting to be discovered.

We're not talking about static well-water; beneath the earthiness of material reality are springs of groundwater, just yearning for the opportunity to burst to the surface. The soul was a vibrant, living piece of God blown into the inert matter of Adam. It's the link to the ultimate Source of all life, the Infinite One. It is a wellspring of living water, hidden beneath the material of the body.

> Everything that exists — every object, person, and situation — has its own innermost point of vitality that defines, animates, and sustains it. Within human beings, it's the soul.

Abraham dug his own wells to draw waters of awareness and belief to the surface so they could be enjoyed by everyone. But after his passing, the forces of a materialistic worldview — the "Philistines" — filled in the wells with earth. The progress that Abraham had made in sharing knowledge of the Infinite One and the soul with the world was in danger of being sealed back up again.

Abraham's wells were the vital waters of loving-kindness; they were touched by his own perfected attribute as they surfaced. But after he left this world, the people of his time lost touch with his way.

Every new generation needs a new wellspring opened for it so it can be spiritually equipped to handle the challenges of its own time. It's the job of the tzaddikim of each new generation to dig those wells and draw up the healing and reviving waters of faith and knowledge.

Isaac had a different way about him; he walked a different path. But it was a path that expanded on his father's great road of loving-kindness. Isaac first only dredged the blocked wells of his father and renewed their old names. But soon enough, he began to open new sources of his own — "living waters" — that he had to struggle to keep open. Isaac gave them new names, each one expressing his determined fight to share his own expanded awareness with the world — one that broadened loving-kindness to include his own capacity for holy restraint.

> Abraham and Isaac dug down through the surface of reality to reveal the Godly spark beneath.

The Philistines eventually absorbed enough of Isaac's truth that they ceased to oppose him. In fact, they volunteered to forge a pact with him — a covenant, a *brit* — because by then Isaac's covenant with the Creator could not be ignored. Isaac was so aligned with the Divine that the people of his time could sense it — and they thirsted for a taste of it.

REACH
HIGHER

THE ANCIENT MASTERS TAUGHT, "EVERY person should ask himself: When will my deeds approach those of my ancestors, Abraham, Isaac, and Jacob?"

But who could be so foolish to think that his actions could ever actually come close to the accomplishments of those pillars of the world? Who are we kidding?

If we look a little closer at the original language of the phrase, though, we'll find that the word for "approach" is *yagia*, and in Hebrew that also means to "touch."

> *I may not be able to reach their level, but I can make contact with their way.*

I can learn what each of those giants has to teach me, what special gift each endowed me with, and do what I can to align myself with those ways. That's a kind of contact; that's my way of reaching them.

I'm not Isaac, and I don't have anything close to the depth of his self-mastery, his upright commitment to absolute justice. But his perfection of his attribute opened a well of living water that I can drink from today.

Every age needs new sources of inspiration, new ways to experience the Godliness that animates all of existence. We explore what has worked in the past, and we examine what doesn't work for us now so that we can develop new strategies in our attempts to connect with the Infinite One.

Isaac didn't dig new wells because he had nothing better to do; a famine in the land forced him to seek sources of water.

The thirst is what inspires us to progress spiritually, to dig new wells.

And after each revelation, a new concealment comes to bring us to a fresh state of thirst. After the work of Abraham comes the new revelation of Isaac. And after the innovation of Isaac there will be the expansion and consolidation of Jacob. This constant tension between revelation and concealment, between satiety and thirst, is the dynamic that drives the evolution of consciousness within every single one of us. It wasn't only Abraham, Isaac, and Jacob thousands of years ago.

It's here; it's now.

It's you; it's me.

JACOB'S GIFT

ACCORDING TO THE **ZOHAR,** ABRAHAM and Isaac worked to reveal their life-giving waters of God-consciousness in the world by "digging wells." Jacob didn't just continue their legacy, though. He didn't *dig* wells; he *was* the well. What do I mean by that? In Hebrew, a well is a *be'er*. But the root also means to explain or clarify something. In the Kabbalistic tradition, the act of *beirur* means penetrating past the externality of something to reach the Divine intelligence that animates it, allowing us to interact with it in an elevated way.

> *The ability to connect with the inner essence of reality is Jacob's gift.*

Jacob was third in a line of spiritual giants, and he began his story with the accumulated influence of his father and grandfather already stamped into his nature. That progression means that his potential exists within every one of his descendants; it's our spiritual inheritance. In fact, the Chassidic master, Rebbe Nachman of Breslov, taught that it's more than just potential — it's our mission statement:

> *We need to always seek out the Divine wisdom that exists within every-thing, to bind ourselves to it, so that it can illuminate the way for us to connect with God through that particular thing. (Likutei Moharan I:1)*

To be a child of Jacob — his spiritual heir — means to engage in this work of seeking the Divine truth and wisdom that lies within everything and engaging with it. It's not something abstract or distant, or only for highly evolved sages and saints. *It is the most basic definition of being a spiritual person*: to always seek the internal essence of a thing or experience, to never be satisfied with what's just on the surface of life.

Furthermore, Jacob synthesized the loving-kindness of Abraham and the self-restraint of Isaac into a new whole — Jacob is the one who arrived at the truth of every matter. We normally think of truth as just being the opposite of falsehood. Either something is true, or it's not. But there's another dimension to truth.

> It is the most basic definition of being a spiritual person: to always seek the internal essence of a thing or experience, to never be satisfied with what's just on the surface of life.

When the desire to *give* (Abraham's gift) is tempered by *restraint* (Isaac's gift) because giving too much is not really good for the recipient, that's *truth*, and it's also called *rachamim*, or mercy. That is Jacob's gift.

For example, when the "no" that's necessary is tempered by a compassionate "not now," or "not yet," or "no to *this*, but yes to *that*," we arrive at the *truth*. Not at one extreme or the other, but at the balanced center that takes everything — all of the factors, inside and out — into account. Mercy isn't unrestricted giving; it's judicious, measured, and appropriate giving. That's truth — it's the truth of what the situation demands, in all of its complexity.

Truth and balance like that are beautiful — and that's another name for Jacob's natural attribute: *tiferet*, beauty or splendor. Just like our ideal of beauty really comes down to perfect symmetry, Jacob's splendor is found in his perfect balance and in his way of relating to the externality of a thing by staying in tune with its internal truth.

Jacob's gift for balance, for penetrating to the inner point of truth within everything, is the essence of the Torah.

In the Torah, Jacob is the "simple, whole man who dwelled within the tents" — within the tents of Torah study. He was called the choicest of all of the forefathers. Jacob wasn't only an extension of the others' attributes, he was their completion, their simple perfection brought to wholeness. And because his nature was that of truth, he was deeply aligned with the Torah even though he lived well before the revelation of the Torah at Sinai.

Jacob accomplished that which the Torah eventually came to reveal — he communicated with the Divine wisdom that animates absolutely everything that exists, the internal dimension of reality that is its *truth*. Not only its truth, but its *life*.

> Jacob's gift for balance, for penetrating to the inner point of truth within everything, is the essence of the Torah.

Jacob's unique gift allowed him to penetrate through the surface of a person, place, object, or situation to connect with its inner truth, wisdom, and vitality. He brought the mentality of the Tree of Life to everything he encountered, and even now he teaches us how to live with that consciousness at all times. We learn from him by carefully studying the story of his life, especially when it's illuminated by the Kabbalistic tradition.

For Jacob, it was all One. When we tap into Jacob's gift that lies within ourselves, we come into contact with that Oneness, too.

THE DOUBLE
BLESSING

JACOB AND ESAU — TWIN brothers — started out like two trees growing from the same root. At first, they could hardly be distinguished from one another, but as they matured their divergent natures were revealed. The mystics taught that the Tree of Life and the Tree of Knowledge of Good and Evil also emerged from a single root — but what different fruits!

Jacob was naturally aligned with the inner life of Torah study and contemplation. He was the "simple, whole man who dwelled *within* the tents." Jacob realm is internal — he was a Tree of Life man by nature.

Esau, the "man of the field," was born to be an achiever in the *external* world of action. He had an innate energy for *doing*, for the sifting and clarifying work of the Tree of Knowledge of Good and Evil. That duality means that you have to *identify* good and evil and *choose* between them. Esau's realm is out in the world where there are always choices to make between that which draws us closer to God and that which drives us further away.

The two brothers were meant to synthesize their paths into a seamless whole — Jacob's life of Divine service would illuminate Esau's work in the world, and the products of Esau's work would sustain Jacob's pursuit of Torah.

The inner vitality and wisdom of the Tree of Life would breathe its spirit into the material of the Tree of Knowledge of Good and Evil, just as it should have from the very beginning. Their story is really our story — everyone has a Jacob and an Esau inside of him.

The ancient sages taught that Jacob had the face of Adam, and that his image was "inscribed on the Divine throne." Jacob's face was like the face of Adam because *he was meant to complete the mission that Adam interrupted.* His image is inscribed on the Divine throne because Jacob is our model of what it's possible to achieve when our Two Trees are brought together, *only this time we eat from the Tree of Life first.* We don't step out into the world of division and confusing choice until we've thoroughly filled ourselves with the wisdom and light that will make that journey a success.

We all have access to the Tree of Life through the soul-nourishment of Torah study, prayer, meditation, and contemplation. And we all have our Tree of Knowledge of Good and Evil — the work we do in the external world where we have to *choose* to bind with the Godliness within everything because we don't see it on the outside.

> *The external world of choice, of sifting out the good from the bad, always needs strong light to guide it.*

Many wonder how Isaac could have loved Esau; we would think Esau would have been the last person his saintly father would have wanted to bless. But Isaac had a natural affinity for the hard work of sifting through the external; he and Esau had a lot in common. So Isaac wanted to give Esau a special blessing of Divine abundance — ample rains, flourishing fields, bountiful flocks — to enable Esau to carry out his destiny. *Isaac loved Esau because his firstborn really did have the potential to bring the Divine plan to fruition.*

We all know it didn't work out that way, though. Esau rejected his own birthright — his share in the partnership — and in doing so, he had already forfeited his blessing before Jacob ever came to take it from him.

Isaac was blind to Esau's unwillingness to work together with his twin. Esau's nature was rooted in Isaac's own attribute of self-restraint; often, it's our closeness and similarity with another that makes it hardest to see them for who they really are.

Esau is our model of a person who had vast potential but wasn't able to actualize it. The Torah tells us he was a man of the field. That means he was an external person who chose to live without penetrating to life's inner essence. Esau had — has — a natural feel for power and influence. Even without partnering with his brother, he went on to become the father of Edom, Rome — Western civilization with all its vast accomplishments in the external sphere.

Jacob could see what his own father couldn't — that Esau was never going to partner with him, and that Esau's hold on the birthright, this spiritual portion from Abraham and Isaac, would only lead to destruction. So Jacob offered Esau a trade — his birthright for a meal — and by accepting it, Esau proved just how little he valued such a precious gift.

In buying the birthright, Jacob really assumed his brother's mission *in addition to his own*. He kept his Torah, but he also took on the burden of working in the world. Without a partner, Jacob became one man with Two Trees to cultivate. So even if he didn't really want Esau's blessing, he would need it; he wouldn't be able to survive without it. By buying the birthright, it was certain that Jacob would have to have Esau's blessing too, by any means necessary.

The Torah offers us a window into Jacob's life more than it does for any other Biblical figure — his life story spans most of the book of Genesis. Why?

> *Jacob is really our model.*
> *His mission is our mission.*

Our work in the world outside — earning a living, having a family, communal responsibilities — can take up every minute of our lives. Being a functioning adult is a full-time job! Yet something inside of us longs for time to think, to pray, to connect...if we didn't have all of these responsibilities, we could spend all day on the inner work that sustains our souls.

But even the most inner-directed scholar has no choice but to go out into the world in some way — that's his mission too. It's all part of the Divine plan. The scholar needs to go out and teach in communities far from home in order to sustain his Tree of Life, but he's actually being sent on a consciousness-raising mission. When he does that, he is doing the work of his Two Trees.

No one gets to cultivate only one tree, no matter how much they want to. We all have to be spiritual and physical multitaskers.

That's what it means to be a Jacob without a partner — your soul is hungry, but your body needs to eat. Your spirit yearns for its heavenly home, but you still have to pay the mortgage. We're all working two shifts, and it's not easy. But just like Jacob, we have the blessing that we need to make that balancing act possible.

After Jacob received that blessing, he left his homeland and headed east to save himself from his brother's revenge and to find a wife. But he stopped on the way for fourteen years to study.

Jacob learned from Shem and Ever — two ancient masters, Noah's son and great-grandson, who taught him the Torah of discovering hidden Godliness long before the Torah was revealed at Sinai. This is Noah's Torah; it's Abraham's Torah; it's the wisdom of cutting through all of the externals to connect with the Divine spark that animates all of existence.

These teachings empowered Jacob to overcome all the trials yet to come. Those fourteen years were his Tree of Life before he entered the world of the Tree of Knowledge of Good and Evil — the next phase of work, married life, and all of the complexity of navigating through a world of hard choices and oppositional people. Without them, could he ever have made it?

Jacob's fourteen years were necessary preparation for his life, and many young people are fortunate to have that kind of opportunity before they marry and begin their lives. It's a chance to center and align themselves with the truth that will be their guide for the lives they're going to build.

But the truth is that this dynamic repeats itself every single day. I always encourage my students to make time for spiritual nourishment on a daily basis, preferably early in the day — you cannot imagine the difference it makes in your life to start each day centered and aligned and only then to go out into the work of your life.

Like Jacob, before we step out into the working world, into the realm of the Tree of Knowledge of Good and Evil, we *all* need to first attach ourselves to the Tree of Life.

A DYNAMIC DUO

EVEN THOUGH JACOB AND ESAU were originally meant to be a perfect symbiosis — each one giving, each one receiving — their partnership never got off the ground. Esau rejected the responsibility that it entailed and chose the path of materialism, the externality of reality instead of the wisdom at its heart. Jacob was left alone to carry both missions, and even though he achieved remarkable worldly success, it still consumed his life.

Jacob had all of the internal wisdom to transform the world, but he really needed someone active on the outside, someone who could reach out to people where they were in the place of externality and bring them in to him. Jacob couldn't be in two places at once — no one can really be fully invested in two completely different realms.

After Jacob had been working for years, marrying, having children, and raising them, his wife Rachel bore her first child — Joseph — whose name means literally, "He will add." Joseph had the potential to carry Jacob's spirit into the world of action. It was only after the birth of Joseph that Jacob suddenly felt that his promised partner had finally arrived.

Jacob and Joseph have been compared to a fire and its spark. Jacob had all of the energy and potential to burn away the husk of externality so that its Divine core of wisdom could be liberated. But it was only in potential. Jacob had it within him, but it was still *within him*, not yet expressed.

Jacob lacked the ability to project that fire out into the world, out into the dark, to really catalyze change on a larger scale. He needed a spark from his fire to shoot out and catch the dry tinder of Esau-type externality.

Joseph was that flame.

Torah cannot survive alone — the inner life cannot exist without help from the "outside" partner, and that means they are of equal importance. The sages taught: "Without flour, there's no Torah. Without Torah, there's no flour." The means of sustaining the Tree of Life can only be found out in the world of the Tree of Knowledge; the means of navigating through the choices of the Tree of Knowledge are only found within the Tree of Life. They are absolute partners, and one cannot exist without the other.

The sages taught: "Without flour, there's no Torah. Without Torah, there's no flour."

Jacob had the potential, but Joseph was going to actualize it. Jacob held all of the needed elements, but they were inert until Joseph came along and catalyzed them. They weren't only partners, they were a *dynamic duo* — a pair who, together, had the ability to bring about movement and change where, alone, it would have been impossible. But it would still take time.

We all know Joseph was singled out by his father, but what set him apart from his brothers wasn't so obvious at that early stage, and that created conflict. Joseph still needed to evolve, and his growth was thrown into high gear (as it so often is) *specifically* through facing the tests of suffering and loss, as we'll soon see.

The sages taught that "everything that happened to Jacob, happened to Joseph." That doesn't mean that their life history was exactly the same; it means that the trajectory of their lives ran parallel. Corresponding challenges, corresponding obstacles. Jealous brothers, homelessness, confrontations with hostile foreign powers. But, together, they were eventually able to continue the original mission of Adam — to draw down Divine mercy — while down in Egypt.

Joseph had true grace and beauty. In Egypt, he wasn't just a spark; Joseph developed into a laser beam that cut right through the externals of every situation, touched its core, *and united it with its ultimate purpose.*

> *Joseph went down to Egypt like a spark invested with all of the light of Jacob's fire...*
>
> *The difference was that Joseph was empowered to travel the distance.*

When Jacob came down to Egypt and reunited with Joseph, the Divine Presence descended with him, and as long as Joseph lived, there was no exile in Egypt. The combined force of Jacob and Joseph illuminated the darkness of Egypt completely. When we live with their gift, the night of exile turns to day.

We're in the dark because our essential selves aren't expressed; they're hidden by layers of external ego, but inside we shine. Our Divine light is incredibly strong, and when we let it out, everyone is able to see our grace and beauty. Then, no matter where we are, we're able to reveal the essential Godliness unique to that place. The world is crying out for an activated spark to burn away its exterior shell and trigger its inner light.

We are meant to be that spark.

TOUCHING
THE CORE

LIFE IS ALWAYS BRINGING US into contact with impossible people — disconnected and unconscious actors with whom we easily get drawn into drama. When Jacob returned to Canaan with his family, Esau came out to meet him with an army, and that was a veiled threat — you don't go to meet your long-lost brother fully weaponized unless you plan to do him harm. Jacob's experience when he met up with Esau again has a lot to teach us, because somehow Jacob managed to transform that potential collision into a moment of reconciliation.

Esau wasn't just a problematic person; he genuinely and deeply hated his brother. What he saw as inequity in their blessings, as Jacob cheating him out of his rightful share, left a deep scar almost certain to result in violence. The great mystic Rabbi Shimon bar Yochai said it plainly: "It's a known fact — *Esau is Jacob's enemy.*"

> So how are we supposed to transform our enemy into our friend? The remedy is to reach inside.

It's because we're operating only on the surface. When we remain at the level of the external, we find ourselves in conflict. The remedy is to reach *inside*. Here is where Jacob's nature has so much to teach us. He wasn't only an inner-focused person; he was a *centered* person. Jacob is a model of how to stay steady and centered even when dealing with people who run to extremes.

The outer self has its own ego-driven agenda that often puts it at odds with others, who naturally have their own motives too. If I can't harmonize with my child (he's oppositional, he's not fulfilling his obligations, etc.), how much of that friction is really about my impatience with him? How much of it is really about me being inconvenienced, disappointed, ego-invested, angry, and afraid for his future? I want to reach my child, but how can I when my externals are clashing with his externals? I'm facing a person who sees me as an obstacle in his way, as his enemy at this moment. And, right now, he happens to be right. When I'm still stuck at the surface of things, I'm in his way and he's in mine.

> *Jacob teaches me that there is a way in...*
> *There is a way to connect.*

When I take that way in, I'm capitalizing on the moment of potential conflict as a means of becoming a more internal, evolved, and conscious person. What could have been all-out war isn't only defused; it becomes a moment of transformation for both of us.

Jacob lifted his eyes and saw Esau marching toward him with four hundred armed men — that's the numerical value of the Hebrew term for the "evil eye."

What did Jacob do? He placed each of the children with their mother and then "he passed before them" and bowed seven times as he approached Esau. The verse is ambiguous, though, about exactly who did this passing. It seems to be speaking about Jacob, but doesn't identify him by name. But we do know that after Jacob bowed seven times, Esau ran to his brother, fell upon his neck, kissed him, and cried.

A complete turnaround. What really happened there?

What would it mean for Jacob to act so submissively before his brother, who really was a wicked and violent man? Is that the lesson we're supposed to learn — that when we're threatened we should just fold before *anyone*, even someone who does real evil? It's clear that Jacob's actions at that sensitive moment touched something within Esau — his core of genuine brotherly love that was plastered over with layers of jealousy and fury.

Were Jacob's actions just submissive flattery, or were they something else?

The Kabbalists teach that what passed before Jacob's family at that crucial instant was the Divine Presence itself. And it was to that manifestation of Godliness that Jacob bowed seven times, in an act of complete elimination of his ego. Jacob would *never* have lowered himself before evil. But the revelation of the Divine Presence made him aware that the only way for him to come away from this meeting whole would be if he *set aside his external self completely*. How does that really work, though? What really happens when you submit before the Divine Will at the moment you're about to clash with another human being? The sages taught: "Make *your will* into *His Will*, and He will make *the will of others* into *your will*."

It happened with Esau — his innermost point of mercy woke up as soon as he saw before him the thing we almost never see: *a human being approaching without an agenda*. Without a

> "Make your will into His Will, and He will make the will of others into your will."

personal, ego-driven agenda independent of God's agenda. There are times we need to take a stand, to say no or draw a line, but what melts the shells around the other person's heart is when we say what we have to say *without our ego getting in the way*.

The truth is, it's possible to relate to anybody. We know of great teachers who could reach the most unreachable student; great masters who could touch the furthest soul. This is *our* gift from Jacob — a natural ability we inherited by virtue of all of the work *he* did — to reach all the way into the core and relate to the essence of every person and situation. Jacob bowed seven times, and he didn't stop bowing until he could feel Esau make that transformation, until his natural cruelty was overtaken by his essence of mercy.

A student once came to me with terrible news. "There's a war going on in my house! My wife hates the forward motion I'm making spiritually. If I make a blessing out loud, she acts annoyed. Everything good I do, she resists."

I asked him, "Well, how do you feel about her?"

He said, "Honestly, it's hard to respect her. All she cares about is the physical aspect of life — she talks with her friends about recipes, loves to shop for clothes for the kids…"

I started to laugh, because the cause of their war was pretty obvious. "If Jacob could see the good in Esau, I think you can see the good in your wife. You look at her externally, and so you can't see the beauty of who she is. What you think is just material is her way of expressing her holy quality of nurturing. And so she naturally hates you for your religious intolerance! Go home...and pay close attention to the beauty of what she's doing. Your war is over."

And you know what? It really was.

PRIMORDIAL TORAH

AS WE'VE SEEN, JACOB WAS already connected with the soul of the Torah, generations before it was revealed at Sinai. In fact, his prime quality *was* the Torah. And all the fathers of the Jewish people lived Torah to a certain extent long before its appearance in the world.

But that leaves us with an obvious question: why wasn't the Torah revealed *to the world* until the time of Moses? The earlier masters refined their spiritual antennae so much that they absorbed a *personal* revelation of the Divine Will, but Moses delivered a comprehensive guide for living to *an entire people*. So what special quality did Moses have that made him the ideal channel for the Torah's descent into the world?

Before we delve into just what made Moses unique, however, we need to take a short detour. We've spoken so much about the revelation of Torah but we're missing an important piece here: *What, really, is the Torah?*

It might seem like a simple question to answer, but we can't assume that our well-worn paths of understanding, sometimes laid down from childhood on, really provide us the insight we need. We've grown, and our grasp of the soul of the matter also needs to mature. So let's go back. We have to remember we're involved in a progression that started at the beginning of Creation itself.

To better understand the nature of Torah, we have to ask an even more fundamental question: Why did the Infinite One wait so long to provide the world with the Torah that sustains it? Wouldn't it have made more sense for Him to share His Mind and Will with the first man, who would then teach it to others as the human community developed? And if we posit that Adam did have a sense of the essence of Torah, why didn't that awareness spread throughout the ancient world?

114

At the beginning of Creation, the Infinite One *did* make His Will known to man, but only just enough to provide a balance between revelation and concealment. The ability to freely choose light out of the darkness, to fill up the empty space, is our most essential human quality. For it to be meaningful, it has to be real. As we've already learned, the space of choice can give birth to knowledge, light, and connection, or breed doubt, distance, and foolishness.

And we get to choose.

At every point along the progression of history, that balance between revelation and concealment has to be maintained. A certain amount of concealment is necessary so that choice stays possible and relevant. If there were no space, no gap or darkness, our choices would become meaningless. Attaining knowledge and developing faith is only meaningful when there's a vacuum of ignorance or doubt needing to be filled. Free will and the space that makes it significant isn't a negotiable principle in reality — *it's the basic condition of all of existence.*

So we've been given all the room we need to exert harmful self-will... or to seek the Divine.

I usually avoid unfamiliar terms if I can so that these essential concepts never feel inaccessible. But sometimes we really need to stick with the exact original word because it encompasses so much complexity. This is one of those times. The God-consciousness that comes to fill the vacuum of ignorance or doubt is called *da'at*. And we'll see that *da'at* is the thread that runs through everything we need to know about Moses.

> We've been given all the room we need to exert harmful self-will...or to seek the Divine.

Da'at is a word with multiple meanings. In the language of the mystics, the purpose of our existence is, "To come to *know* Him," and *da'at* — knowledge — always means *connection*. To "know" in the Biblical sense means to achieve intimate contact with another: "And Adam *knew* Eve, his wife..." (Genesis 4:1). That's the kind of *da'at*-awareness we were designed to achieve: God-consciousness that *unifies* us with our Source.

Maybe God is an optimist — He left humanity with a small but powerful light in a large dark space and allowed people to do their best to see the hidden Divine Will that drives history and nature. And some did — Noah, Shem, Ever, Abraham, Isaac, Jacob, and their descendants. Through great effort, they built on the knowledge passed down to them by the masters who came before them. They sought the Creator's subtle hints to awaken their souls in their lives and in nature, and finally received enlightenment.

But most didn't.

The mass of humanity fell away from its original course of alignment. That spiritual deterioration also had a parallel, though. Even as the human community descended deeper into idolatry and darkness, the line of righteous masters made many gains from generation to generation. The children of Abraham, Isaac, and Jacob went down into a painful but cleansing exile to prepare to receive a *national* revelation. So while the bad got worse, the good *got better*. A small but critical mass of human beings was being primed to receive the means of connection, of bridging the gap with the Divine.

This means of connection is the Torah.

So what is Torah? *It's the da'at-awareness that joins us with the Creator... specifically through the alignment of our thought, speech, and action with the Divine Will.*

BRING
IT DOWN

NOW THAT WE HAVE AN idea of the essential nature of the Torah and its purpose, we need a deeper look at the figure best suited to channel its message: Moses. Only such a connector, such a *knower* who could fill the space of ignorance and doubt, would be able to receive and share the Will of the Creator with an entire nation of millions of men, women, and children.

There never has been any other religion based on a mass prophetic revelation as there was at Sinai. Moses didn't go up the mountain and return with a secret surprise. The mass experience took place *first*, and an entire people then witnessed their leader head off into the epicenter of that explosion of God-consciousness that *everyone* had seen, heard, and felt.

Moses was the agent who set in motion the people's enlightenment — what an accomplishment! And then he returned after a period of private seclusion on the mountain with the *rest* of the Torah. He returned with the *completion* of the nation's experience...not with a private revelation that demanded our blind faith. The Torah rests upon the people's *knowledge* — the experience of connection that can't be denied.

But how did Moses become this channel? How did he become our model of *da'at* — connected and integrated Divine awareness?

To understand Moses's uniqueness, we need to look back to the Torah's depiction of the first phase of his life. Pharaoh's genocidal decree focused on Jewish infant boys, so Moses was born in secret and then sent off by his sister Miriam to an uncertain future. From a basket floating down the Nile, the baby was miraculously saved by a princess and raised among royalty.

The Torah tells us first that "the boy grew," but the very next verse tells us, "*And Moses grew, and went out to his brothers, and saw their suffering...*" (Exodus 2:10–11). Moses grew twice — *as he was growing physically, he matured emotionally and spiritually.*

Most of us only grow in one dimension. But great people grow *and keep on growing*, becoming mature in a multidimensional way. And how do we see that Moses kept on growing? He left his comfort zone — that natural raven-haven of self-interest — to pay attention to the suffering of an oppressed minority in Egypt. How often does a prince go out to identify with the pain of others? The elite are usually only interested in their pleasures. But when Moses saw injustice — in the case of the Egyptian taskmaster abusing a Jewish man by day and violating the victim's wife by night — he took action. When Moses saw two people in conflict, he tried to make peace between them even though it cost him his freedom. He had the essential Divine qualities of *mishpat* — justice; and *tzedakah* — because his mercy drove him to *connect* and to *reach out to help.*

> Great people grow and keep on growing, becoming mature in a multidimensional way.

When Moses became a fugitive, he ran to Midian and became the protector of the weak and exploited, the daughters of Jethro at the well. Moses's future father-in-law immediately identified him as a great man because of the stranger's sense of *justice* — he rebuked the guilty; and *charity* — for putting himself on the line to save the innocent. The greatness his father-in-law recognized was not because of power or position, but because Moses *grew...and kept on growing into greatness.*

Moses then spent years tending sheep for his father-in-law, growing every day in his quality of compassion while caring lovingly for a vulnerable flock. The great mystical work — the *Zohar* — calls Moses, "The Faithful Shepherd." He proved his *charity* and *justice* in small things, and that made him worthy of great things.

We can see how these qualities made Moses the ideal redeemer of the Jewish people from bondage, but how do they relate to his role as the deliverer of the Torah? Let's consider some deeper implications of

Moses's mercy and his unique degree of *da'at* — connected and connecting awareness.

What keeps us locked inside the "raven-haven" of the mind — self-absorbed, fearful, and inattentive to the misery of others? *A limited awareness of the infinite nature of God's love and mercy.* I'm only tight because I'm afraid that if I extend myself for someone else, I won't have enough for myself. But if I'm fully aware and confident that the Creator's mercies are more than sufficient to satisfy everyone's needs, why *shouldn't* I put myself out for a person in trouble?

My ability to be merciful and expansive is a manifestation of my God-consciousness, specifically my awareness of the *infinite* nature of Divine mercy. The mystics speak of Moses's essential quality as *da'at* — applied awareness. That means bringing down consciousness and integrating it fully into the self, and then into the realm of action, and the sharing of that knowledge with others

A person who really has this quality *can't help but share it* — it flows from him all the time, and people just pick up on it. The great sages said, "How foolish people are, that they stand when in the presence of a Torah scroll but not in the presence of a Torah scholar." Because the scholar is a living Torah scroll.

Moses's *da'at* never stopped expanding, and as it grew, his relationship with God and with others expanded. The Torah constantly expands in proportion to the growth of the mind and soul of the one who studies it, and Moses's capacity to *connect* and share his awareness grew so much that it allowed him to bring the Torah to an entire people. This Torah of Moses will continue to flow outward until it has reached everywhere in the world.

An eight-year-old and an eighty-year-old study the same Torah — but it's not the same Torah. It expands infinitely to accommodate the developing *da'at* of those who study it. And as we study it, and more importantly *live it*, our awareness of God's infinite greatness expands too. This was the essence of Moses's mission: to bridge the empty space of unconsciousness with vital, real awareness of God in an active way. Not theory, not ideas, but *Torah*: the drawing of the Will of the Infinite One *all the way down into the realm of action*, in the physical world where we live and breathe.

So redemption and revelation rested upon Moses's *da'at* — his grasp of the Infinite One — and Moses's *mercy*, which filled him with the drive to share that awareness with the world. But there's still one piece missing, one gap in our understanding of how Moses merited to be the channel through which the Torah entered the world.

The Torah testifies that there is one quality Moses perfected: his humility.

The world we live in thrives on self-promotion, self-interest, and self-aggrandizement, so it's easy to get a little confused about the quality of humility. We have a tendency to confuse humility with lack of self-esteem, self-loathing, lack of assertiveness, and even humiliation. But true humility has nothing to do with any of that.

> *"And Moses was more humble than any man on the face of the earth"*
> *(Numbers 12:3).*

With Moses's ever-expanding awareness of God came an ever-diminishing awareness of his ego-self, and the *reliance on self as the solution*. And this actually made Moses capable of accomplishing goals that would have been impossible for those convinced that "self" has to be adequate for the job. Whose *self* could be adequate to transmit the infinite *da'at*-awareness of the Creator? Whose *self* could be strong enough to extract an oppressed people out from under the burdens of Egypt, the most powerful empire in the world?

No one's.

Moses increasingly saw himself purely as an instrument of the Divine. What a human being couldn't accomplish, God could accomplish easily through him, because his ego-self was completely out of the way.

And when Moses saw a gap — an apparent vacuum of kindness or justice that's just a reflection of the original "vacated space" of Creation — he threw himself into that space to serve as a Divine instrument too. For Moses, awareness of the infinite greatness of God also allowed him to see the infinite greatness of every single soul. *Everyone* would be worthy of redemption. *Everyone* would receive the *da'at*-consciousness of the Torah. Without ego-based self in the way, Moses's Divine self — purely an instrument of the Divine Will — had room for everyone.

> For Moses, awareness of the infinite greatness of God also allowed him to see the infinite greatness of every single soul.

Now we can put the whole puzzle together:

Moses's awareness and connection with the Divine constantly expanded;

This growth aroused his quality of mercy and desire to connect and share his awareness of Divine compassion with others;

His expanding God-consciousness brought him to ever-increasing degrees of humility;

And this made him a perfect vehicle for transmitting the Divine message.

Without ego, there was ample space for God to communicate **through** *Moses.*

ETERNAL FLAME

WHO'S NOT FAMILIAR WITH THE image of the burning bush? But it's because we're so familiar with the image that we need to dig deeper. We can't afford to hold on to a cartoonish understanding of such a pivotal moment in the history of the world.

The burning bush wasn't some kind of a Divine flare sent up to get Moses's attention. The Infinite One has infinite ways of communicating a message, so why this particular sign, the vision that Moses called, "The Great Sight"?

As we've already learned, there are dynamics of alignment at work all the time. There had to be something about Moses himself that *invited* this form of communication, something unique to his nature and development. Remember, God doesn't circumvent our free will, so the burning bush had to be a sign Moses was ready for, one that wouldn't automatically force him into acceptance of his mission. He had to be aligned with it ahead of time to receive it in the right way.

The lowly bush was on fire, but it was not consumed. It was burning fiercely, but its material wasn't feeding that flame. *That's* what got Moses's attention. Not a fire in an arid desert; there's nothing strange about that. What caught his interest was that the fire burned without anything to feed it.

That was unnatural; *that* was miraculous.

And if we think about it, we learn something about Moses just from the fact that he even noticed something so subtle. Would we even notice something like that, let alone veer from our well-worn path — our usual way of thinking and doing — to look for a cause?

There's something reminiscent about this, too; it's like Abraham's

122

way of looking at the world, "like a person who saw a castle alight" and knew the owner had to be inside somewhere.

The bush can't burn endlessly without fuel unless it's being fed by some other source.

The castle can't be lit up unless someone is inside tending the hearth.

Someone is keeping the lights on!

According to the laws of nature, fire needs fuel and only burns as long as the fuel lasts. *According to the rules of the soul, however, there are spiritual forms of energy that are not limited in the way physical energies are.* As Moses himself would see soon enough, he would be able to exist on the Divine Word alone during his time atop Mount Sinai, not eating or drinking for forty days and nights. That is another kind of burning bush.

The *Zohar* teaches that there are two kinds of light: "luminaries of fire," and "luminaries of light."

Combustion and illumination.

Now, it's true that fire provides light and heat, but it also can be dangerous, and since it's combustive it leaves behind waste — ash. That's like nature itself: it's both good and bad. We couldn't manage without nature, but it's also a concealer of the direct light of Divinity. It can be useful, but it has its downside; it leaves a residue of confusion about whether nature is all there is.

Light — pure light — on the other hand, just illuminates. It's only beneficial, without any waste left behind.

The mystics speak about night being the time of "luminaries of fire," while day is the time of "luminaries of light." On a simple level, we use combustion to illuminate our nights because otherwise we'd be in the dark. During the daytime that's unnecessary because the sun is shining brightly. But we're not talking physics here; we're talking about spiritual concepts. Daytime represents seeing Godliness with clarity; nighttime represents the "nature-bound" way of thinking that takes over when that clarity withdraws.

Nature — the realm of "luminaries of fire" — is the world of rust and decay. There's only so much fuel to go around, and when it's gone, it's gone. But there's another realm, the world of the "luminaries of light," where it's possible for the light to extend way beyond what the fuel can provide. Moses's burning bush is lit by the Divine light that animated Creation from the beginning, that didn't need fuel but *just was*, fired by the Divine Will alone, before material reality existed at all.

What more perfect sign could there be for Moses, who was worried about taking on a job way too big for him? "Who am I to go...? ...But I am heavy of speech..." he protested. And the Infinite One answered from the flames, "Who places a mouth within man if not *Me*? ...*I will be with your mouth*..." (Exodus 4:11). God was teaching Moses, patiently and thoroughly over a period of many days, that *the mission didn't depend on him being adequate to the task.*

> The burning bush is a message that waits off the beaten path for anyone aware enough to see it.

Yes, you're just a human being and this is a superhuman mission. *But as long as you're holding on to My light, you don't have to worry about the fuel. The truth of My light is that it's infinite. You'll be drawing off a Source **that has no limits whatsoever**.*

The burning bush is a message that waits off the beaten path for anyone aware enough to see it. It teaches us that we too can give and give of ourselves and not be consumed. The limits that intimidate us are literally *self*-imposed; they are the products of our thinking that it all depends on our *self*. But when we're aligned and plugged in to the Source, we find we're able to do everything we need to do, because we're not the source of the fuel that feeds our flame.

THE
CONNECTED
MIND

THE TORAH ISN'T **INFORMATION** — it's the means through which human beings can bond with the Creator and bridge the gap between their finite selves and the Infinite One. To share that kind of knowledge, you need to really have compassion for other people. To redeem a nation from bondage and provide them with *connected minds*, you have to love them and have mercy on them.

What do I mean by that? There are many ways to give, and all of them are important. A person can need a meal, a job, a sympathetic ear, a caring heart...But there's one form of giving that surpasses all of them: to illuminate those whose *minds* are impoverished.

The sages taught, "If you've acquired wisdom, what do you lack? And if you lack wisdom, *what do you have?*"

> The Torah isn't *information* — it's the means through which human beings can bond with the Creator.

The Torah is called *Rachmana* — "Merciful One" — because it came from the Merciful One and because it accomplishes the ultimate act of mercy. It opens our pathways of *da'at* and binds us to the Infinite One through all the channels of thought, speech, and action. Moses was — and still is — our ideal of a leader because his degree of expanded *da'at*, his quality of mercy, and his capacity for sharing Divine wisdom were the greatest in history. Moses didn't just *teach* the Torah — he *embodied* the Torah. He *lived* his *da'at*. Only a person like that is really fit to lead; someone who understands just how much compassion you must have for the person whose mind lacks *da'at*, and how willing you must be to do whatever you can to help them connect with their Source. Every genuine guide and teacher of the Jewish people over history was animated by the soul-spark of Moses.

> "If you've acquired wisdom, what do you lack? And if you lack wisdom, what do you have?"

I'm not talking about just *teaching*; lots of people give lectures. I'm talking about a true leader, a Moses, who spends his whole life trying to do far more than fill people with information. This true leader works to instill transformative *da'at* within his people. He works to *raise* and educate them, to build them into fully conscious spiritual beings active down here in the physical world — integrated and connected, walking the walk and not just talking the talk.

That's the job of every soul-teacher, every parent — of every human being.

If you have children, it's certainly true. You didn't bring children into the world so they should grow into animals in human form. We're interested in raising actualized, connected, aware people. And if you have students, it's not enough to just ply them with information. A true educator works on transformation with his students — on maximizing their human potential.

But as with everything else, we can only give it away if we have it. We need to be living it, to be breathing it. If our *da'at* is genuine, it's joyous, it's connected, and it becomes so easy to share. Because that kind of awakened, expanded, and alive mind is exactly what everyone wants to connect with.

But what about the rest of us? Not all of us are parents, not all of us are teachers.

Or are we?

We exist alongside others, and as soon as we open our mouths to share a concept that can illuminate someone else's mind, we automatically become that person's teacher. And when the other person has something to share that expands our awareness, they become *our* teacher. This natural sharing of *da'at* is the essence of our mission as human beings entrusted with Godly souls that yearn to connect and fill the empty space within the other.

Think back to the burning bush. This world is all combustion; it's all rust and decay unless we find a way to break out of the limitations of death and time. The world is filled with empty spaces crying out to be filled with Divine awareness. Those voids sever the physical world from its eternal Source. If we don't fill those gaps with God-consciousness, material existence turns into a disappointment and a lost opportunity that, literally, goes to waste.

The first mitzvah given to humanity was to have children: "Be fruitful and multiply and fill the earth." Our mission is to partner with God by filling the voids He left for us with *da'at*...not with purposeless bodies. The Divine objective of having children is really the same as having students — even the kinds of friend-students we are to each other all the time, every day. We're making *da'at* deposits into this world that continue filling the voids; in this way, we patch together eternity out of the rusting matter of the world.

The body dissolves to nothingness, but *da'at* lasts forever. It's not about a single generation or even two or three. *Da'at* is the legacy we leave behind that continues to develop and live long after we're gone. Because it's activated awareness of God, it can last forever. That's Moses's legacy — the *connected* and *connecting* mind of Moses that continues to flow through this world and fills it with *da'at* thousands of years after his passing. Moses taught us that our immortality is directly proportional to the degree of Divine awareness we're able to share — mercifully, positively, lovingly — with other minds while we're still here in the world of the flesh.

The purpose of existence is to know God, and the most direct way to accomplish this is through the Torah — the Creator's way of revealing His mind to us and teaching us how to bond with Him here in the material world. Raising children, raising students, *raising each other*, pushes us to really live the *da'at* that we seek. That's the *only thing* that allows us to transcend the limits and loss of materiality and time. *Da'at* — acquiring it, sharing it — is the only thing we leave behind.

DIVINE
ANGER

YOU PROBABLY SAW THE CHAPTER title and thought that maybe you'd skip this one...Who wants to talk about Divine anger? Who even wants to *think* about an angry God? First of all, it's frightening. Second of all, even though it's definitely a Biblical image, it doesn't sound like the merciful and compassionate God we've been talking about until now.

By this time you've probably realized that whenever we come to a concept that raises most people's hackles, I like to really explore it, expose it, and bring it to light. Divine anger is no different. It's just another dragon — a concept that makes us want to run the other way, but is actually a powerful mystical idea. It has wings, and it can even help us fly. I promise you, if we approach it the right way, this idea has the power to take us to a much higher place. So fasten your seatbelts and prepare for takeoff.

We were created to use our free will to willingly connect with our Source — again, to fill the void. That dirty word, "sin," (which in Hebrew really just means to miss the mark) is simply what happens when a person loses conscious connection with God. Negative thoughts, speech, and actions can then arise in this vacuum of awareness. The early masters called this "the spirit of folly" — it's what happens when the connected mind stops working.

Could we, would we, violate the Will of the Creator while in a state of conscious contact? Of course not. It's only in the space that's made by turning away that it becomes possible. We turn away...and the Creator turns away too. What's left is a spiritual void, an empty space calling out to be filled again.

If that void is going to be repaired, *someone* needs to move into that space and refill it with God-consciousness, with *da'at*. Someone needs to turn us back, because Divine anger — the Divine turning away — is only a response to our own about-face. Throughout the Torah we see that Divine anger is a response to the human being choosing to turn away from God. As soon as we return, we find the Creator is already there, waiting for us.

We've already learned that the empty spaces exist to allow us to participate in filling the gap. Of course, there can be endless reasons for the lack, but *from our vantage point*, we need to focus on how it serves as an opportunity for compassionate action and sharing of *da'at*.

> The empty spaces exist to allow us to participate in filling the gap.

Ideally, the state of disconnection should immediately spark our own yearning to bond again with our Source, an immediate *teshuvah* or "return" that would heal the breach. The problem is that the act of turning away and disconnecting makes us less sensitive spiritually. Being less sensitive spiritually can then get us stuck in our process of return.

This is where Moses steps in.

The catalyst for that flow of *da'at* back into the void is a "Moses," a person who also has a *connected and connecting* Moses-mind, as we've already learned. All of us have that potential within us; we all have a spark of Moses — our highest, actualized self — available inside to guide us.

Bearing all that in mind, let's look at the harshest example of Divine anger we can find: the incident of the Golden Calf. It has so much to teach us. The people came down from the heights of revelation and tumbled all the way down into idolatry — is there a worse sin than that? Was there any turning away greater than that?

Yet Moses jumped into the greatest collective breach to bridge the gap between the Jewish people and God. That was the *connected* mind of Moses activated by the *connecting* mercy of Moses.

The heaviest burden in the world is when an intrinsically refined and holy person has to carry the weight of his own transgressions. That's painful. It's more painful than being hungry; it's more painful than being bruised. A sensitive soul feels the pain of the loss of its own sanctity. And what's even worse is when the soul has fallen so far *that it doesn't even feel its own pain anymore.* Then a Moses-minded person — someone who *does* understand the inherent holiness of the soul — just looks on and hurts *for him.*

Moses couldn't stand by without doing whatever he could to bridge the gap, and when he did, the Creator rejoiced. Because even though God loves justice, He loves mercy so much more. The Torah teaches us that Moses was even tested as to the purity of his intentions, and he passed with flying colors. He protested, "If You won't forgive them, then erase me from Your book!" (Exodus 32:32). I don't want a private legacy, I don't want to be the sole survivor and have a new nation rebuilt from my descendants. I only rose to greatness to help the Jewish people, and I won't rest until You forgive them.

If we look to the Torah, we see that God even pointed the way for Moses to see how he could fill the void: "Now leave Me alone, so that My anger will burn against them and I will consume them...and I will make from you a great nation" (ibid. 32:10).

That was a Divine spotlight directing Moses's attention to a moment of opportunity: "*Leave Me alone* so that I can destroy them..." Our sages taught, "From here we see that God opened a doorway for Moses." What's the implication of, "Leave Me alone"? That if you *don't* leave me alone, Moses, *I won't be able to be angry with them any longer, and I will not destroy them!* Moses hadn't even begun to pray, and the Infinite One already showed him the way...Get busy, and don't stop praying, because *it all depends on you.*

So what was the doorway that the sages said God had opened for Moses? "Here's your empty space, Moses. It's up to you to fill it."

When we learned about Noah, we envisioned the scene after the floodwaters had subsided. Noah emerged from the ark and saw the world. He cried out, "God of Mercy, where was Your mercy?"

And the Creator answered, "Noah...where was *your* mercy?" I told you a lifetime ago that this was coming. Why didn't you try to turn people around? Why didn't you at least pray for them? *Why didn't you realize that I was giving you an opportunity to jump into the breach and do your part to reveal My mercy...by asking for it?*

When we look around and see a vacuum of kindness, when we see calamity and suffering, there's nothing accomplished by accusing the Creator of being cruel. We know that God is good, infinitely compassionate, and kind. That space of apparent cruelty is *our* doorway. We are being invited to act as His agents and exercise our own mercy through action, through prayer, and by shining the light of *da'at* into the world so that people can turn themselves around and heal their broken connections with their Source.

Noah was branded the "Foolish Shepherd" — the inverse of Moses, who was the "Faithful Shepherd." The difference between them was how they reacted to the pocket of darkness that opened in front of them. Moses and his family were also offered an ark to escape into, but Moses refused to abandon his mission.

We need to see that Moses was not an isolated individual; he learned from Noah's mistake. He's another point in this transgenerational progression, and he began from where the masters who came before him left off. Moses learned in Noah's school.

This isn't only about the Golden Calf and Sinai and Moses. It's about every single one of us. We all need to learn how to take our *da'at* and our quality of mercy and use them to fill the voids we encounter every day. Everywhere we look, we encounter lack, pain, suffering, injustice… We see these empty spaces in the wider world all over the front pages; we also see them in our personal sphere right where we live.

These are the voids we were created to fill. They're waiting for us to step in and activate our quality of mercy…so that we can trigger the flow of Divine mercy from above.

This was the way of Moses, and it's our path to take too.

THE SECRET
WEAPON

SO WHERE HAS OUR DRAGON taken us, in the end? All that dangerous flaming Divine anger at the sin of the Golden Calf within the empty space...But it aroused Moses to leap into the void and fill it with prayer, *da'at*, and mercy. Moses jumped at the opportunity for that magical moment of reconciliation, of the unity of the restored face-to-face relationship. And at the moment, when he bridged the gap, Moses knew he'd found grace in God's eyes. What did he do at that magical moment? He asked God to grant him a new level of awareness! Moses wanted to grasp the highest degree of Divine mercy and connection possible: "Show me Your glory" (Exodus 33:18). I feel so aligned with You right now, God, please let me see You in the most direct and intimate way that can be.

The Infinite One responded, "No one can see My Face and live...but I have a space *with Me* where you can hide yourself and see Me from behind as I pass over you." The Kabbalists taught that more than just *that space* is "with God" — "I have a space" means that *all space is within God*. No place can encompass Him, but all space is within Him.

Moses jumped into the empty space of Divine anger to heal it, and he was rewarded with a space — a place here in the human realm where the loftiest God-consciousness possible would be made available to him.

What did the Creator teach him during those precious moments?

God allowed Moses to see a vision of God Himself praying that His own higher mercy flow down and be revealed. And God taught Moses the secret weapon of Divine prayer — the magic "buttons" we can press to activate the Thirteen Divine Attributes of Mercy down here, through our words and actions.

That is a gift that can — *and will* — change the world.

These "buttons" can seem like just a formula of words, Names, or aspects, but what they really are is a unified summons of the entire spectrum of God's infinite compassion and forgiveness.

The great mystics taught us, "There's mercy, *and then there's mercy.*" There are two different degrees of Divine mercy. The lower one plays by the rules. If you're worthy of kindness, you get it; if you're not, you don't. But there's an infinitely higher level of Divine mercy where there are *no distinctions, no limits,* and *no barriers.* When we learn of God appealing to His own higher degree of mercy, it's to teach us that there are ways that we too can tap into the Divine mercy that has no limits.

The Thirteen Attributes are that higher degree. And we make use of the tool that Moses revealed *every single day* in the morning prayers. It plays an even stronger role during the month leading up to the High Holidays and culminating in Yom Kippur. These Divine Names are the means we've been given to access that highest level of mercy.

This is a kind of Divine irony. The Jewish people fell to the lowest point, but what came out of that disaster? The highest revelation of Divine mercy. And, not only that, *but we received the main tool we can use to activate God's mercy for the rest of human history.* This wasn't only a one-time event; that moment returns every time we encounter an empty space within ourselves, in our lives, in our world.

At those moments, we draw off this *da'at* of Moses — "God, *I know You*, and I know Your mercy is never-ending…that You can do absolutely anything…*even if it means forgiving the unforgivable and having compassion on the hopeless.*"

So now we can really understand the completion of the *da'at*-cycle (which never really ends):

- You transcend your natural self-interest and reach out with compassion;
- This expansion of self then helps to open your mind to a greater grasp of God;

- You internalize the awareness and make it a part of you and then you further bring it down by sharing it with others whose minds are constricted;
- You now have new space within yourself to receive the next level of perception;
- Which then deepens your compassion and ability to connect with others;
- And the *da'at*-cycle continues.

Moses's mercy and self-sacrifice on behalf of the Jewish people *drew down* into the world a Divine gift that's the expanding nature of this *da'at*-cycle.

Now, instead of just talking about the Thirteen Attributes, we need to really take a good look at them one by one, to understand them better. I'm just going to follow the sages' basic understanding of the distinction between these Names, and bear in mind that the first Name that we pronounce "*Adonai*" ("Master") is really written as the four-letter Divine Name known as *HaVaYaH* — "Existence." That Name also expresses God's quality of loving-kindness.

Adonai: You were a *loving and merciful God* before I did anything wrong...

Adonai: ...and *You are still loving and merciful* even now, after I've made my mistakes and want to repair them.

El: You are the *force of mercy* accessible to me here in this world.

Rachum: *Merciful*...

V'Chanun: ...and *compassionate One*,

Erech Apayim: You are *patient*, and give me time to return to You.

V'Rav Chessed: You even provide *great lovingkindess* to those who don't really deserve it all that much...like me.

V'Emet: You are *true* — faithful to reward those who do Your will.

Notzer Chessed: You *guard kindness* by remaining ever aware of the good I've done...

L'Alafim: ...for *two thousand generations*. You are so much more attentive to my good than to my bad!

Nosei Avon: *You forgive rebellious sins*,

Va'fesha: and *You forgive purposeful sins*,

V'Chata'ah: and *You forgive errors,*
V'Nakeh: and *You cleanse!*

We'll revisit these Attributes later in the book, when we learn about other ways to activate Divine mercy down here in our world, but these are the root.

These Thirteen Attributes are the gift that keeps on giving...forever. Some say that even though the merit of our ancestors is vast, it has an expiration date. These Attributes, however, never lose their power. In fact, as time goes on and the world is in ever-greater need of God's mercy, they become even more powerful. That's because the greater need for mercy helps to reveal that Divine mercy is *infinitely* great (more about that toward the end of this book), and more than sufficient to help even us, no matter how undeserving, how limited, and how far away we are or feel. "God's prayer" bridges the gap between us and God when nothing else can.

> These Thirteen Attributes are the gift that keeps on giving...forever.

SECTION THREE

THE TORAH MASTERS

IN THIS SECTION, WE JOURNEY THROUGH MORE THAN THREE THOUSAND YEARS OF EVOLVING TORAH REVELATION. WE BRIDGE THE AGES BETWEEN MOSES, THE FIRST REDEEMER, AND THE MESSIAH, THE FINAL REDEEMER.

THE TORAH UNFOLDS

IF WE SEE THE TORAH only as a book of rules, then it would make the most sense for Divine revelation to be a static, one-time event, without any flex or fluctuation as its message rolls through time. But when we understand that the Torah is a means of bringing humanity into alignment with the Divine Will, *which is constantly unfolding throughout time,* it's clear that the vibrations of spirituality that resonate through each messenger will emerge differently.

Every great teacher transmitted the same essential Torah, but each one transmitted it in his own way, with emphasis and elaboration on the concepts most needed for his own phase of the progression. But it's not only about teachings and concepts. It goes deeper than that.

> *Each master plays a unique role in the transformation of the world and in the evolution of its consciousness.*

The Torah testifies to the unparalleled stature of Moses as a prophet — "There never arose another like Moses among the Jewish people..." Nevertheless, throughout history, sages have each done their part to catalyze the rectification of the world, each in his own irreplaceable way.

Each had a unique reflection of Moses's unsurpassed degree of *da'at* — integrated God-consciouesness.

At the same time, certain figures throughout the ages served as paradigm-shifters. The advances in Divine awareness they brought to the world made it a completely different place than before they did their work. So even though the teachings of all of the sages are worthy of study, we'll focus on those unique figures who completely changed the prevailing state of spiritual development in the world, stage by stage.

Each came on the world scene at a crucial historical juncture, bearing the message and teachings that would provide all the tools the world would need to grow into the next phase of development. Each revealed the extent of Divine mercy to an ever-greater degree.

Let's watch it unfold.

REVEALING
THE HIDDEN

THE KABBALISTIC TRADITION HAS ALWAYS existed, just like the Infinite One has always existed. And just like the Creator keeps Himself well hidden to preserve the integrity of our own free will, the teachings that explain the mechanics of His ways were also kept very quiet. Even righteous and scholarly people throughout the ages were not necessarily privy to their mysteries. In every generation, those secret vital seeds of the Kabbalistic tradition were only entrusted to the disciples who proved worthy and able to guard them carefully to plant them into the future.

In our Internet-fueled information age, it's hard to imagine there was ever a time when there were secrets. I don't mean secrets in the personal sense; I mean the *purposeful concealment of an entire system of spiritual development and consciousness*. The Kabbalistic tradition was hidden in this way because the world hadn't yet developed to the point when it could be revealed to a broader audience.

Nearly two thousand years ago, Rabbi Shimon bar Yochai — author of the *Zohar*, the great ancient text of Kabbalah — rose to greatness in the north of Israel. And the Divine light refracted through him in a different way than it had through Moses, revealing new dimensions that had been hidden until then.

When pure, white light flashes through a prism, a whole spectrum is revealed...but all those colors were really hidden within the beam of white light all along.

Kabbalah isn't about *knowing more*; it's about sharing a sense of the meaning of existence so that our lives are transformed. The mystical tradition isn't metaphysics, it's the reorientation of our minds and hearts to focus on the inner dimension of reality. It's the soul of the Torah...the Tree of Life.

When we understand that revelations of the secrets of Creation and Providence aren't about *information*, but about *connection*, the evolution of the Kabbalistic tradition assumes a whole new meaning.

Rabbi Shimon bar Yochai's revelations were rooted in his *compassion*, because there's no greater act of compassion than to help another human being understand the purpose of his existence.

Where did Rabbi Shimon get his knowledge of this tradition? He certainly had teachers; he was one of the main students of the great sage Rabbi Akiva. But we see from his history that his light only really began to shine after he went through an ordeal. Rabbi Shimon's struggle to unearth the hidden Torah took thirteen years of constant effort, near-constant physical deprivation and suffering. If it's hard for us to imagine that there were ever secrets, it's far harder for us to imagine the kind of self-sacrifice it took to gain the privilege of revealing the hidden Divine light of compassion in the world.

> There's no greater act of compassion than to help another human being understand the purpose of his existence.

THE HOLY
FIRE OF
RABBI SHIMON

AFTER SPEAKING OUT AGAINST THE *Roman occupation,*
Rabbi Shimon and his son Elazar fled to a cave outside the
Gallilean village of Peki'in. There, they subsisted on carob fruit
and water, and studied Torah in great deprivation and solitude
for twelve years. But those twelve years transformed Rabbi
Shimon completely.

Throughout those years, the prophet Elijah came to study with
him; he received a flow of Divine information that came from
a much higher Source. They were on fire, Rabbi Shimon and his
son, and when they emerged from the cave after the danger
had passed, the fire in their gaze was so powerful that it would
incinerate everything it hit upon. Looking out on a mundane
world of fields and crops and people tending to their everyday
concerns aroused their judgment — "How could you waste
your lives on such fleeting concerns? What about your spiritual
lives?!" But a Heavenly voice called down: "You left your cave to
destroy My world? Go back!"

They spent another twelve months in the cave, but this time
their garments were in such tatters that they had to bury
themselves in the earth so they could cover their nakedness and
continue to study. They had to go down into the earthiness they
had scorned and scorched to make a repair.

Later, Rabbi Shimon and Rabbi Elazar met up with Rabbi

> *Shimon's father-in-law, Rabbi Pinchas ben Ya'ir. Wrapped in rags, their skin covered with sores from the earth that had covered them, Pinchas ben Ya'ir was devastated at seeing how debilitated they had become.*
>
> *"Woe is me, to see you this way!" he cried.*
>
> *Bur Rabbi Shimon answered serenely, "No — you should be saying, 'Happy am I to see you this way!' Had I not suffered the way I did, I would never have succeeded to unearth such treasures of Torah!"*

Every year, on the anniversary of Rabbi Shimon's death, anywhere between half a million and a million people travel north to Meron to pray and celebrate at his gravesite. The vast majority of these visitors are not scholars or mystics, or even necessarily all that religious. What brings them there? And what keeps them coming back, year after year?

What happens at the annual celebration is rooted in a very deep mystery, one that people don't need to articulate to themselves because *they're just drawn to the place* without necessarily being able to explain why. On some very deep level, people realize that the inner essence of even Rabbi Shimon's most obscure teachings *does* include them — but it took the work of later sages to reveal just how.

RABBI SHIMON'S LAST DAY

WHEN WE THINK ABOUT THE arc of a person's life, we can get trapped in a limited, materialistic view. If our focus is on physical accomplishments, life can look like an upward climb from birth until adulthood, peaking around the prime years of strength and productivity, and afterward declining into old age and death.

But when spiritual evolution is our focus, we see how life can be a gradual upward motion that *culminates* in the moment when the soul is ready to rejoin its Source.

Rabbi Shimon's life reached its high point just as it was poised to end.

> *On Rabbi Shimon's final day, only the closest disciples were permitted in the house. Outside, the humble dwelling was surrounded by fire. Angels descended from heaven to hear the teachings; no one could draw close to the building as it was encircled by blinding light and flame.*
>
> *Rabbi Shimon took his closest students and arranged them around him according to the cardinal directions. It was just as the tribes had been arranged around the Tabernacle in the desert, and just as Jacob had instructed his children to arrange themselves around his coffin to carry it back from Egypt to the Land of Israel for burial. Rabbi Abba, filled with fear and trembling, was instructed to record the final gathering. He wrote down Rabbi Shimon's every word. And Rabbi Shimon bar Yochai spent the last day of his life revealing the nature of God's Thirteen Attributes of mercy.*
>
> *Before he began his final discourse, Rabbi Shimon said, "God's*

Presence is with us, and this is a sign that now is the time to reveal the Torah's deepest secrets. I refuse to go to the Next World ashamed. All of the secrets that I held close until now, I'm going to reveal before the Divine Presence. And then it will not be said in paradise that I died incomplete." No one will be able to say that Rabbi Shimon left his secrets unsaid.

Rabbi Shimon left nothing unsaid; his intent was to get all of his teachings set down in a way that both revealed them (so they could be accessed by the wise) and concealed them (to keep them safe from the unworthy). Since his time, successive teachers have — and this is the greatest Divine mercy — revealed more and more of this tradition. With *connection* and *compassion*, they have literally drawn it down into the atmosphere of this world, where you and I live and breathe.

A UNIFIED
LIFE

MOST OF US SUFFER FROM a dysfunctional kind of thinking. We're not focused, because we're in the world of multiplicity. When we're "bound to this world," we tend to feel fractured, because this world is a place of fragmentation. We're pulled in endless directions, driven by numerous and shifting desires and motivations, assailed by endless distractions and temptations. Yet, before Rabbi Shimon left this world, he summed up the essence of his life:

> *All the time that I was bound up with this world — all the days of my life — I was, in truth, tied with a single bond to the Infinite One.*

Even when Rabbi Shimon and other tzaddikim like him are "tied down" here because they're living in a physical body, they remain bound up with the Infinite One. They're focused on the Divine Will and they stay aligned with it. And then all their human experience is also bound up with the unified Will of the Infinite One. The multifaceted life can be tied with a *single bond* to the Infinite One.

So what was Rabbi Shimon bar Yochai so determined to share before he left this world? What was the essence of the teachings that he had his student, Rabbi Abba, commit to writing in the *Zohar* itself? It's really the encapsulation of his tzaddik-mentality, his way of seeing and being, informed by the Torah's secrets.

> Rabbi Shimon teaches us that it's possible to be bound here in the physical world and still be unified with the Infinite One.

His final lesson was on the Infinite extent of God's mercy.

With an internal landscape formed by these teachings, it's possible to leave the natural state of fragmentation and bind ourselves up with the Infinite One. It's possible to live in alignment, in unity.

When our minds let go of the racing and the self-will, we come to a kind of clarity. We can imagine that our minds are like the pressings of grapes that are still fermenting; thoughts run in all directions, bubbly and clouded. But if we've received good influence from minds more clarified than our own and we give it time, the lees start to settle and our thinking begins to clear too.

The unified mind is serene; it's no longer self-seeking. All it wants is the Infinite One and His teachings, and since the Infinite One is available to us at all times, in all situations, the external focus of all human striving starts to become less relevant.

> The unified mind is serene; it's no longer self-seeking.

It doesn't matter so much if I have a lot of money or I don't have a lot of money, whether I have a large apartment or a small one — conscious contact with the Infinite One is available to me no matter what my circumstances.

Instead of striving, I can be serene. Instead of being driven by dissatisfaction, I always have a reason to rejoice. Because I'm *bound up with a single bond* — my life is unified to a single purpose, to a single Will, which is infinitely merciful.

BUILDING ON THE FOUNDATION

WE'VE ALREADY LEARNED THAT, WHEN it comes to history and the development of spiritual consciousness, we are involved in a *progression* — a process unfolding over time.

Even though Rabbi Shimon bar Yochai reached lofty levels of Godly perception, there was still a limit to how much he could share those perceptions with others. That's because a teaching relationship isn't only about the master's grasp of a concept; it also depends on the student's ability to receive that knowledge.

Teaching doesn't only mean sharing the information that you have. Your student also needs to have the tools to process what you have to give.

Rabbi Shimon bar Yochai expended his last energies on earth ensuring that every drop of Divine awareness he'd gained during his lifetime would remain down here with us *in some form*. He was successful, but what he left behind was a kind of code. His own students could understand it, and their few students throughout the generations were able to glean something from those recorded teachings that form the *Zohar*. For most of us, though, that book is sealed.

> Teaching doesn't only mean sharing the information that you have. Your student also needs to have the tools to process what you have to give.

You and I can browse online for great books on relativity, but unless we have strong backgrounds in higher mathematics they're not going to make much sense to us. We can stare at diagrams and formulae until our eyes give out, but unless we already have a lot of prior knowledge of the subject, we might as well be reading a foreign language.

About five hundred years ago, after another deep historical trauma — the expulsion of Spanish Jewry — a new light arose in the Holy Land. Rabbi Isaac Luria, also known as the "Arizal" — the "Divine Rabbi Isaac" — was determined to bring healing to the Jewish people and to the world. He did this, mainly, by taking the code of the *Zohar* and providing us with its Rosetta Stone, its key.

Where Rabbi Shimon seemed obscure, Rabbi Luria discovered a system. Where Rabbi Shimon sounded cryptic, Rabbi Luria revealed a pathway.

Rabbi Shimon bar Yochai was the father of Kabbalah, but it took another fifteen hundred years until Rabbi Isaac Luria became the father of modern Jewish mysticism. Every significant development in Torah since then had its foundations laid by him.

Kabbalah is the revelation of the Torah's inner dimension...its soul.

Our tradition describes the process of birth as one that begins from pure spirit, and which later takes on the form of flesh.

The Torah's soul was given expression by Rabbi Shimon's teachings, but it wasn't fully born into the world until more layers and garments — a kind of body — could clothe it. The Arizal's teachings are that body.

THE MAN
OF GOD

BUT WHAT WAS RABBI ISAAC Luria *like*? What kind of a person do you need to be to serve as a conduit of such powerful Torah? Rabbi Chaim Vital, Rabbi Luria's main disciple, once came out and *asked* the Arizal what he had done to reach such lofty levels of understanding. Contrary to what we might have thought, the Arizal did *not* reply that it was through fasting, self-mortification, or nonstop study.

Rabbi Chaim Vital describes the greatness of the Arizal in an introduction to one of his works:

> *Today, I'm going to share the Holy One's secrets with you...*
>
> *God always illuminates our path in every generation by way of unique teachers. In His compassion, he has sent us "an angel descended from heaven" — my master and teacher, Rabbi Isaac Luria Ashkenazi — who was a scholar of every dimension of Torah. He was a master of the full Kabbalistic tradition. He knew the language of the trees, birds, and angels. And, like Rabbi Shimon bar Yochai, he knew one's future and inner workings and thoughts just from looking at one's face.*
>
> *He knew the future, and also had knowledge of events taking place all over the world.*
>
> *By candlelight and firelight, he came to know of wondrous things...*
>
> *He knew each person's soul-history, the incarnations they had already been through and their particular mission in life. He knew all of this without resorting to practical Kabbalah [the use of amulets, etc.] or immersive meditation. There has been*

no one of his caliber since the time of Rabbi Shimon bar Yochai.

His knowledge, as well as communication with the souls of great sages throughout the ages, came to him naturally, after many years of personal purification and intensive study, without having to exert himself in mystical meditation. Elijah the Prophet himself came to teach him the inner mysteries of Torah...

Yet when Rabbi Isaac Luria answered Rabbi Chaim's direct question, "How did you come to the heights you've reached?" the Arizal answered, "Through performing the Divine Will with *joy*."

At first glance, that might seem overly simplistic. But when we remember that the mitzvot are individual channels of connection and alignment with the Creator, the Arizal's answer starts to make more sense.

To carry out God's Will with joy means taking hold of a mitzvah, of every connecting channel that presents itself to me based on my nature and situation, and using it mindfully. I don't have to think about what was, or what's going to be. I just have to be present in this magic moment of the mitzvah...*and enjoy it.*

> To carry out God's Will with joy means taking hold of a mitzvah, of every connecting channel that presents itself to me based on my nature and situation, and using it mindfully.

Rabbi Isaac Luria is pointing us toward the gateway to prophetic connection with the Creator. Yes, you need to refine yourself; yes, you need to study. But the thing you need most is to take hold of that perfect instant of opportunity for connection with the Infinite One with a deep understanding of its cosmic importance.

In other words...with *joy*.

SOUL REPAIR

ONE OF THE MOST FUNDAMENTAL cosmic truths is that the Infinite One is in constant communication with His Creation. God waits for us to reach out and make conscious contact with Him. He sends us reminders of His presence in every situation we encounter.

> *Everything we see, hear, think, and experience is a manifestation of Divine Providence. It's God's way of saying, "Here I am."*

Those calls are what we call Divine Providence.

Sometimes, the Divine calling cards are magical, connected moments. But sometimes the workings of Providence — Divine supervision and orchestration of events — are beyond our understanding. The world is full of suffering, and even genuinely good people can, and do, suffer.

> God waits for us to reach out and make conscious contact with Him. He sends us reminders of His presence in every situation we encounter.

Everything rests on our belief that the Creator is good, and does only good — so it's natural for people to find their faith tested when they see evil in the world.

One of the Divine concepts Rabbi Isaac Luria brought down to the world was his grasp of the reincarnation of souls. The teachings he shared weren't innovations of his — they were already part of the tradition — but they were generally unknown until he spoke of them openly.

Sharing a fresh perspective that broadens our understanding of Godly compassion is one of the greatest acts of mercy a person can do. An entire book detailing the workings of soul reincarnation entered our world because of the Arizal's great compassion for us — it's called *Sha'ar*

Hagilgulim, "The Gate of Incarnations." It's a tapestry of teachings that open our minds to one essential truth: The Infinite One leads us all on a path of individual and collective soul-repair, with the greatest providential exactness, *out of His love for us.*

The concept of reincarnation — especially when it's interwoven with the ability to know the workings of Providence *on the individual level* as the Arizal did — was vital nourishment for the faith of the Jewish people. It undoes the idea of meaningless suffering. When we're able to see the full story of an individual soul — where it's been in the past and where it needs to get to in the future — a picture of purpose takes form in our minds and hearts. This is the antidote to the erosion of faith that has become so widespread. In the story below, we can see how an awareness of the dynamics of soul-repair can make a genuine and immediate positive impact on the way we live our lives every day.

> The Infinite One leads us all on a path of individual and collective soul-repair.

A man came to visit the Arizal of Safed with a personal problem. He and his wife just could not get along. Although he had spent years trying to appease her, his wife sniped at him constantly. He, in turn, would fire back; their home was a battleground. Maybe the great sage would be able to offer some advice so that his home could be peaceful?

When the man entered the Arizal's room, the sage immediately looked up and said: "The woman you're married to makes you suffer so because you have a debt to repay. In your previous incarnations, it was you who made her life a misery. She is merely God's instrument to bring about your soul-repair. You must do your best to accept her harangues with love. Be grateful that your repair involves nothing worse!"

The man went home with a completely changed attitude. When his wife began to berate him, he nodded calmly and wouldn't respond. If she brusquely ordered him around, he would think, "I'm sure that this is repairing the damage to my soul that I caused before!" These thoughts made his life bearable, even happy.

After days of this changed behavior, the man's wife decided she wanted some answers. It was hard to fight without a sparring partner! She said, "You've been different since you went to see the rabbi. What did he tell you?"

When her husband was reluctant to divulge their conversation, she pestered him relentlessly. Eventually, he told her the truth. "I have no complaints, because when you fight against me you're actually helping me. I will love you exactly as you are, whatever you do, unconditionally."

The wife was so incensed, she cried out, "Help you?! If being hard on you is helping you, then from now on I'll be all sweetness! So much for your soul-repair!"

The following day, the man ran back to the Arizal. "Holy Rebbe, my wife has starting being so good, but it's only from spite. She won't cooperate anymore in repairing my soul!"

The sage smiled and said, "No, she is being kind because you've finished your rectification. Now you can go home and live in peace."

EXILE AND REDEMPTION

ANOTHER REVOLUTIONARY CONCEPT INTRODUCED BY the Arizal relates to the nature of the exile. The Jewish people were exiled from their land for the last time two thousand years ago. During that long period, they were driven throughout the world by expulsions and forces beyond their control. For much of that time, they suffered oppression, forced conversions, and mass murders. Until recently, the exile — which we started to call the diaspora when it got easier — was the collective accumulation of our trials and tribulations.

Then Rabbi Isaac Luria came and explained — patiently, compassionately — that exile isn't an arbitrary punishment for sins in the past. Because punishment is a lot like revenge, and the Creator doesn't exact revenge for our past misbehavior.

What He does is arrange for repair, for redemption of a bad situation.

The Arizal explained that Adam's choosing to eat from the Tree of Knowledge of Good and Evil fragmented reality into the state of multiplicity, of perceived distance from the Infinite One. Every bit of reality would appear to be separated from its Source, in a state of independence and disunity, with no "cosmic glue" of Godliness to hold it all together. From that point on, the power of faith would have to be harnessed to experience unity with the Source; it wouldn't be automatic.

> The Arizal revealed to us that exile isn't punitive — it's the key to our soul-repair.

In the teachings of Rabbi Isaac Luria, exile is the *necessary condition* of spreading outward into ever-increasing fragmentation — both individually and collectively — in order to bring God-consciousness to *absolutely everywhere*. Exile, then, becomes a story of a mission, a complex and ongoing process to gather in all of the sparks of Godliness that have been dispersed throughout Creation.

The Jewish people weren't exiled as much as they were *sown* throughout the far reaches of the globe. And all sowing is a necessary investment for a future harvest.

With these teachings, and others like them, the Arizal infused a suffering Jewish people with hope

> The Jewish people weren't exiled as much as they were *sown* throughout the far reaches of the globe.

and healing, and a new focus on *redemption as it unfolds and evolves right now, through us and within us*.

THE
SHATTERED
JUGS

THE ARIZAL DIDN'T ONLY TEACH in theory, using the traditional tools of word and text. He took his students on the path of transformation through action — the most genuine learning experience there is. Rabbi Luria taught his disciples about loving-kindness by gathering them to live with their families in a single courtyard, with household goods shared in common. Through refining their small circle, he knew they could change the world.

> *Once, the great spiritual master Rabbi Isaac Luria was in the fields surrounding the mystical city of Safed, teaching Kabbalah to his inner circle of disciples. All of a sudden, he stood up mid-sentence and appeared to be completely engrossed in a matter far from the subject that had so mesmerized his students a moment before. In a kind of frenzy, the great master broke away from the circle and began to run back toward the town, with his students trailing behind in wonder.*
>
> *As the Arizal ducked through the narrow stone alleyways of the ancient city, the disciples could barely keep pace with him. Suddenly brought up short, they found the saintly rabbi bent over an old water-carrier who was lying on the ground, surrounded by his smashed earthenware jugs. And the poor old man was crying bitterly.*
>
> *Rabbi Luria helped the man to his feet, gave him a warm embrace, and spoke a few words to him quietly. He reached into*

his pocket and handed the man five valuable coins to buy new jugs, then turned to retrace his path back out to the fields beyond the city. Still in a state of wonder, the small group of disciples followed their master back to their spot in the grasses. The questions began to flow from their lips. "How did you know?" "Why was it so important to interrupt our lesson in the middle to carry out this act of charity?" "Doesn't Torah study take precedence over everything else?" "Could you not have sent one of us to take care of him? Why did it have to be you?"

The Arizal patiently explained, "These earthenware jugs were all that the old man had; there was no other way for him to make a living, and a meager one at that. When he slipped and they shattered, he was broken to pieces. At that moment, he began to weep and hate his Creator for having ruined him. Right in the middle of our lesson, I could feel that his tears, his claim against God, had triggered a heavenly decree that would have destroyed the entire world. One man's pain can destroy the world! I had to run and find him...and let him know that God had not abandoned him!"

> The Arizal shared a new awareness with his students — that small, human-scale acts of mercy have the power to overturn the harshness of a Divine decree.

The Arizal shared a new awareness with his students — that small, human-scale acts of mercy have the power to overturn the harshness of a Divine decree. He implanted in their consciousness that acts of kindness *down here* are an accessible means of mitigating the heavenly judgments that can afflict our world.

THE MYSTICAL
MITZVAH

ONE OF RABBI LURIA'S GREATEST contributions to the evolution of spiritual consciousness was his marriage of the mystical and the mitzvah.

What I mean is that the Arizal succeeded in introducing customs rooted in Kabbalah into our daily practice as Jews. One beautiful example of this is the prayer service that inaugurates the Shabbos. On the cusp between Friday afternoon and Shabbos evening, we have a custom — initiated by the Arizal, although it is hinted at in the *Zohar* — to sing a series of psalms and special prayers as a way of ushering in the Shabbos Queen.

Rabbi Luria knew that the structure of mitzvah as legal code might be factually accurate, but it is *actually* lacking. Kabbalah always has been the soul of every mitzvah and Torah verse.

Mysticism isn't naturally separate from mitzvah practice.
It is the hidden, inner soul of the practice that vitalizes it.

> Mysticism isn't naturally separate from mitzvah practice. It is the hidden, inner soul of the practice that vitalizes it.

By breaking down the apparent barriers that existed in people's minds between mystical and mitzvah, he allowed the vital essence of mitzvot to stream into their outer forms so that we could access that life-giving spirit.

We'll see, though, that although the Arizal *began* this process, it would still take hundreds of years for it to really flourish and spread throughout the world.

THE
REGRESSION

HISTORY, FOR US, IS ABOUT witnessing the unfolding of Divine mercy through distinct stages of spiritual evolution. At each stage, certain historic figures served as catalysts of radical shifts in human consciousness. All of those changes were actually about revealing the Divine mercy that vitalizes Creation to an ever-greater extent, stage after stage.

To understand the next important figure in the historical progression — the founder of the Chassidic movement, Rabbi Israel Baal Shem Tov, the "Master of the Good Name" — we need to first take a look at the historical backdrop. Although this isn't a history book in the conventional sense, we can't really grasp the role he played if we don't understand the empty space he came to fill.

The truth is that everyone has a mission, and in a certain way it's about filling in a gap, a kind of cosmic *empty space* like we learned about at the beginning of this book. There's a hole in the fabric of reality that no one can fill except for you. When it comes to a master like the Baal Shem Tov, his destiny was to fill a spiritual void that had plagued generations of suffering souls. At every major stage of spiritual evolution, certain historical figures served as catalysts of radical shifts in human consciousness, and the Baal Shem Tov was perfectly suited for bringing the changes needed in his time.

In the year 1626, on the ninth of the Hebrew month of Av — a day that's been set aside for mourning the losses of exile for two thousand years — a man named Shabbtai Tzvi was born in Turkey. Brilliant and charismatic, an iconoclastic student of Kabbalah, Shabbtai Tzvi soon rose to unimaginable influence in the Jewish world. A messianic cult formed around him, which ultimately led to further fracturing of the Jewish community and mass despair when his messianic project failed miserably. (Many books have been written about the movement and its ramifications, and the subject is beyond the scope of this book.)

For our purposes here, it's important to know that Shabbtai Tzvi twisted the Arizal's teachings to form a new and dangerous doctrine. He claimed that *willful* descent into sin or exile of the spirit would be the key to redemption. And so he and his followers adopted anti-Torah practices — the exact opposite of alignment with the Divine Will that brings connection and blessing.

Shabbtai Tzvi was arrested and pressured by the Ottoman authorities to convert to Islam. He eventually died in exile, leaving behind a traumatized and altered Jewish world. Despite a hundred years of the flourishing of Kabbalah and significant change ushered in by Rabbi Isaac Luria, the wounded Jewish world became allergic to mysticism.

If Kabbalah could produce a force as destructive as Shabbtai Tzvi, the rabbis reasoned, then it would be better to send its light back behind the curtains until some far-off future. Until then, the inner dimension of Torah would remain the province of a very select few scholars. Certainly, it was too dangerous for the masses. It was toxic. Radioactive. So after seventeen hundred years of slow but significant progress since the time of Rabbi Shimon bar Yochai, the Jewish world went into a sudden tailspin.

THE MASTER
OF THE
GOOD NAME

IN 1698, THE FATHER OF the Chassidic movement, the Baal Shem Tov, was born in a forgotten corner of Ukraine, and, before long, he managed to reignite the dimmed soul-spark of the Jewish people.

So, what is Chassidism? It's essentially the work of bringing down the light of Kabbalah — the soul of the Torah — and translating it into tools of thought, speech, and action that can be used by anyone. It's the transformation of the highly esoteric ideas of Kabbalah into a way of life. These concepts breathe energy into the performance of religious rituals, have the power to infuse mundane activities with infinite spirituality and, since they began to spread nearly three hundred years ago, they've completely altered the Jewish world.

Like the Arizal, the Baal Shem Tov was a master mystic. In those times, a "Baal Shem" was a Kabbalist who could perform miracles — a master wielder of the Divine Name for the sake of helping those who suffer in body and spirit. Israel Baal Shem Tov spent the first part of his life in poverty and obscurity. He worked as a simple laborer, sometimes as an assistant teacher with the youngest children. Israel Baal Shem was interested in staying close to the people and having time and privacy to pursue his mystical studies.

Later, he began to share his knowledge locally, but outside of his immediate circle he was still a mystery. Only at about age forty did he begin to allow others to know of his qualities and abilities. Eventually his light started to shine so brightly it could no longer be hidden. Even though he kept his scholarship a secret, Providence conspired to make him known far and wide.

With a glance, the Baal Shem Tov knew everything about any supplicant or student who came to him for help. When he prayed in the field, even the goats stopped grazing and got up on their hind legs to pray with him.

The Baal Shem Tov had angelic mentors in addition to his earthly masters; his teachings ran the gamut from absolute simplicity, the most down-to-earth for the earthiest person, to the highest and most subtle discourses for the most advanced disciple. The common people loved him; the scholars came to study at his feet. He was a wonder-worker, a Kabbalist, a healer of bodies and hearts and souls.

The new master's way of transmitting those seeds of the inner vitality of the Torah was completely different from Rabbi Shimon's and the Arizal's. Yet it was perfectly suited to the spiritual, emotional, psychological, and physical needs of his time. The Baal Shem Tov was sent to the world to teach the value of simplicity to the sophisticated, and to share the Torah's inner light with the common man. He taught his elite students the value of the simple people, and how beloved they are by God.

> The Baal Shem Tov was sent to the world to teach the value of simplicity and to share the Torah's inner light with the common man.

The founder of Chassidism made it his mission to find a way to drip the Torah's secrets into the veins of ordinary Jews until their regular practice of Judaism was transformed into a vital connection with the Creator. His goal was to revive the nation with a revolutionary way of understanding the nature of the mitzvot.

> The Baal Shem Tov's mission was to transform our grasp of mitzvot from rules to channels of connection.

Instead of seeing the mitzvot as mere rules that bind, the Baal Shem Tov wanted all Jews to realize that they are channels of vitality, portals for coming into contact with Godliness, for drawing Godliness into this world of action. And this can revolutionize not only Jewish life, but all life, everyone's life.

To follow the Baal Shem Tov's path, one doesn't have to be living on the loftiest level; what you do have to do, though, is connect yourself to the people who are.

TWO HOLES

DUE TO THE "ALLERGY TO mysticsm" brought on by Shabbtai Tzvi, a new personality emerged — a type the Baal Shem Tov would come to call, "The Depressed Torah Scholar."

The Baal Shem Tov said, "The only reason I came to this world was to help fix the depressed Torah scholar." Who could be in greater need of help than someone who spends his days and nights studying Torah, the Tree of Life, *and doesn't feel any vitality from it*? What a hole, what a vacuum that was in the world! To be immersed in Torah and still feel empty? That was a space the Baal Shem Tov came to fill.

> The Baal Shem Tov said, "The only reason I came to this world was to help fix the depressed Torah scholar."

But that first empty space gave birth to another hole. It was the widening gulf between the learned — many of whom were missing that all-important spark of Divine connection — and the simple Jews who lived (barely) by petty trade and manual labor. And those simple people happened to be the vast majority of Eastern European Jews.

During that time — really, throughout Jewish history — Torah scholarship was *everything*. People made unimaginable sacrifices to ensure their children were properly educated. For centuries, when the only non-Jews who could read and write were either nobility or clerics, the Jewish people had an almost universal literacy rate.

Torah had always been a great unifier and equalizer. But when economics, politics, and steady persecution made it harder and harder for the poor to focus on Torah study, they became like a people apart from the learned. Another gaping hole appeared in the fabric of reality.

The Baal Shem Tov said toward the end of his life, "I suffered my whole life long from two holes in my heart because of Shabbtai Tzvi." While he didn't elaborate on the nature of these two holes, perhaps we can say that he meant these two gaps that the false messianic disaster precipitated.

The first hole was the distance between the outer Torah and its inner soul.

The second hole was the space between the learned and unlearned among the Jewish people.

DESTRUCTIVE CRITICISM

HERE WE HAVE A WELL-KNOWN anecdote about the Baal Shem Tov's early mission. It gives us a clearer picture of exactly what the "two holes" we've learned about would lead to...

> *One midsummer, while the Baal Shem Tov was still living in quiet obscurity, he went to visit a certain town, but when he arrived he found the entire community in a sorry state. The area had been suffering from drought for weeks and all of the crops were on the verge of collapse. Filled with compassion for his fellow Jews, the Baal Shem Tov invited a number of his fellow hidden tzaddikim to the village to join him in his prayers for rain. Not long after they gathered to beg the Infinite One's mercy, the skies opened and rain began to fall.*
>
> *The people of the town were overjoyed — the rabbi and local leaders decided to devote that Shabbos to special prayers of gratitude and community-wide celebrations in recognition of God's kindness. The Baal Shem Tov and his students, rejoicing together with everyone else, decided to stay in the town for the Shabbos.*
>
> *During those days, rabbis didn't really give sermons to their congregations on Shabbos throughout most of the year. The custom was that traveling scholars would go to different towns and be paid to deliver fire-and-brimstone sermons in the synagogues as a way of bringing the community members to repentance. The Baal Shem Tov disapproved of the practice; weren't the Jewish people already suffering enough? Did they also need*

to be made to feel so bitter over their failings, most of which weren't even really their fault but the result of circumstances beyond their control?

That Friday, an itinerant preacher came into town, and he headed straight to the synagogue to make arrangements with its president for his sermon that Shabbos. This time, however, the president was stuck.

The community had already decided to use the traditional sermon time of late afternoon for the public recitation of psalms in celebration of their local miracle. He tried to explain the matter to the preacher, but the man became very defensive, even a little offensive.

The visitor stated firmly, "Do you realize what a credit to your town it is to have me here to uplift your community? I'm famous for bringing entire communities to genuine repentance just by speaking to them for a single hour!"

When the president tried to beg off by telling the preacher that the usual speaker's hour was, this week, designated for the public recitation of psalms of thanksgiving, the visitor browbeat him.

"The people here have time for eating and sleeping on Shabbos, but not for repentance?!"

Not knowing what to do, the synagogue's president said that he would like to discuss the matter with the town's rabbi. "Let us go together to him, and we'll see what he says."

The visiting preacher bristled. "It's a disgrace to the Torah's honor for me to go to your local rabbi; proper form dictates that he should come to me!" The synagogue's president ran off to bring the rabbi.

Once the local rabbi arrived, the visiting preacher completely bulldozed the town's quiet scholar. "You should consider it an honor that I have chosen to come to your town! One hour with me will change their lives here!" The rabbi agreed to amend the schedule for Shabbos, and the two sat down to discuss Torah matters. Indeed, the visitor was a profound scholar, with mastery of vast reaches of Torah wisdom.

Once Shabbos arrived, the Baal Shem Tov and his fellow tzaddikim were overjoyed to see the way that the villagers had outdone themselves in expressing their gratitude to God. The women lit an extra candle on Friday night; they wore their very best and prepared more than the usual complement of special Shabbos dishes. The children were given special pastries and told that it was in celebration of God's kindness. Men assembled in the synagogue for extra recitation of psalms. All in all, a beautiful Shabbos.

Shabbos afternoon, the entire town assembled in the synagogue to hear the itinerant preacher's lesson. He rose to the podium, and began, "There are seven kinds of heavenly punishment..." Within minutes, everyone in the synagogue was reduced to tears.

The preacher thundered about the punishments that awaited them in this world and the next for failing to be sufficiently God-fearing. He threatened them with drought, crop failure, death, and destruction. Panic mounted in the synagogue, and some people even fainted dead away.

Just then, the Baal Shem Tov entered the synagogue and saw how the townspeople's joy had been reduced to rubble. He walked up to one of the tables and knocked on it, hard, to be heard over the cries and groans that filled the room.

"Rabbi," he called to the preacher, "surely you know that when the Jewish people were on the verge of destruction, God invited Moses to argue on their behalf and save them. Who are you, then, to come and rebuke the people so harshly when all they've done is serve their Creator with faith and joy?! It would have been your job to pray on their behalf when there was no rain, and now that God has shown them compassion, you should be encouraging them to continue to serve Him faithfully!"

The entire congregation shouted, "Amen!"

LOVE OF
THE PEOPLE

ACCORDING TO CHASSIDIC TRADITION, THIS incident of the itinerant preacher, or something like it, was what drove the Baal Shem Tov to eventually reveal himself. For how long would a suffering Jewish people be subjected to such a harsh model of leadership? Their souls needed to be uplifted, or they were in danger of being extinguished altogether. The time had finally come for a paradigm shift.

The natural question is: How could it be that genuinely great Torah scholars believed that the path to improvement of the Jewish people was by way of the stick of rebuke?

It's imperative to know that the entire Creation pivots on unity.

Unity doesn't only mean everyone getting along, the way it's often invoked now. Unity means a deep and integral oneness among a spectrum of individuals; they all need to have the sense of their absolute interdependence. The Torah only descended to the world when the Jewish people were in a state of just that kind of unity — like a single, organic whole.

So when it comes to other people and their flaws and failings (and our own, from the perspective of other people), we have a mutual responsibility. Because we're not each one for himself; we are actually our brothers' (and sisters') keepers.

The ancient sages described the relationship as follows:

> We're all sailing in a single vessel when, suddenly, someone on the ship takes out a drill and starts to bore a hole beneath his own bench. The person sitting next to him gets up, shocked, and says, "Brother, what are you doing?! You're going to sink us all!"
>
> The guy with the drill keeps at it and says, "Mind your own business. I'm only making a hole under my own place."

That kind of answer might work if he was all alone in own little boat, but when the ship is filled with — in our case — millions of people, that little hole is going to impact a lot more individuals than just him.

So it's a mitzvah to give specific and constructive correction to a person who will be receptive to it. But, like we've said about all mitzvot, they are *connectors*. If you have to set someone else straight, it has to be from the place of compassion. It has to be delivered respectfully. It has to be in the way of connection — to connect the person with the natural goodness of his soul, with the natural vitality of contact with the Creator.

Two thousand years ago, the great Rabbi Akiva said, "I doubt if anyone in this generation is capable of giving rebuke." Did he mean that the great scholars of his time didn't know what to say?

No. He meant that they didn't know how to say it.

A scholar is always potentially at a disadvantage when trying to set people straight. Even with the best of intentions, the receiver of rebuke is almost always going to feel diminished in the process.

"I'm a Torah scholar, and that's why I know better than you do how you ought to be living. I'm right, and that automatically makes you wrong."

How is it possible to work on the collective spiritual health of the Jewish people — which needs correction — in a way that doesn't diminish them? In other words, "How do you help a person change without breaking him?"

> The question that the Baal Shem Tov came to answer was, "How do you help a person change without breaking him?"

That's what the Baal Shem Tov came to accomplish.

Through love, through compassion, the Baal Shem Tov succeeded where generations of teachers and preachers had failed. He came to the Jewish people armed with infinite Divine love — the love that can overlook faults and flaws.

The love that can *heal* faults and flaws.

He saw the people's hidden good, their hidden strengths. And this empowered even the simplest people to begin to grow into their better selves.

THE
THIRD MEAL

THE BAAL SHEM TOV CAME to teach the world that even the earthiest individual can be a bridge between the material and the spiritual. Even a simple person can shine the light of the soul into the place of the body, because that soul is a piece of God, and it is capable of carrying out the loftiest work *wherever it goes*, even if it's to the fields and the workshop.

The Baal Shem Tov took the teachings of the Arizal and drew them way down to the soil itself. He taught people how to infuse that soil with soul and how to think about the Infinite One while plowing a field or greasing a wagon wheel.

> Even the earthiest individual can be a bridge between the material and the spiritual.

The Baal Shem Tov's greatest students needed to learn this lesson, and so do we. The mission of the person who has optimized his spiritual potential — one who is truly aligned with the Divine — isn't only to serve as a mentor to the great. He isn't here only to encourage the downtrodden, either. His purpose is to bridge the higher and the lower. A figure like the Baal Shem Tov teaches the scholar and mystic that he still knows nothing, and he proves to the person in the lowest place that God is with him right where he is.

The Baal Shem Tov's custom was to share words of Torah at the third meal of Shabbos, on Saturday afternoon toward evening, when only his students were in attendance. The simple folk were invited to eat with him on Friday nights, but they had no way of understanding the depth of those lessons taught during the third meal. So, as Shabbos drew to a close, the regular workingmen would retire to the synagogue to recite psalms.

On one Shabbos, the Baal Shem Tov had shown special favor to the non-scholars, and the closer disciples didn't look upon it too kindly. The following afternoon, during the third meal with his inner circle, the Baal Shem Tov reached out his hands to the students to either side of him, and he began to lead them all in a stirring wordless melody. As they circled, the group entered a kind of trance, and together they experienced an uplifting of the soul — a collective rising to a higher plane. At this elevated state of consciousness, the group began to hear the sounds of angels, a multitude of perfect voices merging in the most exquisite harmonies, and the whole universe seemed to be resonating with this otherworldly singing. What they were hearing was not the melody of the Baal Shem Tov — it was an echo from a much higher world that brought them to a state of bliss.

They stayed there at that lofty peak for what seemed like an eternity, and then the Baal Shem Tov slowly lowered his hands and broke the circle; all of the disciples descended back into the world they had left not long before. The students begged to know what heavenly chamber they had been blessed to enter; where had the master taken them on high?

The Baal Shem Tov answered, "This is the just the sound of our neighbors' psalms in the synagogue. This is what they sound like in the upper worlds. Like angels...You have no idea how much God loves them, no idea at all."

HERETICS
AND REBELS

WITHOUT MODERN MEANS OF COMMUNICATION — no Internet, television, film, phones, or even newspapers — the teachings of the Baal Shem Tov spread like wildfire throughout the Ukraine, Russia, and Poland, and revolutionized Eastern European Jewry by word of mouth. And, soon enough, the Baal Shem Tov's students began to build new and beautiful structures upon the foundations he had laid.

The way of a true master is to teach each individual according to his potential and abilities. So these transmitters of the Baal Shem Tov's teachings — great souls, each and every one — were each a novel channel of their own. They were — and we are — like a *shofar*, the curved ram's horn we use on the Jewish New Year to proclaim God's Kingship, and the Infinite One blows His breath through us. Just as no two shofars are exactly alike, each of us has a completely unique shape, so that Divine sound emerges in some measure differently from within every one of us.

> The way of a true master is to teach each individual according to his potential and abilities.

While all the early Chassidic teachers were great spiritual masters, one of the Baal Shem Tov's own descendants stands out as a unique and striking figure: Rebbe Nachman of Breslov. I am not going to do a treatment of his life in these pages, but I do want to make clear how Rebbe Nachman has served — and still does serve — a crucial role in the progression of the revelation of the Torah's inner soul. More specifically, he has been instrumental in our evolving understanding of the infinite extent of Divine mercy.

When we look at the work Rebbe Nachman did within this historical dynamic, his teachings and statements assume a fresh significance. We can see that Rebbe Nachman provided a pathway for the Torah's innermost, life-giving essence to reach everyone, even those who feel furthest from the Source.

Earlier, we learned that each of the major paradigm-shifters of Jewish history — Moses, Rabbi Shimon bar Yochai, the Arizal, and the Baal Shem Tov — arrived at critical historical junctures. *The pressures of their eras did not only make their appearance possible, it made it necessary.* When we look at Rebbe Nachman's era, we see he lived on the cusp of modernity, and he came to address the changes those new conditions brought to the world.

Born in 1772, Rebbe Nachman entered a world in flux. Everything was changing. The industrial revolution was in full swing; the Enlightenment movement had introduced an alternate vision of Judaism that flew in the face of traditional norms. Instead of the simple farmer of the Baal Shem Tov's time, Rebbe Nachman would spend his life with one eye trained on a new tribe of Jews: *heretics and rebels.* Although the face of Eastern Europe hadn't yet changed all that much, Rebbe Nachman had the vision to identify the deep cracks in the facade of the Jewish world. In his words, "We are at the cliff's edge of Jewishness."

Perched along this edge — which not everyone could see at the time — Rebbe Nachman flowed with fresh teachings that had the power to speak as vividly to the scholar as to the despairing and the faithless. He too came to fill a vacuum, but instead of the vacuum of knowledge and connection that the Baal Shem Tov filled, Rebbe Nachman came to fill the space that goes dark when faith itself is gone.

In this new world of alienation and Godlessness, Rebbe Nachman emphasized concepts and pathways of action that help us stay connected with the Creator *no matter what.*

Throughout this book, we've mainly focused on his teachings about the raven, the pathway out of the cruelty and tightness of the disconnected life. In this brief section, though, I want to share a few concepts that cut to the essence of Rebbe Nachman's work, and explain how they fit into the model of cosmic progression.

As we've already learned, there are many ways to be compassionate: you can extend financial help, you can provide emotional support, exert yourself physically on someone else's behalf. But the greatest act of mercy is to share a life-changing perspective with the person searching for answers and wisdom. The spiritual masters who put themselves on the line to raise the consciousness of other, suffering human beings are the most merciful of teachers, and they are the catalysts of the final redemption. The prophet said, "He shall lead them in mercy…"

> *Genuine leadership stems from the qualities of mercy and compassion.*

The history of Chassidism is studded with magnificent figures — learned, wise, giving, and devoted — but Rebbe Nachman's light shines in a different way. Although the Chassidic leader left this world over two hundred years ago, he is more popular today than ever.

Those who count themselves among his students come from every imaginable background, and his pathway is shared by way of the broadest coalition of teachers, in multiple languages, via every format and platform possible. Although he didn't leave behind a successor or a dynasty, his teachings have reached millions of people, Jews and non-Jews, religious and non-observant — more and more people every day — all over the world.

The real surprise is that two hundred years after Rebbe Nachman explained to his followers just how important it is for them to be with him for Rosh Hashanah, the Jewish New Year, tens of thousands of people come to his burial site in Uman,

> Rebbe Nachman didn't leave behind a successor or a dynasty…yet his teachings are reaching more and more people all the time.

Ukraine, to pray and study together for those days, and the annual gathering is only growing. Why? Because the gateway of mercy and access to the Divine that Rebbe Nachman opened is palpable there. Uman on Rosh Hashanah is like entering into the beating heart of the Jewish people while it receives a yearly renewal of vital energy and Divine compassion.

Rebbe Nachman's path — and his Rosh Hashanah — was a gift that was sent from the Infinite One specifically to us, the souls on the verge of the redemption. We are the ones who are going to walk from the deepest darkness into the brightest light. And *how* are we going to cross that gulf? We're going to do it with the power Rebbe Nachman taught us how to value and to wield...the force of will and desire within the soul.

THE ESSENCE IS WILL

MOST OF US WOULD SAY that our actions define us, our words pinpoint us, and our thoughts tell us who we are. But Rebbe Nachman of Breslov would say, in his usual counterintuitive way, that *will* is really what counts — it's really the only thing that matters. Your intentions are in your *will*; your deepest yearning and desire is in your *will*. What's most important to you is going to be found in what your *will* seeks.

The *essence of the soul is will*, and if you want to know who you really are, if you want to change who you are, you need to develop a means of communication with this deepest and truest part of yourself. But in a world of surfaces, it's all too easy to miss the stirrings of our will, the yearning of the soul.

"Don't let this world fool you!" cried Rebbe Nachman of Breslov.

> The *essence of the soul is will*, and if you want to know who you really are, if you want to change who you are, you need to develop a means of communication with this deepest and truest part of yourself.

Earlier in this book, we learned about how the Creator weaves the forces of nature and physical matter into a garment that hides His Presence, all to preserve our free will. Material reality isn't a figment of the imagination. The illusion is that *that's all there is* — that there's nothing behind the veil, beyond the curtain, beneath the garment.

The world of matter is finite; it's dead and empty unless it's constantly being infused with vitality from the Source. When we're in tune with that inner vitality, we also feel alive and vibrant. But if we're only scratching the surface of the material, it never satisfies us. *It fools us.* We fall for the external shell of the material, and then suffer for it.

We can look inward and follow the same dynamic. We're also a composite of material and spiritual. The body alone is just flesh, blood, and bone. While we're alive, the soul animates the body, but we're still so easily fooled. Just like we might miss the Source behind the veil of material reality, we're also liable to relate to ourselves as just physical beings and fail to recognize our innermost, most essential and vital self.

Human beings have the ability to be active in different ways, each more internal than the next. We can *do* — carry out action in the physical world. We can *speak* — communicate ideas and emotions, bridging the inner world of thought with the outer world of action. And we can *think* — the mind is the birthplace of the speech and actions manifest in the outside world.

But there's another power of the soul, closest to its essential nature. It's the will itself, the capacity to *want*, to *desire*...to feel yearning and longing.

The soul is called "a portion of Godliness from on high." The Creator is Infinite, so we're not talking about a mathematic subdivision of infinity — that's impossible. What the ancient mystics meant when they spoke of the human soul's relationship with the Source is that it is an analogue of the Infinite One — every soul possesses the same basic attributes as the Divine Essence.

> The force that's closest to the essential nature of the soul is your will...your ability to feel desire, yearning, and longing.

And the highest of them all is Will.

What does the Creator want? What is the essential Will that drove all of reality into existence?

It was, and still is, the unfettered Divine desire to bestow good and reveal the infinite extent of the Godly nature — compassion and loving-kindness. It's the Creator's Will to connect with another (that's *us*) and share the greatest good.

This is the key to understanding ourselves and to making real changes in our lives.

What drives us, at the root, is this will, this deep-seated desire to connect with others and with the Creator. Our underlying drive is to also *be* connectors — to use all of the other aspects of the self (thought, speech, and action) to gather up all of physical matter and experience, and unite it with its Source. This is the mystic joy and unity every soul seeks when its deepest longing and desire is known.

The body's actions can get derailed; words can fail to express what we really mean; our thoughts sometimes betray us. But the *will*? That innermost will to connect? It's the essence of the soul, and it is always seeking complete alignment with the Divine Will.

To help clarify the point, let's take a look at something everyone is always chasing...that *everybody* wants.

Money.

Is money real, or is it an illusion?

Everyone chases it, so it must be real, right? But we still find that people can work their whole lives and run after money, and in the end they're left with nothing. Rebbe Nachman even asks this poignant and strange-seeming question: "Where is all of the money that people have been chasing since the beginning of time?"

> What drives us, at the root, is this will, this deep-seated desire to connect with others and with the Creator.

Clearly, it's not with them, since no one leaves this world with any money. Either people's money gets used up and disappears, or the money stays here but the person dies and leaves it behind. In either case, there is something illusory about it. That's what Rebbe Nachman meant when he cried out, "Don't let the world fool you!"

Of course, money is real in the physical sense. But when it's pointed out to us, we can also grasp that something so seemingly solid, something we're all so intimately concerned with, can give way when we examine its significance in the long term, in eternal terms.

Meaning, it's only *really* real when we get in touch with its inner vitality, when we push the curtain aside and realize that, until money is spiritualized through the activation of *our own will and intent*, it's just inert, dead weight.

Your *will*, your intent — and *only* your will and intent — has the power to take dead matter and make it come alive with soul and purpose.

THE POWER
OF "AS IF"

SO WE'VE SEEN THAT THE vital force that animates every thought, word, and action is really the will. If you want to influence reality, you need to reach to the root, to that core. If you want to transform the realm of the material into channels of spiritual connection, your success will depend on *what you want*, on where your desire and yearning is focused.

That's true on the physical plane. If spiritualizing my eating, my financial life, and my relationships — really all of my material experience — is important to me, then the place where I have to do the work is within my own *will*.

I need to begin at the root, and allow myself time and space to *feel*, to *want*, to *yearn*, and focus my heart and mind on touching the innermost point of vitality that enlivens all of material reality. My soul has a desire — a powerful and innate need — to reunite with its Source in the Divine. Normally, my conscious mind is disconnected from that wellspring of *will*, of yearning, because I'm busy with all the distractions of my life. I need to reach for it, since it isn't visible on the surface.

But what about spiritual pursuits? Since actions like studying Torah, prayer, and carrying out mitzvot are by their nature spiritual, how much does our will and intent — what we call *kavanah* — play a role in them? Isn't it enough to just do them?

Characteristically, Rebbe Nachman turns our assumptions on their head.

> *"When it comes to serving God, I don't know who can say that he serves God as befits His greatness.*
> *Of course, everybody serves God...but not as befits His greatness."*

God's greatness is infinite, and all creatures are limited — even the great forces of nature, even the laws of physics and the most spiritually evolved individuals. And certainly that's true of people like you and me.

> "...It's just that, when it comes to serving God, the essence is will."

When it comes to spiritual pursuits, to the service of God, the main thing is *wanting* and *yearning* just like it is with physical pursuits? But why? Hold on tight, because the answer needs close attention...

> "...And not all wills are equal..."

The degree of your desire to join together with the Creator is always in flux. There's a spectrum of yearning that differs from individual to individual, and even within the same person, from moment to moment.

Rebbe Nachman said that making money — the everyday work that feels *so real* to us — is just *"as if."* It's just an illusion, an appearance of accomplishment. And now he tells us that all of our *spiritual* acts *are just as illusory, unless they're fueled by* **will**, *by* **desire**.

> "The main thing, then, is will...to always yearn for God.
> In the meantime, we pray, we learn, we carry out the mitzvot...
> But all of that is really like nothing. It's all just 'as if'..."

Even the greatest number you can imagine is like nothing compared with infinity. *Anything* of a quantity, within the realm of limits, is as nothing when compared to the infinite. So what separates me from the spiritual master, or me from the wicked and empty person? Only the quality of my desire and yearning to approach the Infinite. We're all creatures of limitation, but of all our capacities, our will is the one that comes closest to transcending our limitations.

You can carry into action far less than you can say. You can speak less than you can think. Our mouths might sometimes feel like they're running a mile a minute, but the flow of our thoughts is much, much faster than that. And, even so, your thoughts are more confined than your desires. Thoughts are still articulated in some way. But desire, yearning, longing...it can sometimes fill your whole world all at once.

> It turns out that what we thought was real — thought, speech, and action — is flimsy. But the will? That's where all of our force lies.

And so we're all living in the world of "*as if*." When it comes to our means of spiritual connection — prayer, study, mitzvot — we're really in the same situation as we are in the realm of the material. We're not the masters of our reality, and so our physical actions are not fully in our control. I might wake up in the morning with the best intention to align with the Divine by devoting myself to a righteous action, but I'll only know if I've succeeded after I've finished, because my good intentions don't determine my physical reality. Everyone knows that.

And I might be determined to pour my heart out in prayer, speaking eloquently and passionately before my Creator...But what can I do if the words just don't flow well for me today?

And I could be committed to focusing my thoughts on the words I recite from my prayer book today, but what will I do if my lack of sleep, having eaten too late last night, and just general fogginess means my mind is muddled and the words that barely crawl out of my mouth are empty and lifeless?

My body can fail me, my speech can get stuck, my thoughts can get bogged down...but my will is always mine. The *Zohar* teaches: "No good desire is ever lost." My yearning for God is *real*. It lasts. It's powerful.

> The *Zohar* teaches: "No good desire is ever lost."

I need to know that when it comes to the *externalities* (thought, speech, action) of spiritual pursuits, we are all acting "*as if*." We're all — sages and regular people too — in the world of limitation, and none of us can ever really serve God in accordance with the truth of His greatness.

When I understand that, I begin to realize the power that is in *my will*, in my desire.

My deeds may fall short...but so do those of the greatest sages.

My words may be insufficient...but so are the heavenly songs of the loftiest angels.

My thoughts cannot grasp God's Infinity...*but neither can anyone else's.*

What within me is the most unfettered? Where can I really be free? *In my desire to be closer to God, in my longing to align.* This is the part of all of us that is the least limited, and, as the least limited, it's the closest part of us to Godliness. This is what we really mean by "free will."

We all know that you can't always get what you want, *but you can still always want.* That, at least, is free.

What makes a person righteous, then, isn't so much *what he does* — since we're all acting *"as if"* — but *how much he wants.* And when a simple person like myself is in touch with this deep wellspring of desire for the Infinite, it means I am also in touch with my highest possibilities.

> We all know that you can't always get what you want, but you can still always want.

This is really such a revolutionary idea — the externalities of difference in levels of observance can be deceptive. If we put all of our attention there, we risk missing the point of it all, that innermost point of burning desire for God that unites all the worlds of thought, speech, and action with their Source.

Even so, the importance of carrying out spiritual intentions into the world of action can't be minimized — that would be like saying you can have the spirit of a thing without a body to contain it. A body without a soul is dead flesh, and a soul without a body is just a ghost. To really live, we need both.

But the emphasis on the inner spark of will is necessary...because the externals are what we see, and the inner desire is hidden from us. We can't get so caught up in what's obvious that we miss the essence, the hidden potential of the will.

That's the power of *"as if"* — working from the inner point of the will, and knowing the will is the force that drives everything else.

PRAYING "AS IF"

I WANT TO SHARE WITH you a beautiful story with a powerful message that helped to open my mind to the possibilities of "*as if.*" This story inspired me to start working on incorporating the principle into my own spiritual life...

> *There once was an elderly Jewish couple that rented land from the local nobleman. Although they had married young, this couple was only finally blessed with a son in their old age. The couple was very poor, and barely eked out a meager living from their small plot of soil. They had a very good relationship with the landowner, though.*
>
> *Poverty and infirmity took their toll, and the boy soon lost his beloved father. Not too long afterward, he was orphaned of his mother, too. The local nobleman, however, was kind of heart and had a soft spot for the child. With no children of his own, he took in the Jewish orphan and raised him like his own beloved son. Time passed in the village, and people more or less forgot about the strange origins of the nobleman's heir.*
>
> *One day, when the young boy was playing in the square with other lads, one of them shouted in a moment of anger, "You Jew!" The nobleman's son was devastated; why would his friend call him a Jew? The boy had no idea of his history; he believed he was the nobleman's very own son. And so he ran home to his father, sobbing.*
>
> *The landowner held his beloved child close and soothed him. "They're only children. Don't pay attention to them." But the*

boy felt that his father held something back from him, and he pressed him until the story of his birth came out.

"Your parents were very fine people, two elderly Jews who were very poor, and they lived on my land. When they died, I took you in..." And the wealthy man unlocked a chest off to the side, and took out a small book and a little sack. A prayer book for Yom Kippur, and a little velvet sack with an old prayer shawl inside. "This is all they left you, my son," said the nobleman.

The little boy didn't know what the objects were, but he knew they'd belonged to his lost parents, and so he cherished them. The boy hid his inheritance away in his room and grew up in the nobleman's house, the master's son in every way.

Years went by, and the treasures remained in the drawer. But one day in autumn, the young man spotted a Jewish family in the square, loading up their wagon, clearly heading out on a journey.

Feeling friendly, he approached them and asked, "Are you going to a fair? I didn't know there were any in our area now. You must be going far!" The husband stopped in the middle of his task and said, "No, there is no fair now. We're traveling to our Rebbe for Rosh Hashanah...for our New Year."

The youngster asked, "Even if it is a holiday for you, why can't you stay here for it?" The other man looked at the nobleman's son and said quietly, "Rosh Hashanah is the Day of Judgment for the entire world. We need to be with our Rebbe, to pray with our brothers."

And he left it at that, not wanting to get in trouble for preaching to the landowner's son. They finished packing and headed out on the road. But the boy's curiosity was piqued, and his mind kept returning to the words, "Jews...Rosh Hashanah... Day of Judgment..."

That night, the boy had a dream, and in the dream his father came to him and cried, "Yossele, Yossele, it's not too late. You also need to go and pray with your brothers." He woke up in a state of turmoil. The nobleman who had raised him never called him Yossele, but he knew that it was truly his father's soul that had come to him.

The next night, his mother came to him in tears. "Yossele, my Yossele...Don't give up! It's not too late to join your brothers." He woke up, wild-eyed.

Truly, the nobleman had been the best of fathers to Yossele as long as he could remember. The boy felt suddenly that he was being torn in two. Such powerful dreams — his own lost parents had come, begging him to follow those travelers back to his roots — but how could he leave the noble-hearted man who had raised him?

The very next day, Yossele's foster father announced that he was going on a journey, and the boy was left at home to his own devices. As if driven by a force he could not deny, Yossele grabbed the book and the bag and ran into the forest.

He ran for many days until he arrived at a distant city toward evening. Exhausted from his journey, he took hold of the first person he came across and asked the way to the synagogue. He opened the doors and walked inside, not knowing what day it was.

The Yom Kippur evening prayers were about to begin. He barely had the strength to stand, and he was thunderstruck by the vision of a hall filled with pious Jews, all in white, wrapped in their prayer shawls.

At that very moment, far away in the little village of Mezhibuzh, the Baal Shem Tov paced back and forth in the synagogue, deep in thought. The community, and especially the master's closest disciples, looked on in confusion.

"What could be wrong? Why won't the tzaddik begin the prayers already?" Yet the Baal Shem Tov continued to pace back and forth, rubbing his furrowed brow, eyes closed in concentration, saying nothing. Back and forth, back and forth. At long last, a smile bright as day broke out across the master's face, and he signaled that it was time to begin the Yom Kippur prayers.

At the close of a full night and day of Divine service, the Baal Shem Tov's inner circle asked the sage to explain why the opening prayers of Yom Kippur had been delayed. The Baal Shem Tov then told them the entire story of Yossele the orphan.

He added, "You must know, my beloved students...I was there in spirit with that orphan boy when he walked into the services, which seemed to him so foreign and fearsome. He saw that wall of white — all of those holy Jews in their glory — and he very nearly walked right back out the door, never to return.

"Yossele looked down into his father's worn and tearstained prayer book and saw letters he'd never set eyes on before. He yearned to pray, but he didn't know how. He was filled with so many feelings — longing, frustration, love, fear — and his heart overflowed with so many questions. 'Do I really belong here? Can I really come back? Are these really my people? Does God really want me to pray with these strange and crooked letters?' It was impossible...he barely believed that he was Jewish.

"Just then, Yossele raised up his father's prayer book to heaven and said, 'Master of the Universe, I want to pray but I don't know how! But I believe...I do believe that this book has all of the prayers I need to say inside of it. May it be Your Will that it will be as if I prayed them all!' And the young man hid his tearstained face in his prayer book and cried and cried."

And when the Baal Shem Tov finished the story, his students all broke down and wept.

The master ended, "Remember this story, dear ones, when you pray. For who can say that he truly knows how to pray? Who among us can say that he prays according to the mysteries of those holy words? We're all like orphaned, ignorant children, just praying as if. But the secret of as if is powerful enough to carry our prayers up to heaven!"

THE SECRET
OF "AS IF"

ONCE I REALIZED THAT THE concept of "*as if*" had the potential to completely change the way I pray, the way I *live*, I began to see hints of it everywhere I looked.

The mystics suggest that before certain prayers and mitzvah-acts, we recite "For the Sake of Unification," a statement of spiritual intent.

It helps us to stay in tune with the intent of the act: that the Presence of the Infinite One should be revealed through this finite motion down here below.

Right at the end of it, I say: "May it be Your Will...that what I am about to do will be '*as if*' I had carried it out with all of its details and its mystical intentions..." I've shared this secret with numerous students, and they've all told me what a difference it made in their daily lives.

"*As if*" means that although I'll do my legwork as well as I can, I'm limited. I'll learn as much as I can about the mitzvah, but I'm not a Kabbalist. But when I know that I'm just acting "*as if*," I leave room to feel the power of my will and desire for the act to be complete. I might be limited, but my *will*, my *desire*, my "*as if*" inspire me to feel close; they leave space for me to just *want* to be able to fulfill the mitzvah fully.

> I start from my state of limitation, my normal human inadequacy, and then my yearning acts as a bridge to the infinite.

I start from my state of limitation, my normal human inadequacy, and then my yearning acts as a bridge to the infinite.

Yes, I'm going to do it imperfectly, but my longing to do it perfectly bridges the gap. And I know that when I send my will upward,

I bring joy to my Creator; I'm reaching up with the most precious part of myself.

As we've learned, the mitzvah is a channel of connection. My innermost desire to carry it out in its fullness actually allows me to reach perfection even though the deed is going to fall short. The perfection of the mitzvah is what I would achieve, if only I could have what I *really* want.

Now, if we were to look carefully at that statement we'd find that it doesn't really say, "Your Will"; it just says, "May it be '*will*' before You..." Without understanding the secret of "*as if*" and the concept of alignment, it's hard to make sense of the literal meaning of the words.

> *What we're really saying is, "May this uplifting of the will — of my own will — align with Your Divine Will."*

It's as though, through the awakening of my inner will alone, I reach up to the Infinite and say, "You, God, want me to fulfill this mitzvah perfectly...and so do I. We both want the same thing. I might not be able to do it, but at the level of *will*, we're both in exactly the same place."

And, on the level of the essence, that's how I accomplish it — through the wanting.

THE WILL TO TRANSFORM

SO WE'VE SEEN THAT **WILL** is really the essence of the soul, it's the core of our innermost self. And since we're free to choose to *want*, we do have genuine free will — even though the outcome is so often out of our hands. It's not just *called* free will...it really *is* free.

Rebbe Nachman went one step further and taught us that yearning and desire is actually the *most important* part of spiritual work. That was a new idea for the world, and as time goes on we see just how crucial it is.

Let's go back to an idea that came up in our discussion about the Baal Shem Tov — the concept of rebuke. Rebuke is really too harsh a word; it's simply that when you see another person acting in a way that's problematic, you have an obligation to set them straight so that they can correct their behavior. Not because you're the expert or because you're any better, but because we're all in it together. The Torah binds us all into a unity of mutual responsibility; if there's a breach somewhere, it's my problem too. Remember that image of the person drilling a hole in the bottom of everyone's boat?

> The Torah binds us all into a unity of mutual responsibility; if there's a breach somewhere, it's my problem too.

Rebuke isn't meant to be punitive or insulting; it needs to be done respectfully, appropriately, and in a way that empowers...Now, how easy is that?

Not very.

It's the easiest thing in the world to take an earnest desire to improve the world (by improving someone else) and allow it to become an ex-cuse to let my judgmental nature take over. Seeing the negative — even when it's for what appears to be the right reason — just comes naturally to most of us. And that negativity tends to color what we say and how we say it.

That's why it's no surprise that our best intentions and efforts to improve a situation often fall short of the goal. So how are we supposed to work toward positive change with others when it's so easy to trip over them or ourselves on the way?

There are so many potential pitfalls along the road to communicating a corrective message — causing embarrassment, making the other person feel judged, self-righteousness, an error in judgment altogether about the nature of the situation, too harsh an assessment, too unsym-pathetic a delivery...How am I supposed to reach the other person when it's genuinely necessary and constructive, in the best possible way, without causing any harm to that person's spirit?

If I work externally, in the world of words and actions, it's easy to make mistakes. But if I begin the work from the *inside*, from the inner-most point of *will* that propels all of the rest of the levels of thought, speech, and action, I have a better chance of accomplishing my goal.

> *I need to be able to touch the other's innermost will...*
> *and I do that by activating my own will on that person's behalf. Yearning*
> *and desire for the good is the most important part*
> *of spiritual work.*

When I willingly stoke myself with yearning for the good, the joy, the wholeness and spiritual completion of the other person — especially if I express these feelings in prayer — I begin to work at the deepest level, from the root. I can only really do this when I'm able to focus on the powerful good points *already* within the other.

It's so tempting to focus on the negative, but a little bit of light drives away a lot of darkness. If I focus on the light within the other — the Godliness and goodness — it's going to expand and together we'll find a way out of the darkness. If all I see is the flaw, we'll both remain with it. The flaw is the problem, not the solution.

When my attention is on the good within my friend, I'm filled with desire and longing to see that good expressed more fully. That's not passive work; it's active. It's an act of faith in the essential goodness of the other, and trust that goodness gives rise to more genuine goodness.

The obligation to offer corrective guidance doesn't only come into play in our interpersonal relationships. It's also how we get ourselves back into alignment when we're out of balance. Self-correction is a kind of rebuke, as well, and we need to be as careful with ourselves as we are with other people. All of those pitfalls I mentioned lie along the path to our own self-transformation too. With ourselves, too, we work through the *will*.

This is the best foundation for my relationships with other people, and it's also vital to my relationship with myself. I need to activate my free will and *choose* to see the good within myself and build from there. Just like it's natural for us to focus on the negative in others, we're often drawn to focus on the negative within ourselves, and this is a paralyzing, spiritually deadening way of dealing with ourselves. To avoid that kind of self-defeating negativity, we need a consciousness-shift.

That good point — within myself and in others — is really the spark of Godliness inside, and the way to access it is through the will...the will to transform. It's the will to connect to the Source. This isn't just belief in the Divine origin of my soul, but an *activated* faith that knows it's possible to reach upward and connect through the action of *will*. I can do it with myself, and I can do it with other people.

But the subtle connections between all souls are so deep that, truthfully, this inner work has an effect on other people *even when we don't articulate it to them*. The truth is that we do communicate our *will-to-transform* work with others even if we don't tell them what we're up to — it comes across in how we relate to them, in how we speak to them, and in how we feel about them.

This is true when I seek change in the world around me, and when I seek change within myself. I focus my attention on the good and on the Godly and on its expansion, I express that deep desire in words, and I bring my own *will* — the highest part of myself, bound up with the Divine Will at its root — down into the world of action.

Was this really something new when Rebbe Nachman first started to speak about it? Could it be that, until about two hundred years ago, *no one* knew about the power of the will and its potential to transform our relationships and behaviors? No. Every spiritual master had to be aware of the power of the will and become expert in refining it to accomplish all that they did!

A central idea of our work lies in seeing how the development of fundamental spiritual concepts, their revelation in the world and availability to people like us, involves a progression. What one master could achieve in one era becomes the foundation of further development during the next era. While it's true that the essential power of the will was certainly known about and utilized by spiritual giants throughout the ages, the teachings about exactly *how* to accomplish that were not available to people like you and me.

As we've already learned, Abraham fulfilled all of the Torah's mitzvot, but he still only served as the channel of revelation of a *single* mitzvah: circumcision. The wisdom of Kabbalah precedes Creation, but Rabbi Shimon bar Yochai had the distinction of being the channel through which it was codified into a system of teachings for the fully developed student.

Rebbe Nachman didn't innovate the power of the will; he served as the conduit for revealing to the world that developing your will to transform is a practice that needs to be taken up by *everyone, every day*. He shared with us that it is something without which we *cannot function fully as spiritual entities*. Rebbe Nachman surprised us by using a very contemporary kind of idiom when discussing this teaching. He said, "You have to *go with this one all the time*."

And he also provided us with models and techniques as to how to carry this out.

THE CONVERSATION

MY WILL IS FREE TO me at all times; the power generated by yearning and desire is always accessible if I only choose to take hold of it.

Rebbe Nachman shared new concepts that help us crystallize the power of our will and express it within the world of action. And, *above all*, he emphasized the practice called *hitbodedut*, establishing it as a daily practice. The Hebrew word literally means to consciously seclude myself. It conveys the need to make space to speak to the Creator in my own words, on a regular basis, and express my innermost will to transform and draw closer to my Source. This isn't prayer from a book; it's a call from the soul itself.

Speech is the articulation of my innermost desire, and the way I can take something limitless and provide it with form. The words become a vessel that can then contain the good I yearn for so it can materialize. The will is the vital force that drives the whole, and personal prayer is the key to unlocking its potential. Longing and yearning bring those empty words to life.

When you speak out your deepest yearnings for Godliness, for goodness, for connection and communion, your words do more than just provide a form of expression.

Your words are the building blocks of your soul. They're the means of articulating where you want to go next in your spiritual life; without them, your soul stays where it is, landlocked by the raven-state, tight and doubtful about the world of possibilities right in front of you.

Yearning for more and expressing your deepest will to change and grow reinvigorates your spirit so you can keep on moving. You ascend on the wings of your *will*, embodied within your *words*. This is how you grow your soul.

We all know that conversation is vital to any relationship. If we want to get connected and stay connected with another person, we have to devote the time to communicate and speak our hearts out to each other.

It's no different when it comes to our relationship with the Infinite One. Even if we're not able to hear actual communication in return, the Divine Will is communicated to us through the

> Yearning for more and expressing your deepest will to change and grow reinvigorates your spirit so you can keep on moving.

Torah, through our experiences, through every word we hear, everything we see...they're all manifestations of the Divine Will.

When Adam hid in the Garden, the all-knowing Creator reached out to him with a question, "Where are you?" The only reason He did this was *to engage Adam in conversation.* God knew where Adam was; the question that radiated outward was, "Do *you* know where you are?"

In my own life, too, the Divine Will calls out to me through the situation I'm in at this moment, right now: *"Where are you? I want to speak with you, I want you to reach out to Me."*

The Torah tells us that God communicated with Moses "face-to-face." The Infinite One has no physical form, so the description indicates some inner reality. It means that the communication was prophetic and, most significantly, *direct.* But it also means that Moses was able to speak with his Creator at any time, too, without barriers.

Learning how to speak freely is an art. Even though natural aptitude can take a person a long way, the development of all art depends mainly on *practice.* Personal prayer is a practice that helps us raise our attempts at soulful, soul-building speech to a high art.

Whenever I share this idea, people often say, "But God actually *spoke* with Moses. He doesn't answer me!"

So I remind them, "How many conversations do you think Moses initiated with God until he was answered face-to-face? This was his lifelong practice; the Creator didn't speak with him until he was eighty years old! *Practice, practice, practice.*"

By "high art" I don't mean something flashy; this kind of prayer isn't elaborate. Quite the contrary — Rebbe Nachman emphasized that the main thing is to speak face-to-face in our own words, like we would to our very best friend, with immediacy and honesty. That's the beauty of this art — speaking the truth of the will, the truth of the self, simply and straightforwardly.

> Personal prayer is a practice that helps us raise our attempts at soulful, soul-building speech to a high art.

The great spiritual masters spend their lives searching for the Divine Will in the Torah and hidden within worldly experiences. The focus of their own free will is on aligning with the Higher Will, and this makes them into conduits of transformation...even miracles. But we'll see that this dynamic also applies to regular people like us.

The Torah provides us with 613 "pieces of advice" — the mitzvah-channels of connection and vitality. But we are still always in need of more guidance so that we can actually grab hold of these conduits. The guidance is made available to us when we activate and express our will to align with the Divine, our desire to get connected and stay connected.

People say, "Where there's a will, there's a way." For us, this means that when we choose to activate and express our *will*, the *way* and the *means* to reach our goal will be made clear to us in time.

And when we reach our spiritual goals and change, and when we refine our own natures, that's a miracle too. If a spiritual master can draw down miracles through prayer, what could be more supernatural than a stuck person actually changing?

All prayer is valuable, but prayer-conversation has a big advantage over formal prayer. The prayer books were compiled by great spiritual masters, prophets even, but their accessibility is also their disadvantage. The prayers can become too familiar, too well-known. Their pathways are like a well-marked trail; they might be well worn and easy to walk along, but we're also vulnerable to any bandit who lies in wait along heavily trafficked roads. It's easy to get distracted in words that aren't our own.

Spontaneous, personal prayer is like striking out through the wild on your own. You might have to hack your way through — the path won't necessarily look pretty — but no one's been here before. The words can be raw, but they're *yours*. They've never been said before, and they're expressing the precise need of this moment in time, never to be exactly repeated again. It's hard to lose your train of thought when you're clearing the path for the very first time.

Of course, sometimes the words might not flow. Rebbe Nachman taught that that's okay too; you can take the single phrase or word that expresses your will at that moment and repeat it again and again, as many times as necessary, for as many days as it lasts. The power of personal prayer is that when your heart and will are really invested in it, you feel that your soul, your very life, is on the line.

And that's the essence of prayer. Your will is on the line, your yearning is on the line...and you uplift the essence of yourself in your own trusting, outstretched hands.

> The power of personal prayer is that when your heart and will are really invested in it, you feel that your soul, your very life, is on the line.

WILL
OF WILLS

YOU'VE LEARNED THAT YOUR WILL is the highest part of yourself, the truest and deepest *you*. The Infinite One provided us with the means of drawing forth the most powerful essence of the soul by placing us at the *furthest possible distance*.

Distance is what makes us yearn; it inspires longing.

Rebbe Nachman would say, "It's the *thirst* that makes drinking such a pleasure." If you don't experience the distance and the thirst, you can't enjoy the reunion, and the water won't taste nearly as sweet.

> "It's the *thirst* that makes drinking such a pleasure."

Such yearning is the peak of human possibility...to long for connection with the Source, to yearn for the Infinite One. It engages the highest faculty of the soul, something the direct gift of closeness with the Creator could *never* accomplish. Yearning can reach the Infinite One because the will has no limits on it — the will is untethered and free.

And it wants to grow; it's the essence of the life-force, and it always seeks more, better, greater closeness and ever-higher attainments. The will's upward striving is the path of all life...if you're not busy growing, you're atrophying and dying.

That's just the way it is. Wanting leads to fulfillment, which leads to the next level of wanting, and so on, until infinity.

So we find that the spiritual masters didn't reach some kind of a plateau and stay there; they continued their upward path until their last moment. The greatest example we have of this is Moses himself. His prophecy was the clearest, the most direct, and yet he never let go of his desire to draw ever closer to the Infinite One. *He always wanted more,* and so his life culminated in a merging of his upward-reaching human will with the Divine Will.

The mystical works speak of this state as *Will of Wills* — the highest peak of yearning and desire for the Divine.

You might think that these concepts are so beyond us that they have no relevance to the way we live our lives down here, in this world, but the sage I learned from told me once, "Just take in the words, swallow them and try to digest them. If you just let them in, they'll do what they're meant to do."

We can be deeply affected by teachings that seem way above us as long as we're open to absorbing their message. And their impact is all the more powerful when we seek the parallels to them in our own lives and inner development. Spiritual processes are universal; they're only particular in how we apply them.

Like Moses, no matter how much we know, we haven't yet begun to know. No matter how much we've felt, we haven't yet begun to feel. And so our desire is constantly stoked with fresh fuel, because no matter how close we feel we've gotten, we know that the Infinite remains always...Infinite.

When describing the heights of will and desire, Rebbe Nachman would say, "It's the feeling of, *'I want, I want...I don't even know what I want!'*" That's the height of yearning, because it's so upward reaching that it can't even be articulated — it's just *pure longing*.

Rebbe Nachman would say, "Never get old! I don't want you to be even an old sage, I don't want you to be an old disciple!" He didn't mean that we shouldn't live long lives. He meant that we mustn't lose our freshness, our yearning to continue growing and changing, our faith that there's always further to fly.

> We mustn't lose our freshness, our yearning to continue growing and changing, our faith that there's always further to fly.

We're always wanting something. But instead of spending the precious coin of desire on things that never satisfy us — food, money, sex, property — we should put it where it provides endless fulfillment. We should invest it in our search for ever-increasing connection with the Infinite. That way, the distance that appears to lie between us is transformed into the means of attaining closeness; the thirst is its own satisfaction.

TODAY!

TOWARD THE END OF REBBE Nachman's life, he began to speak about his *Teachings of the Messianic Era*. These concepts are consciousness-shifters that can bring us into alignment with the nature of the future world even before the dawn of that era comes in action. Rebbe Nachman was already in the grip of his final illness by that time but, nevertheless, he insisted that those concepts were enlivening him, literally pumping him with life.

As we've learned, the spiritual masters can live profound and lengthy lives of connection with the Infinite One in what passes for a brief time in this world. Consciousness — immersion in the ever-present Now where God is to be found — is what determines the passage of time in the most important sense.

But what did Rebbe Nachman mean that these are teachings of the Messiah? How do we learn lessons from a teacher who hasn't yet become manifest in the flesh? To make the matter clearer, we'll look to an ancient narrative recorded in the Talmud...

> *Rabbi Joshua ben Levi met Elijah the prophet near the entry to the cave of Rabbi Shimon bar Yochai. He asked Elijah, "When will the Messiah come?"*
>
> *"Why don't you go and ask him yourself!" Elijah replied.*
>
> *"Where can I find him?" Rabbi Joshua ben Levi asked.*
>
> *"He is sitting at the entrance to the city of Rome," Elijah replied.*
>
> *"And how will I recognize him?"*
>
> *Elijah answered, "The Messiah is sitting among the poor and the suffering. You'll know him by the way he changes his bandages. All of the stricken remove all of their bindings at once, tend to their wounds, and then re-dress them, but the Messiah*

only changes one bandage at a time. He has to be ready at every moment for the redemption."

Rabbi Joshua ben Levi went to Rome and found the Messiah exactly as Elijah had described.

"Shalom, my Master and Teacher," Rabbi Joshua ben Levi greeted him.

"Shalom, the son of Levi," the Messiah answered.

"When is the Master coming?" Rabbi Joshua asked.

"Today!" the Messiah told him.

Rabbi Joshua ben Levi went back to Elijah to tell him what the Messiah had said.

"But he lied to me," Rabbi Joshua concluded. "The Messiah said he was coming that day, but that day came and went and he still hasn't arrived!"

"You misunderstood his words," Elijah replied. "He meant that he was coming today — in the sense of, 'Today!...If you'll listen to My voice.'"

There's a kind of call-and-response line from Psalms that incorporates a big concept: "When are we the people of God?" — *"Today, if you'll listen to My voice."* Being aligned isn't about some point in a theoretical future. It's *today*, if you'll only get attuned to the message I'm sending you.

So let's examine the anecdote to see what it has to teach us about the Messiah, and about time.

> Being aligned isn't about some point in a theoretical future. It's *today*, if you'll only get attuned to the message I'm sending you.

The first thing we discover is that when Rabbi Joshua ben Levi asked the prophet for information about a long-awaited event he expected to come in the future, Elijah told him the Messiah was already accessible to him. That's the first surprise, since Rabbi Joshua ben Levi clearly wanted to know about something he assumed was only tied to the future, not to the *now*.

So if we wondered how Rebbe Nachman spoke about these *Teachings of the Messianic Era* when that era hadn't yet arrived, we now have our answer: these teachings *already exist and are accessible.* If the Messiah can be reached by Rabbi Joshua ben Levi, it means his teachings are already here. We're just not aware of them.

We're not talking about the physical redeemer in the flesh — we're talking about a state of mind.

The narrative tells us that a great master like Rabbi Joshua ben Levi only realized the present nature of messianic consciousness after receiving guidance from a prophet — this level of awareness was rare and known only to a select few. But Rebbe Nachman wanted to bring this state of mind to regular people like us, to propel us forward into a new world of possibility. He did it by helping us to realize the vitality and connection that lie right here, in the present moment — in Today.

So the message of the Messiah sitting among the poor and suffering in Rome is that freedom and redemption are always at hand *the moment that your mind expands.* The Messiah dresses his wounds one by one; he is always ready, because this shift in consciousness can be activated universally in an instant.

"When will I arrive?" the Messiah asks. *"Today!...*As soon as you learn how to live in the present moment fully."

Personal redemption from all of our challenges and pain is waiting to be discovered right now, right here. Living our *now*, right here where the Creator is to be found, provides an infusion of energy and strength. When we do, it will be as though our own private redeemer has already arrived.

BEYOND TIME

THE TORAH OF THE FUTURE is really about time.

To be more exact, it's about moving *beyond time*.

But how are we supposed to move beyond time? As physical beings living within the nexus of time and space, we don't experience anything outside of those limits.

Or do we?

We're not only bodies caught in time and space; we're also souls unrestrained by either of them. Some part of us *does* have access to the transcendent. When we open our minds to the guidance of those masters who did live with transcendent consciousness, we can follow them up to the state beyond time.

So we begin with a simple question — what is time? And what does it mean for us to live bounded by the limits of time?

Before there was a human being, an animal, a plant, or a stone... before there was a universe as we know it with its planets, suns, matter, and dark matter...there was only the Infinite One.

Within the all-encompassing Self of the Infinite One, there were no Divine attributes or Names, there was no space or time, nothing *other* than the Infinite One.

With the awakening of the Divine Will to bestow, to give, and to reveal its loving-kindness and mercy upon an *other*, there was a withdrawal of the Creator's Infinite Light to create a conceptual space. That primal constriction, the *tzimtzum*, is the beginning of time and space.

This, as we learned at the beginning of this book, is the most basic dynamic of Creation.

So time and space arose from the constriction and concealment of the

Divine Presence. They are what came to fill the vacated space, where the Infinite One is unseen, unknown. In this world of time and space, we have free will, and we have the conceptual room we need to exist and act.

The Infinite One is beyond time and space, but we can grasp Godliness by harmonizing our own actions with the Divine Will. Everything good is rooted in God. When we're engaged in a righteous action, *and when we're attuned to the Source of that goodness*, our limited act unites with the Infinite that vitalizes it. When we're aware of the opportunity to use aligned action as a gateway of transcendence, we rise up out of our normal state of consciousness and enter the consciousness "beyond time."

Although we operate through the limits and medium of time, our moments of aligned awareness give us access to the realm of the Infinite. It is specifically *through* the boundary of time — because that's the only place we can operate — that we have the opportunity to touch that which is beyond time altogether. Full focus on the present moment of contact with

> Full focus on the present moment of contact with the Divine transforms what would otherwise be an earth-bound, time-bound action into a gateway to infinity.

the Divine transforms what would otherwise be an earth-bound, time-bound action into a gateway to infinity.

To the enlightened, time and space are just very sophisticated illusions. Our reality of time and space that appears so solid to us is, to them, like the life of a dream. It feels substantial; you can eat and drink in the dream, sleep deeply, live out days and years filled with action and interest...and, still, you wake up to find that only an hour has gone by since you fell asleep.

For the spiritually evolved, the state of "beyond time" — what people call "The World to Come" — is the actual wide-awake and pulsing heart of our dream reality, just like your body and mind are fully alive, sustaining you there in your bed while your imagination weaves its dreams.

> *The life of the World to Come is not exactly the future…*
> *It's a time that is always coming, always happening,*
> *deep within the core of our visible reality.*

Our goal is to just plug into it. We don't need to pitch forward into the future; we need to dig deeper into the *now*.

There are people who live long lives, but they're not growing or changing, and so those years have no vitality no matter how long they last. We can waste our whole lives, all of our energies, build up social structures and industries around physical desires that we enjoy for a few minutes and then they're gone. It's like taking a lifetime of seventy-odd years and compressing it all into a quarter of an hour of pleasure — is that really living a full life?

If I spend my entire adult life working to earn money…so I can pay my mortgage to safeguard my possessions and my body…and pay for the food needed to feed it…so I'll have energy to get up and go out to work again tomorrow and do it all over again — is that really living? If I do this for years and years just so I'll have enough to retire on, to spend my summer vacation somewhere cool and my winter break somewhere warm — is that called living?

We also find people who live relatively short lives, but their days are long — bursting with vitality and expanded awareness. They have managed to enter the world beyond time. They have gone beyond time, in the *now*.

In fifteen minutes, they can reach states of conscious contact with the Infinite that other people don't attain in their entire lives. And they do it again and again, quarter-hour after quarter-hour, for days and years, as their minds and souls expand and blossom. That's really living.

Their state of consciousness allows them to transcend the strict limits of minutes, hours, days, and years. They're in tune with the pulsing heart that lives at the epicenter of every moment. Each instant is an entirely new creation. We experience freshness and presence in our lives when we follow their path.

When we're untethered from the harsh limit of time, possibilities for radical change open before us. We can change; we can experience genuine revolutions. What's happened until now doesn't determine our future. Our habits don't have to box us into a fixed cycle of action and reaction like they've always done. The past is gone — we let it be. The future is unknown — we don't speculate.

Going beyond time is our means of release and transformation.

LIVE YOUR NOW

At this moment in time, the Infinite One is accessible to me...as long as I remain in this moment in time together with Him. For the Infinite One, past, present and future all exist within the all-encompassing Now. If I want to be in conscious contact with the Infinite One, I have to let go of my thoughts of the past and the future, and stay present...in the present.

The Infinite One created the universe in order to provide us with the highest possible degree of good. He uses that energy to recreate the universe from instant to instant, filling it anew with life and vitality.

> At this moment in time, the Infinite One is accessible to me...as long as I remain in this moment in time together with Him.

Our lifeline to the Infinite One exists in this present moment, because that is the point of communication between the created universe and its Source. All good flows through that point of contact, and when I touch down right there, I'm standing at the wellspring of energy and joy.

The mystical works explain that the wellspring of Divine abundance renewed at every moment is surrounded by a shell; even though the entire universe derives all its life force from its link with the Infinite One, not everyone manages to break through the hard exterior. Staying stuck in yesterday or agonizing over tomorrow leaves me on the outside of that barrier, that fence. In fact, *those thoughts of past and future are the fence* that keeps me separate from the flow of goodness at the heart of every moment.

We can only think one thought at a time. Allowing our minds to move into the past or the future pulls us right out of the present, our only sphere of action and choice. All we really have is this moment right now. So thoughts of the past and future just rob us of our *now*, the only space in which we really exist.

That doesn't mean that the past is entirely off-limits. Sometimes, the work of the present moment involves a careful examination of the past, but not as a way of reinhabiting dead history. *I immerse myself in the past only as a means of correcting my path at this moment in time.*

> All we really have is this moment right now. So thoughts of the past and future just rob us of our *now*, the only space in which we really exist.

And it's sometimes necessary to plan for the future, and *that can be the work of the moment, too.* But the past and the future aren't meant to be endlessly looping movies in the multiplexes of our minds, where we wander from one showing to the next, without ever getting out into the vivid daylight of today.

It's part of human nature to be drawn toward the negative, to pursue unproductive and toxic thoughts and patterns. So it's not a surprise if you find that your mind comes up with a lot of very good reasons why you can't delight in this moment in time. The weather is crazy, your health is worrying you, you're too busy, the economy is depressing, your marriage is disappointing...you name it.

But, the truth is, at this moment in time, you're reading these words, holding an actual or virtual book in your hands, presumably not starving, naked, or exposed to the harshness of the elements. You're breathing; you're alive. Everything you need at this exact moment in time is available to you. The abundant flow of Divine love and energy is pulsing through you, providing you with existence and vitality. Take this moment to feel it.

Just like I have a choice to fill my mind-space with the past or the future, I also am free to reorient my thinking on a moment-to-moment basis so that I'm focused on the now and not anywhere else.

In Psalms we find an affirmation that we can always work with:

God said to me, "My child, I have given birth to you today."

When I'm living my now, I'm here with the Creator in a universe being recreated from instant to instant. If the entire universe is receiving a fresh influx of vitality every moment, *why am I stuck in the past that's gone? Why am I fixated on a future that doesn't yet exist?*

The Infinite One tells me I've just been born; shouldn't I wake up and flow with that reality?

It's not only a matter of *thoughts* of the past and future. The negative habits of the body and its toxic emotions are also a function of time. Let's use a common example of a harmful habit: overeating.

How many times is overeating rooted in trying to get away from the present moment? What people call comfort foods are often those foods that feed an emotional need of the past, or soothe an anxiety about the future. And it's possible to eat so much of these foods because the overeater is often so busy taking it in, he's not even really experiencing the food as he eats it.

The simple acts of slowing down, feeling grateful to the Source of your nourishment, enjoying the taste as you receive it, and really experiencing the pleasure of the food make eating *timeless*, joyous, an act of connection that satisfies on every level. That kind of presence in eating makes it very hard to eat too much.

And the inverse has a lot to teach me, too. If I find myself falling into the negative habits of body and emotion, it's a good indicator that I've lost the thread of the present. So while it's important to talk about the flow of our thoughts, the other expressions of the self also have to come on board. It's not enough to talk the talk...we want to walk the walk too.

PAST AND FUTURE

SO WE'VE SEEN THAT THE essence of reality is only the constant flow of the present. The Jewish mystics invested themselves in plumbing the depths of the *now*, using the framework of temporal life as a way to touch the Infinite that vitalizes every single instant. This is how they achieved transcendent consciousness.

As I began to explore these ideas in my own life and meditated on how to integrate them, I became increasingly aware of just how much of my mind-space was given over to thoughts about the past and the future.

As I started to pay more attention to my own thought processes, I was taken aback by how much I was allowing the present to slip through my fingers. But I didn't allow this new awareness to discourage me — change only begins when I realize just how prevalent an unproductive pattern is. Only by recognizing that something isn't working can I repair it.

> Only by recognizing that something isn't working can I repair it.

So, late one night — or early one morning, depending on how you look at it — I started to consider just how much of Judaism appears to focus on the past or the future. How could I reconcile my newfound understanding of the need to live in the now with what appeared to be a focus on my people's historical experiences and its aspirations for the ultimate future?

And then a new window of understanding opened for me.

There's a traditional anecdote about a meeting between the prophet

Jeremiah and Plato, the philosopher, after the ruin of the First Temple in Jerusalem.

> *Plato came across Jeremiah weeping bitterly and lamenting over the loss of the Temple. The philosopher approached the prophet with two questions...*
>
> *"They say you are a great sage," said Plato. "Why, then, are you crying over the destruction of sticks and stones?"*

Meaning, you're a wise man, and so you must know that Godliness isn't confined to a structure built of physical materials. What is there to cry over?

> *His second question was, "Why are you crying over the past?"*

Once the past is gone, it's done. Why cry over it now? Why live in the past when the point is to live in the present?

These questions may make Plato sound more like the Buddha than an ancient Greek, but they're going to help us to understand our Torah concepts of time, and our relationship to the past and the future.

Let's translate these questions in terms more relevant to us right now. "Why don't you Jewish people move out to Western Canada, go find yourselves a nice mountaintop where no one will bother you, and get on with your lives? Why are you still stuck on Jerusalem, concerned with your Temple Mount, and the endless story of your historical collective suffering? Why not just let go of your national baggage and your painful past, and plug into the now? Why not just transcend it already?"

And the question *is* relevant, because the Jewish people do engage in collective mourning over historic losses during certain cycles of the year, reciting Jeremiah's own *Lamentations*. At the other end of the time continuum, we find that a focus on the redemptive future is a basic part of our belief system. So where do these values fit in with the need to stay in the present and connect with the Infinite One in the Now?

Let's go back to the ancient story...

Instead of answering Plato's questions immediately, Jeremiah stated, "They say you are a great philosopher. Do you have any unanswered questions of your own?"

Plato answered, "Yes, many. But I've despaired of ever receiving answers from any human being."

Jeremiah said, "Ask, and I will answer them for you."

Plato presented a series of very challenging questions to Jeremiah, which the prophet answered without hesitating. Astonished, Plato asked, "Where did you learn such wisdom?"

Jeremiah answered, "From those sticks and stones. And as far as your second question goes, I cannot answer it. You would not understand me."

So what's the difference between a philosopher and a prophet? A philosopher harnesses the potential of human reason to answer the great questions of existence. But human reason is limited; human beings are only creations, not Infinite Creators. A prophet, on the other hand, receives his flow of insight from the higher Source, but it can only be accessed through spiritual alignment.

A prophet has to be wise, but the wisdom he shares isn't the product of his intellect alone. Jeremiah was a conduit for the flow of Divine insight — and the "sticks and stones" of the Temple served as the focal point of this flow for the hundreds of years it stood in Jerusalem.

The Temple was a channel, just like the structure of every mitzvah with all of its details is a constriction of the Divine Will into a small package of action in the realm of space and time. The Temple was built along a particular plan of design; its vessels were of particular dimensions and materials; every part was a concretization of the Will of the Infinite One.

The Temple was a place of paradox, where heaven and earth kissed, where the infinitely spiritual somehow became manifest within the world of limits and dimensions. God constricted Himself in cosmic humility and allowed the Presence to be contained in such a finite vessel. It wasn't something you saw; it was something that you perceived, that you felt. And the entire world flocked to Jerusalem to experience it, indescribable as it was.

"For My House shall be called a house of prayer *for all the nations*" (Isaiah 56:7). The Temple wasn't only a gift to the Jewish people; the Temple was a gift to the world.

So Jeremiah's statement, that those sticks and stones were the well from which he drew his wisdom, was really his answer to Plato's first question. "I shouldn't cry over sticks and stones like *those* now that they're gone?"

But when it came to the second question — what is the purpose of revisiting the painful past if it can't be altered? — Jeremiah said he couldn't give Plato an answer that Plato could understand. There are different ways of explaining that response, but I have my own view.

There are four basic types of people who have suffered traumas. The first are those who never really left their painful past. Their thoughts and emotions are still in the pain-place, and it taints their present. Survivors of major disasters and wars, victims of abuse, those who still grieve over old losses are all liable to carry their trauma with them indefinitely.

The second type — and that's most of us — learn how to live with it, but they're what I'd call "functionally dysfunctional." Meaning they're fine until something triggers their old pain. Some spend their lives in therapy just to navigate through it.

The Buddhist, or Plato of our anecdote, has an answer for the sufferer: Drop those pain-filled suitcases. You can become one of the third group of survivors — you can transcend the pain-place. To do this, you must let go of the baggage of the past. Live today; live now. There is only the present moment; the past is irrelevant; it's gone. It cannot be retrieved, and you don't really want to retrieve it anyway since it cannot be repaired now. Let go of your legacy of Jewish suffering.

> We aren't here to *transcend* the world; we're here to *uplift* the world.

But Jeremiah has a fourth option for us — the one he cannot explain to Plato. He can't explain it because it touches upon the innermost heart of Judaism. It's a secret, not easily shared.

We aren't here to *transcend* the world; we're here to *uplift* the world.

We're not here to forget our past; we're here to transform the present through allowing ourselves to experience the pain of the past. The past is revisited so we can redeem our present.

Experiencing the pain of loss of those sticks and stones brings me to feel a yearning for what is possible, for what has been and could yet be. That's not called living in the past or even waiting for the future — it's a transformation of my *now* through the activation of my will and desire.

We aren't seeking to transcend this world; we want to experience heaven on earth. Not a new earth, and not hell on earth...heaven on this earth. And we access it through our yearning and the expansion of our Divine awareness, because it's always already here.

The World to Come is the beating heart of all that exists, just like the soul is the hidden vitality that gives life to the body.

Jeremiah can't explain this to Plato, because it's the secret of Judaism itself. If something exists — the pain of the past or the challenge of the present — it exists so that I should elevate it back to its Source in Godliness through the force of my awareness.

> There is no situation that cannot become a tool of transformation.

There is no situation that cannot become a tool of transformation

A WORLD
BEYOND TIME

SEVERAL YEARS AGO, ON ONE of my trips to the West Coast, I lectured at a friend's home. One of the participants was a doctor who ran a rehab center for recovering addicts. Afterward, he asked me if I could speak to a group of his patients; he was interested in sharing spiritual tools with them to help them in their recovery.

I opted to speak with them about the same concepts we're learning about right now — the teachings that help us stay in the present, move out of the toxic past, and not get overwhelmed by the future.

One of the greatest challenges facing addicts is negative thinking about the dead days that can't be recovered. But what might be even more daunting is the prospect of time looming ahead — "Am I *never* going to be able to use again?" *Never* is such an endless mountain to climb. Learning how to take it one day — or one hour or one minute — at a time is the foundation of recovery.

And no one says you have to hit rock bottom before you change your life. The same tools that bring new life and hope to a person who has nowhere to go but up are more than powerful enough to infuse your own life with a whole new spirit.

But it's not really just about you or me. Let's start thinking about what it would be like to live in a world where everybody's *now*-consciousness has been turned on. Can you imagine a world that isn't stuck in its old, dysfunctional way of thinking and being? Where individuals, branching out into whole societies, tap into the joy and potential of the now without being drowned by a toxic past? Where our present isn't eviscerated by our fears about the future?

That's the job of the Messiah — to wake up the world so that we can, together, achieve a higher state of being focused on the infinite potential within every moment, maximizing the vital flow of Divine energy that enlivens every instant. We'll be centered and serene, secure and joyous.

In 1971, Ram Dass published his awareness manifesto, *Be Here Now*. At that time, his ideas were completely novel to Western readers. But forty-five years on, we're awash in a super-abundance of bestsellers — TED talks, seminars, podcasts, and books — all about "The Power of Now." When we look around, we see there's a gentle revolution going on. As these concepts spread — from meditation centers to the psychologist's office, to schools and corporations — the world is easing into messianic consciousness.

It's the wave of the future, and it's taking place right here, right now.

When I look around and see how these ancient concepts have suddenly become — in different forms, through diverse channels — the cresting wave of a shift in consciousness all over the world, I stand in awe. These are a reflection of *The Teachings of the Messianic Era* that Rebbe Nachman shared. And they're flowing out into the world at an unprecedented rate. It's truly a new era.

YOU AND ME

NOW IT'S TIME FOR US TO TAKE EVERYTHING WE'VE LEARNED UNTIL NOW AND CARRY IT OUT INTO THE WORLD OF ACTION. BECAUSE **LIVING ALIGNED** IS REALLY ALL ABOUT **YOU AND ME** — WHAT **WE'RE** GOING TO DO TO MAKE THIS WORLD THE PARADISE IT WAS MEANT TO BE.

YOU
AND ME

UNTIL NOW, WE'VE LEARNED ABOUT the gradual revelation of the Divine Will going back to the first impulse of Creation. Together, we've traveled down through time and seen how the great figures and sages — from Adam through Moses and until the Messiah — have contributed in their own way toward the full revelation of Divine mercy. Each of these spiritual masters opened unique channels so that the plan of the Infinite One can unfold down here, within this world of action, to *you and me* today.

Despite all their superhuman efforts, though, we still find ourselves in a less-than-perfect world. It's only natural for us to ask the question: If the work hasn't been completed yet, *is it really possible that it will be accomplished in our own time*? We look around and don't seem to see any figures on the horizon that are of the caliber of Rabbi Shimon bar Yochai or the Arizal or the Baal Shem Tov. If *they* didn't manage to complete this cosmic project, how are *we* going to do it?

The essence of the messianic era is the consciousness of "Today!" The changes we want to see in the world are the accumulations of the apparently small steps we take, from moment to moment, day to day. The progressive revelation of the Divine Will is happening not only all around us, but *through* us. Cosmic shifts are catalyzed by the incremental shifts in consciousness made by people like *you and me*. Even relatively simple people like us are going to catalyze the final phase of human development and the repair of our world.

Let me share a story with you, to make it all clear...

THE
WALL

ONCE UPON A TIME, THERE *was a great city, and it was surrounded by an insurmountable wall. Every king wanted to conquer this city and each one tried with all his might, but none succeeded. Their forces fell victim to the arrows shot from the city's wall.*

Later, a very wise king came to examine the wall itself. He

> Our hidden acts of compassion — no matter how small they appear — complete the spiritual work of the ages.

understood that if his best troops were to drive against the wall in a rush, they could take it down. Nevertheless, all of his troops fell from exhaustion. He sent wave after wave of fighters, but each one retreated after battering themselves against the obstacle. The king remained alone.

He walked around the wall to see if it had sustained any damage during the attack, and it had. The inner wall was almost down, and the outer wall only appeared whole; in reality, it was riddled with cracks. The king realized that if he were to call up even the elderly, the ill, the weak, and the children, they would topple it completely.

The king immediately gathered together everyone left to him. An army of the frail and tired rushed the wall...and broke it down completely.

Together, they conquered the city.

So let's think about the parable in relation to what we've learned so far...

Who really tore down the wall? Even though it appeared as though the warriors who came first didn't succeed and the infirm who came afterward managed to topple it, we know that's not exactly true.

Together, through all of their combined efforts at different times and in different ways, they broke through the barrier.

What's the barrier, though? What kind of war are we fighting?

The battle is in the realm of consciousness. The barrier is that which divides us from the fullest revelation of Divine mercy and Will, from experiencing the absolute unity of God.

If the giants who came before us didn't manage to break down that stone wall, how can we? First of all, we need to stay aware that *the lion's share of the hard work has already been done.* We're not alone in the task, and what remains isn't nearly as overwhelming as it appears.

The Kabbalistic tradition is clear that the purpose of Creation is to reveal Divine compassion: to give, to share. When *you and me* — as we are right now, without preconditions, without perfection — align ourselves with that essential Will by activating our own Godly gift of compassion, we become partners with the spiritual masters throughout the ages and with the Infinite One in bringing Creation to its goal.

Throughout this book, history itself has been the lens through which we've watched this process unfold. At times, the concepts have been new and challenging and required a lot of clarification. At other times, I focused on the pathway of a particular master in a more general way, without going into great detail about the working ramifications.

At this point, it's time to get practical with this system, basing ourselves on the Kabbalistic tradition that draws together all these threads. We'll revisit the basic concepts, this time with our focus on translating them into *tools for everyday living.* Because the essence of cosmic truth lies in bringing it down into our world of action.

The Creator has left pockets of emptiness, small vortices of need, down here in the world of action *for us to fill.* The great sages of the past have already done their part...now it's up to *you and me* to welcome in a new era of consciousness. Our small, hidden acts of compassion turn out to be not small or weak at all. They're game-changing, earth-moving acts of alignment that complete the work that's been progressing since the beginning of time.

We *can* take down that wall. And we will.

And this is how we're going to do it.

YOUR HEART'S
DESIRE

FOR **YOU AND ME** TO set this new era into motion, we need to be in the right state of mind and heart and, most importantly, we need to operate from the place of desire and *will*.

Earlier we learned about the transformative power of desire and yearning. The Kabbalistic tradition teaches us that will is our very highest force, the part of ourselves that best expresses the essence of our soul. The Divine Will is the guiding force of all of Creation, and within us it's the spark that initiates and carries to completion everything we accomplish.

Anyone who has tried to quit an addiction like smoking knows that when we're not working *with* our will, we work *against* ourselves. If I make the behavior an enemy rather than making freedom from the behavior *an expression of my own free will*, I'm setting up obstacles to my own progress. Rather, I must discover the purpose smoking has served in my life, and how my will can find other channels for its desire that aren't self-destructive. If I don't, my relationship with the addiction becomes *more pronounced*, *more dependent*, and *more entrenched*. The negative associations I have with smoking in my mind become walls that surround and *protect the habit*.

That's not the way to freedom.

To really reach our potential, we need to be *inspired* — literally filled with an enlivening *spirit*. Our actions are powerful when they're *in-spirited*, when they're invested with soul. How do we do it, though?

> We instill our actions with the spirit of life by filling them with the
> highest aspect of our soul...
> Our will, our desire.

227

The Kabbalists teach that we each have a unique mission in this life, a story of repair and redemption that is ours alone. Our desire — the work we love to do, the act of service that calls to us — is the key to understanding our unique contribution. Our hearts summon us to the place where our investment is most needed, where it's our destiny to shine. To discover our mission, we have to listen, to open our eyes and hearts and be sensitive to who we really are.

> Through knowing what we really want, we come to know ourselves fully.

Through knowing what we really want, we come to know ourselves fully.

Are we really listening to our heart's desire? Do we give ourselves the necessary space and time to figure out what really motivates us, what we really love to do, what we really *want* to do?

So many of us just go through the motions...We do what we do because we *have* to do it. Or we're just getting pushed along by the current of our families, friends, neighbors, and communities. I'm not knocking being a responsible member of family and society, but within the framework of our duties, *how soul-invested do we feel*? Life is a gift, it's precious...it's the most valuable thing there is. How can we expend so much of it where we're not really engaged and present, where our desire and will aren't invested?

Let's look at a really simple example. When it comes to food, we all have our cravings and our aversions. I, for instance, can't stand liver. My son tells me it's because of my blood type, but I know it's really because of my *soul* type. Certain foods draw me because I have spiritual work to do with them. This doesn't necessarily mean I should eat them; maybe my spiritual work with them is avoiding them because they're not healthy for me. Maybe the work with them is that I need to experience a desire for something material and translate that into feeling more yearning in my relationship with my Creator. Whatever the case, it's a fact that I have spiritual work to do there, otherwise I wouldn't be drawn to those foods. And the opposite is also true. Foods I don't like are a hint that I don't have spiritual work to do with those particular foods.

There's a full spectrum of thoughts, words, and acts that are intrinsically righteous, that connect me to my Source — they're called mitzvot. But within that broad spectrum, I have choices about where I really immerse myself, where I find the maximum contribution to make. To discover them, I must follow my heart's desire. Not my parents' desire, not my spouse's desire, not my friend's desire.

> *My own desire.*

Let's say I have a genuine longing to alleviate other people's suffering — that's a great place to put my energy. But there are so many ways to help, so many possibilities...How can I know which direction will put me in the greatest degree of harmony with my Source? *I need to look inside myself and develop sensitivity to my subtlest feelings. I need to discover what path of service has the greatest pull on my heart.* That pull is no less than my Creator's way of communicating with me; it's His way of guiding me toward my mission.

I want to fill my mind with new concepts that expand my spiritual life, but there's so much to learn. What subjects should I focus on? *The subjects that draw my heart the most powerfully* — those are my guides, and they're gifts.

The Rebbe of Kotzk — a holy man whose clarion call was absolute truth at all costs — once asked, "Why did King David pray to be saved from *all* of his enemies, and also from Saul who was his pursuer? Why wasn't Saul included among the collective 'all'? Shouldn't that term be all-encompassing?"

> The subjects that draw my heart the most powerfully — those are my guides, and they're gifts.

The master then taught a deep truth, "The path of Divine service is filled with obstacles, but the *worst* is borrowing. The name Saul in Hebrew is *sha'ul* — to borrow. King David knew he had many enemies, but the greatest barrier to his alignment with the Infinite One was the temptation to walk someone else's path, to follow and to borrow without taking the courageous step of discovering *his own unique direction.*"

The greatest obstacle to real spiritual growth is found in the tempta-tion to impersonate others.

The holy Kotzker Rebbe would say:

> *If **I am I** because **you are you**...*
>
> *And if **you are you** because **I am I**...*
>
> *Then **I am not I**, and **you are not you**.*
>
> *But if **I am I** because **I am I**...*
>
> *And **you are you** because **you are you**...*
>
> *Then **I am truly I**, and **you are truly you**.*

While these words encourage us to be more self-directed in our own spiritual life and identity, there is a potential negative side to being that attentive to your will and desire...you might make the mistake of confusing an *aligned will* with plain old *self-will*.

> The greatest obstacle to real spiritual growth is found in the temptation to impersonate others.

When I'm inspired and pas-sionate about what I'm doing, there's power in my actions. It's magnet-ic; I find that things fall into place, and people also pick up on it. There's a lot of talk about the "law of attraction," and focusing your will and thoughts on getting what you want out of life. The reason these ideas have so much traction is because they do have some underlying validity. The great masters knew that the will and mind are powerful forces that can be harnessed to activate changes within the self and the world.

When we hear about books that promote the "law of attraction," they resonate with us because it's only natural that, as physical beings living in a material world, we'd like to see our wishes materialize. It only takes a little thinking to realize, though, that *not everything we want is good, or even really good for us personally.*

There's a whole world of spiritual work involved in practicing discern-ment — choosing a goal, a focal point of will and desire, that's aligned with the Divine Will.

That's our original Divine Dance step of *judgment* — creating a limit and a space so the good has a place to flourish.

What I'm really seeking is that point where the Divine Will and my own individual desire unite. It's at that point of contact — and there's not only one, there are potentially endless points like that — where I am filled with yearning and desire for this act of alignment.

So, when you wake up in the morning and you're ready to begin a new day of choosing the good — positive and present thoughts, meaningful and honest words, aligning actions — *head toward the good that is your heart's desire with passion!* Your innermost heart's desire is really the longing of the soul to be in contact with its Source, and you have so many ways open to you every day to make that contact.

How, though? It's natural to wonder just how much impact our "small" actions are going to have in the great scheme of things. One of our challenges in this world is that, when we look at the expanse of humanity and the vastness of the world, our actions — no matter how good they are — can seem kind of small, a little insignificant. But I've seen so many times in my own life that a small act — inviting someone for a Shabbos meal, or passing on a book that helped me overcome a challenge — can have profound effects on someone else's life.

So if we really want to stoke our will and desire to animate our actions, we can focus on the cosmic significance of those acts of alignment. They aren't only a personal opportunity for connection with the Infinite One — they open a channel that brings life and abundance to the entire world. They help to bring Creation one step closer to its final repair.

If we were to imagine ourselves always at a cosmic balance-point, where *one more positive, connecting act* could tip the scales and change the world, how much desire and will would we invest in that act?

When we know that it's really up to *you and me*, we're able to fully invest the best part of ourselves in every positive act that we do. And when our hearts are really in them, *those acts will accomplish their highest purpose.*

STAY
CONNECTED

IF DESIRE AND PASSION — soul-investment — are so important, are there touchstones that speak to all of us? What really drives us? What fulfills us? When I work with students and clients, I always ask them, "What's the most important part of your life? What makes you happiest?" The answers are always similar:

> *Relationships. Connection. Sharing. Giving.*

Why is that? Is it just because we're social creatures? Because we like to feel generous? No...it goes so much deeper. It's the bedrock of our existence and the deepest foundation of reality. It's the driving force of Creation itself. The will to connect, to share, and to give is an expression of our Divine soul, because it's the core of Godliness trying to express itself through us, into the world of action.

The Infinite One's Will was not expressed until He created a universe with which He could share. Remember, God didn't *need* us...He *wanted* us, because the highest good is to share good. God chose not to exist in a state of self-sufficiency and absolute good. He chose to introduce an *other* — this universe, and us — in order to express the *highest good*, which is giving. So it's natural for us to want to connect, to feel enhanced by sharing...*just like the Creator takes pleasure in our relationship with Him.*

> The Infinite One's Will was not expressed until He created a universe with which He could share.

A good friend once took me out to dinner at a really upscale restaurant in Manhattan. By the time we were done, the bill was ridiculous. We had a fantastic time — the food, the wine, the ambience...

Now, what would it have been like if I'd been sitting there alone? *God didn't want to be alone either.*

Let's make it even clearer...The Infinite One didn't want to be alone, *and that's why we don't want to be alone either.* It's not about feeling lonely, or the fear of being alone. Human beings want to *be* with others; we long to share, to connect, to give. And we don't only have an innate yearning to connect with our family and friends. Relationships aren't just a positive enhancement to our lives. *They are a basic human need.* We're always, always reaching — whether we know it or not — for contact with our Source, the Infinite One. This isn't just a facet of life; *it's life itself.*

So let's think about starting our days from the place of connection.

Imagine what it's like rolling out of bed in fight-or-flight mode — or maybe you don't have to imagine it, because a lot of us do exactly that every single day! When you're in fight-or-flight, you start off at war with your alarm clock, frustrated with your spouse for interrupting your sleep the night before, annoyed that before you can even get yourself going, you have to prod sleepy children out of bed so they can make their school bus.

And it just gets worse from there...The boss is out to get you, your coworker won't cooperate, and you're being asked to work overtime on a day when you have a family obligation. All day, it's you against *them.* What kind of life is that?

Now let's imagine waking up with the certainty that *every single person I meet today* is another member of my team, playing a different position, and *together* we're going to accomplish the cosmic plan for the coming twenty-four hours. It's not me against them — it's *you and me*, and together we're moving toward the goal.

> Every single person I meet today is another member of my team, playing a different position.

Every morning, we focus on moving away from ego-based anxieties

— fears of scarcity, of diminishment, of infringement — that lead us to keep a distance from the people in our lives. We commit to letting go of defining ourselves by way of separating from others. To paraphrase that great sage, the Kotzker Rebbe, "I can *be* because I'm *me*, and not just because I'm distinguishing myself *from you*." My success doesn't make you a failure, and your competence doesn't mean that I'm a loser. *You being right doesn't make me wrong.*

Adam and I learn regularly by web-conference, and sometimes when he faces challenges I try to help. Adam is highly intelligent, very motivated, and successful. He was hired by a big company in another state to spearhead a large, complex, and very expensive project. During one of our sessions, I asked him, "How's it going down in Florida?"

Adam answered, "Everything's good, except that my head personnel guy — Mike — is problematic."

"Can you pinpoint what's bothering you?"

Adam thought. "On a personal level, I don't like that he treats me like a peer. I'm his *boss*."

I asked, "Well, how old is he?"

Adam admitted, "About twenty years older than me."

But he went on, "As far as work goes, I feel bogged down by Mike. We can't do anything without him because he's the point man for all of the hiring on the project. He makes poor decisions and won't take responsibility for them."

Adam sounded angry, anxious, and frustrated. He was at an important juncture in his career, locked in with a problematic employee.

Adam continued, "And now this guy is taking a four-day vacation, and we're totally dependent on him. The worst part is that on Friday, I realized that he was leaving and I still needed some information from him desperately, so I called him. He said, 'I'm on the runway...I just have to finish up something and then I'll get you what you need.' About ten seconds later, I got a text that was clearly meant for his wife or something: *Adam, that jerk, he's impossible, what a—* " [From here it gets unprintable]

"So what did you do?" I asked him.

Adam said, "I sent him a text: *thanks.* Half a second later I got one back: *...oops.*

I took a good look at Adam and saw his frustration just spilling out of him, but it was more than that: He was afraid. Adam had to make this relationship work, and it wasn't. He wasn't only angry; he was scared. Mike *could* sink his project, and Adam *couldn't* just fire him.

It's like they say: can't live with him, can't live without him.

Adam took a breath. "You always tell me to focus and stay centered, so I thought about what you might suggest. Maybe I should just let him explain himself when he gets back?"

Very gently, I said, "Even if you don't say anything at all, he's going to come back very defensive."

I went on, "You need to find a way to cut through all of this and *connect with him.* Right now, you're on offense and he's on defense. Whatever you say will push him further away. So why not go against your instincts and his expectations? How about saying, 'Mike, when I got that text, I was really hurt, but not for the reason you might have thought. I said to myself: *What am I doing wrong as a leader of this project to make you feel this way about me?*'"

Adam decided to try it and got back in touch a few days later.

With real excitement in his voice, Adam said, "You cannot believe what came out of this, Rabbi. I followed your advice, and Mike's first response was, 'I was sure you would fire me.' But then he clarified where he felt the breakdowns at work had begun, that he'd made some bad choices initially and they just kind of spiraled out of control. Mike shared his background with me, *and I really connected with him.* I was able to understand him. And I believe that he also understands me better now, too."

Instead of destroying the relationship, the dark and stuck situation became an opportunity to build a *far better* relationship. I'm pretty sure that, damaging as it would have been to the project,

> A dark and stuck interpersonal situation is an opportunity to build a new and better relationship.

Adam would have found a way to fire Mike had their relationship not shifted into a new gear.

So the darkness is an opportunity, a portal to something new and better — and now we can better understand the Infinite One's relationship with us. We can take Adam's story and go one step further with it.

What do I mean?

Ever get a bad text from God?

We all have. Whenever a situation isn't going the way we want it to, the way we *need* it to, it can feel like a Divine slap in the face.

But can you fire God? Do you have a way out of this relationship? No. You have to make it work. So you ask yourself the question: *What am I doing that's putting me so far out of alignment?* And then take this paradigm with you everywhere you go.

Every relationship has to work, even if it's just to keep the peace.

The beginning of being able to connect and make it work is in realizing that everyone has good intentions, even those people who appear to be ruining my life right now.

From that basic awareness, I can always find words to connect us. Most of us are just stuck in feeling alone and afraid; no one taught us how to connect. We think it's supposed to just come naturally. And maybe it does for highly evolved souls...but most of us tend to get stuck. Something within gets twisted, and it's hard to bond two convoluted surfaces.

So we want to straighten ourselves out, get into alignment with our essential self and with others. Again, where there's a will — when we want to enough — there's a way. And we find the words and the means that bridge the space between us. I've seen people revolutionize their relationships by focusing on the point of connection between them. It begins by letting go of seeing others in an adversarial way.

Why am I fighting with my spouse? Because we're in an adversarial dynamic; we're not connected, *we're not aware that we're on the same team.* We may be playing different positions, but we're really on the same side. And it goes way beyond my spouse — *we are all in this project of life together.* Even when it seems like we're at odds, we're all playing on the same team. We're not antagonists at the level of our essence.

And our essence is the place from which we want to act.

SIMPLE
ONENESS

WHAT IS THE FOUNDATION OF all of Judaism? Our belief in the absolute Oneness of God. But what does that really mean for us, on a daily basis?

It means that God is absolutely simple. Oneness is simplicity. The Infinite One doesn't have complex parts, needs, or desires. Oneness means there is essentially one Will, one Mind, one Being.

This is why the ultimate statement of Jewish faith is the *Shema*: "Hear O Israel..." We live with it our whole lives, and die with it on our lips. That statement could really be translated as:

> *Listen carefully, Jewish people...*
> *The Infinite One, our God, is absolutely One.*

But what does this really mean? It means that the forces of nature — that often seem independent, rooted in multiplicity — *all* emerge from the Eternal Merciful One, from that single, unified Will, which is all goodness.

Human beings are naturally attuned to that Will, as long as our own self-will is set aside. That means that if we're in doubt about what course of action to take and are willing to be fully honest with ourselves, we too should be able to tap into that unified Will.

Sit quietly, set aside your own conflicting desires and motivations, and ask your heart and your soul this very simple question: *Does the act I'm about to do align with the Divine goodness, with the simple Will of the One?*

If the answer is yes, then do it. If not, don't.

It's that simple.

THE
FLOOD

THE PARABLE BELOW, DEPICTING THE End of Days, was Rebbe Nachman of Breslov's way of illustrating just how essential this quality of simplicity is, especially as the world grows ever more complex.

There was once a king who went out hunting with his courtiers and officers. To better enjoy their sport, the king dressed as a commoner. Suddenly, in the middle of their outing, a storm blew in — literally a deluge — and each of the king's men scattered, seeking shelter for himself among the trees.

The king was left alone, in danger of his life. He wandered deep into the forest in his search of refuge. Soaked to the skin, frozen, and exhausted, the king stumbled upon a shack in the woods in which lived a simple peasant.

The cottager brought the stranger into his modest home and offered him the plainest of foods — hot groats. The poor man lit the pot-bellied stove and laid the bedraggled king on his pallet on the floor.

The king thought he had never had such a sweet sleep in his life. The groats had filled and warmed him, and his exhaustion made that night on the pallet indescribably pleasurable.

Meanwhile, the rain stopped and the royal ministers went in search of the king. They finally came to the cottage and discovered their king asleep on the floor, near the stove.

"Your Majesty!" they cried. "Let us take you away from this place, back to your palace!" But the king refused them.

"None of you tried to rescue me from the flood; when it came,

each of you thought only of saving himself. But this man, this simple peasant, saved my life. Here is where I spent the sweetest moments of my life. So he will be the one to bring me back to the palace...in his plain wagon, in these clothes. And he will sit with me on my throne."

As is often the case in the Chassidic parable, the king represents God, and his throne is the means through which the Divine Presence — His Kingship — is made manifest down here in the world of action.

In the story of The Flood, we see that the king's ministers — all of whom were accomplished and wise — fell into confusion and dispersed when the moment of danger arrived. The hyper-sophisticated and complex people who seem closest to God tend to lose their way under pressure. In the parable, all of them lost sight of their single simple duty — to safeguard their king. When the king finally made his way to the peasant's cottage, the poor man might have only been able to provide the simplest of fare and lodgings, but it was sweeter than anything to the king. Straightforward loyalty and devotion to God is the highest value, and is the one that can be relied upon.

We may not be much when compared to the spiritual masters of earlier times, but it's simple people like us, doing our earnest and modest best, who will return the King to His throne. Our contributions might be plain, but they are very beloved by the Infinite One.

THE SOUL'S
MISSION

THE ROMAN GENERAL TURNUS RUFUS once asked a challenging question of the great Rabbi Akiva, one that comes to mind for many of us, even now: "If God loves the poor, *why doesn't He feed them?*" If the Creator is so merciful, why is this world filled with poverty and lack?

Rabbi Akiva answered, "The Creator leaves pockets of need in the world so that those who *have* can give to those who *don't.*"

Turnus Rufus countered with what the "raven mind" would consider a logical argument: "But if the poor suffer by Divine decree, *who are you to tamper with the running of the universe?* If the poor person is like a servant fated to be punished, you shouldn't alleviate his suffering!"

Rabbi Akiva answered that such a belief rests on the assumption that we're only servants of the Creator. "But we're called *children* of God, and even when a parent is harsh with his child, he still appreciates when someone steps in to take care of that child's need." God *wants* us to step in and take care of His children's needs. He's waiting for us to do our part.

So what really is the nature of our contribution? What are we really here to do? Is there a universal mission for *all* souls to carry out, some purpose that applies to all of us, individually and collectively?

We discover the answer to these questions within these last words of the great spiritual master, Rabbi Shneur Zalman of Liadi, the founder of Chabad Chassidism, committed to writing just hours before he left this world:

> *The soul's mission lies in the Torah's practical application —*
> *both in studying it for oneself and in sharing it with others —*
> *as well as in performing acts of material kindness. This includes*
> *lending a sympathetic ear and offering advice to others about*
> *mundane matters...*

Even though the Divine attribute, or "angel," of truth argued
against man's creation because he is full of falsehood, neverthe-
less the Divine attribute, or "angel," of kindness responded that
man should indeed be created, because he is full of kindness.
And the whole world is built upon kindness...

In these short paragraphs, Rabbi Shneur Zalman summarizes the *soul's*
mission — that means your soul and my soul — the universal directive.
And what is it?

> *The soul's mission is the expansion of consciousness (which he called "the*
> *study of Torah") and to share it with others. That, and performing acts*
> *of material kindness.*

We'd normally think of acts of material kindness as helping someone
financially, sharing a meal, or helping a struggling person to cross the street
— any one of the endless ways you can engage your body in a compassionate
and giving act. These are all great examples of acts of material kindness, but
Rabbi Shneur Zalman defines it also as *lending a sympathetic ear* and *offering*
advice by providing emotional support and the benefit of our own experience.

The forms that kindness and mercy can take are endless, meant to
express the ways in which each soul is drawn to give. For example, giving some attention to a person who is neglected; smiling at a person
who feels down; seeing the physical need of another and using the gifts
you have to fill that gap. The cosmic holes in existence were created to
give us the opportunity to mirror the Divine. Our lives are filled, every
day, every hour of the day, with openings so that we can carry out this
mission, the purpose of our existence.

Not long ago I bumped into my old friend Binyamin and I told him
that he is my Rebbe — my spiritual mentor and guide — when it comes
to good deeds. I reminded him of the following story:

Close to forty years ago, I was living in the mystical city of
Safed in northern Israel. Binyamin arrived, fresh after getting

married, and he was so young, he looked about fifteen years old — not a single hair to his beard. I knew him from Jerusalem but I was curious as to why he had moved up north; in those days Jerusalem was still affordable and it was the norm for a young couple to live in the wife's town.

He looked at me with eyes wide open, like he was seeing something in the future, and said the following words:

"Baruch, in Jerusalem the big work has already been done. Wherever you turn there is another charitable organization to fill another need. But here in Safed, it's a new frontier — wherever you look, it's wide open, there are gaps everywhere!"

From that young age, Binyamin started his "career" of giving — looking for the places of need and working to fill them. As his giving grew, his financial life flourished. Today he is a well-known businessman remarkable for his generosity.

But *why* is *giving* "the soul's mission?" Is that really the sum total of our purpose in life?

Yes, it is.

If we understand that our souls are extensions of the Divine Will, and the essential force of that Will is to give, to share, then we start to grasp just why performing "acts of material kindness" down here in the material world is the essence of our mission.

> Follow your heart's desire and seek the form of giving that speaks to the root of your soul. The opportunities are, literally, endless.

The Infinite One's giving is the expression of His essential nature. The Creator shared His essential self with us — that's the soul — and so *our essence also needs, wants, and yearns to give...to connect through giving.*

So you follow your heart's desire and seek the form of giving that speaks to the root of your soul. The opportunities are, literally, endless. Just follow Binyamin's example and open your eyes.

BEYOND
NATURE

WE'VE ALREADY SEEN THAT OPPORTUNITIES for giving are infinite, and the general guideline is to follow your heart's desire. The form of compassionate action that resonates with you — with your nature, your resources, and your circumstances — is the best place to begin. But when we talk about the heart's desire, we're leaving out another important element of giving — *transformative giving.* They're not always the same thing.

As we discussed earlier, when giving transforms you, you're also *receiving a gift.* It's your opportunity to leave the state of *stuckness* and stagnation that's like spiritual death. Because if we're not growing and changing, we're dying. Transformative giving is what keeps us alive and vital, dynamic and fluid.

> When giving transforms you, you're also *receiving a gift.* It's your opportunity to leave the state of *stuckness* and stagnation that's like spiritual death.

If the *entire universe* is a different place than it was an instant ago, then why should we be so stuck? The entire universe is constantly experiencing endless shifts and fluctuations of matter and energy — stars are born and die; my cells divide, multiply, breathe, and die by the millions and trillions. Why shouldn't I be able to follow the universe's lead and change too? Why shouldn't you?

The stuck person gets up in the morning, boxed-in, stuck within self-imposed limits. He needs to break out to really live.

When you start your day looking forward to the new opportunities for growth and change heading your way, you're living in a universe that's alive, that's being vitalized constantly, and you're tapping into that flow of Divine energy. When you live that way, you exist in the absolute present, savoring every moment. Every day is a new world. You don't stumble through your life thinking, "This time last year? Now, that was living. But today just isn't a real day. Today I had to go to the bank, I had to go to work; it was just the same old, same old. Next month, next year, I'll really get to live. Today, I'm just surviving. I'm just trying to scrape through."

Every day presents endless new openings to know the Presence, to reveal it, and to develop a relationship with the One. You break out of the cycle of nature, the sleepy and predictable way of being, and the best way to do it is by *breaking out of your own nature*. And there are endless ways to become transformative givers.

If reaching into my pocket and giving someone a few dollars is no big stretch for me, the transformative act can be the choice to stop and engage that person in conversation, make eye contact, smile at them, ask if I can grab them a cup of coffee since it's cold out. If reaching out in a humane way does come fairly naturally, then it could be that my transformative charity can involve giving the benefit of the doubt to someone I resent — to choose to be less judgmental, more charitable in my opinion of them.

Where I find myself feeling tight is my guide to where I need to exert a little stretch.

And now we're back to our original idea, that the greatest flow of Divine mercy — that's Divine vitality and energy — really gets going when the individual does the transformative act. Because the transformative act — in this case, giving — is proof you're awake and alive, participating in a dynamic energy system fully capable of expansion and change.

Stretch past your usual limits, past your raven-state, and see what kinds of changes unfold.

SHARE
YOUR MIND

KING DAVID SAID IN PSALMS: "Fortunate is the one who enlightens the poor; God will rescue him on the day of evil."

Wouldn't it be better to say, "Fortunate is the one who *provides for* the poor?" Not necessarily, because by using the word *enlighten*, King David hints that the greatest gift you can give is that of expansive consciousness. And it's a gift that will give back much more than we realize.

Believe it or not, it's quite possible to follow all of the religious rituals and requirements and still lack God-consciousness. It's possible to pray every day and still be missing the vitality that comes with truly knowing that the Infinite One is good and does only good. Sharing this awareness with someone who lacks it himself fills the dark pockets in the world and brings the universe to a greater state of completion.

It is our human duty to expand our consciousness. This is genuine wealth — knowing and feeling deeply that Divine mercy is an endless reservoir. When one is attuned to it, the channels open. Then it's possible to meet the needs of anyone you encounter because you are only an instrument of the Divine Will. You can give and give and not feel strained by it, because you're drawing from an infinite account. When you give that way, the recipient also is touched by a new awareness of the endless nature of Divine generosity.

What are you really trying to get across to yourself, and to everyone else you meet? That there is only one God, and this Infinite One is full of love and compassion; all that He does is good even when it appears to be the exact opposite. It's how we break out of the raven-state. The mind ceases to be a haven for the raven; instead, it's like a sanctuary of expansive mercy.

You're fortunate and blessed when you're able to illuminate the mind of a person whose consciousness is impoverished, who's stuck in the mindset of limitation and lack. If you can share a fresh vision of Divine mercy and loving-kindness with someone, you've given them the key out of poverty, since the primary poverty is that of the mind, constricted consciousness.

The end of the verse promises, "God will deliver him on the day of evil." When you help someone else to readjust his perspective, you've got a Divine assurance that, down the line, it will come back to help you.

Our attitudes tend to be in flux, however. Even though one day we're infused with the awareness of the Creator's compassion, a day will come when our mind closes down again and all we can see are the shortages in our life.

That's the "day of evil" — the day (or days) when everything goes back to looking bad. We'll be saved from the day of evil by working on expanding other people's consciousness even when ours is constricted.

But how are you supposed to share something at a moment when you don't have it? If you're in the prison of the mind today, how are you supposed to get someone else out of jail?

This is how you break out of your own poverty of the mind: you act like a giver even when you don't feel you have much to give, because there's always someone else who needs a perspective adjustment even more than you do. Relative to his constricted state of mind, your awareness is very expansive. When you realize how much you can help another person even when you're feeling limited, your boundaries get blown wide open. The other person's constriction provides you with insight into the more subtle nature of your own limitations — the areas where you also need to do work — and you'll find that this insight saves you on your own personal "day of evil."

> When you realize how much you can help another person even when you're feeling limited, your boundaries get blown wide open.

In my own life, this has been my greatest pathway to growth. Whenever I've invested time and energy in trying to help another person out of a state of small-mindedness and limitation, I've always found their dark place to be a mirror that helps me examine my own stuck places. By walking through the constricted consciousness of another person, I've been given the gift of insight to find my own way out of a similar state in myself.

I've seen this happen over and over again.

When you really know there's only one God — when you know that even what we consider to be a harsh manifestation of Divine justice is only mercy and compassion garbed by the pockets of darkness — then you know the most important fact there is. When you share this awareness with another, it is reflected back to you as a gift, expanded and in full bloom.

SWEET CONSOLATION

THERE ARE COUNTLESS WAYS TO share expansive consciousness with another, but one oft-needed form of spiritual giving is *consolation*. To console means *to mirror Divine compassion by alleviating the suffering of another*. Expanded awareness of Divine mercy and compassion is the path to genuine consolation. Compassion means, literally, to expand beyond your own boundaries of self, your "raven haven," so you can genuinely feel the pain of the other and respond.

There are many ways to demonstrate compassion, and offering consolation is one of the highest ways to truly be there for another person. You can help another financially, materially, or emotionally, but truly relieving suffering means that you bring meaning to the pain. You don't only help — you *console*.

When we hear the word "consolation," we naturally assume that some tragedy or trauma has already taken place. The unfortunate truth is that life is full of its own pains, regardless of any particular trauma.

Life begins with the pain of birth. You have to sweat to earn your living; raising children is great but sometimes it's excruciating; aging brings its own pains; and finally, there's the pain of the separation of body and soul — death itself.

The sages point out that all pain is really just a product of the soul's life in the body. A dead body feels no pain, and a disembodied soul has no means of feeling pain. So pain is really just an often unavoidable part of life.

As they say in the world of twelve-step recovery: "Pain is inevitable, but suffering is optional."

Pain is what we experience; suffering is how we *interpret* the experience. Pain is actual and factual; suffering is a product of attitude and mind. It flourishes when we're disconnected from the knowledge that Divine mercy is the orchestrator of all that occurs.

When I see a person in pain who is also suffering, I want to do

> "Pain is inevitable, but suffering is optional."

whatever I can to bring relief. I may not be able to do anything about the pain, but I can help relieve the suffering by shining meaning into it, by sharing some greater awareness of Godliness.

Our awareness and knowledge of God is what unites us with the Infinite One. As one of the great sages said, "If I knew Him, I would be Him!" Since God is the essence of good and perfection, the more we are living aligned with the Divine, the more wholeness and good we experience.

So even though pain is inevitable, the suffering that's the result of our limited perception of God *can* change. The prophets promised that, in the ultimate future, all of the universe will be filled with knowledge of God, and *because of that awareness*, suffering will cease.

So how do we tap into this kind of consolation? How can we learn to transcend suffering and *transform* it?

We've already spoken about people responding in one of four basic ways to their own past traumas, but this time I want to reenter the model with a different focus. We need to see how to apply these ideas in our efforts to reach out and help people, to console them and relieve their very real suffering. So now we're on the outside, looking in.

The first, and lowest reaction to pain is where one endured pain in the past and his injuries have thoroughly followed him into his present. The old pain (which is past and gone) constantly activates present suffering. The person relives his painful past in his mind, and suffers deeply and persistently. This will result in serious *dysfunction*; no one who is constantly pained and suffering can lead a normal life.

The second response is similar to the first, with an important difference. The pain is there, but it's been fairly well repressed. The sufferer couldn't deal with his pain, so he managed to bury it. He functions, but his pain and suffering haven't gone away. They sit beneath the surface of his awareness, waiting for some new event to break through. You say the wrong thing, or too much of the right thing — it's sometimes hard to identify the trigger — and in floods the old pain and its accompanying suffering all over again.

So the second response produces what I like to call *functional dysfunction* — a life that seems to work except when, suddenly, it just doesn't. Such sufferers seesaw between living in their old trauma and "setting it aside" — repressing it, forgetting about it, burying it. Unfortunately, a lot of people live this way; more, perhaps, than we'd like to admit.

Our third response — definitely a step in the right direction — is *letting go of the suffering*. That's the argument attributed to Plato earlier in the book; it's the advice of the Buddhist. Live in your now. You can transcend your past by letting go of it. Cultivate detachment, and leave behind the places and people with whom your pain and suffering are enmeshed. What's done is gone, it has ceased to exist altogether. You can live free of it, because it's as though it happened to someone else.

This might be a kind of *transcendence*, but it enforces full disconnection from the past in the present. It denies that it's possible to redeem and heal — even elevate — the old pain and suffering.

Which brings us to the fourth and most elevated response: a full transformation of the pain of the past, so it no longer serves as a source of suffering. How does this really work, though? We've already stated that pain is certainly real, and in some cases unavoidable.

To keep it really simple: if a child is pained by going to sleep in a dark bedroom, you have to admit that the room is dark. Could there be a monster in the room? Well, theoretically it's possible because the room is dark and maybe something's lurking there. I've never seen a monster in broad daylight, but in the dark? Maybe something's hiding. So I can go into the room and tell that child, "Here, I'll check all of the nooks and corners and closets in the room. I can show you that there's nothing hiding there."

I can shine a little light of my mind, of my awareness, into the dark corners to alleviate the suffering. The dark will stay, but the fear and suffering it breeds will go.

Although pain has a beginning and an end, our suffering mind convinces us it has always existed and that it will last forever.

Although pain has a particular magnitude, our imagination blows it up into something overwhelming we cannot tolerate for even a moment.

Although pain can also spark growth and necessary change, our imagination tells us it's pointless.

And that's really where the suffering peaks — when we see our painful experiences shear away from the purpose of existence and Divine goodness, when we fall into doubt.

But if I am filled with genuine awareness of the limitless and absolute nature of Divine compassion, I can share that and provide relief.

If I can demonstrate to the sufferer my deep and powerful awareness that everything that happens is Divinely purposeful no matter how painful, I can console. It's not a matter of just telling a person, "You know, sometimes you need to go through illness to build your immune system; sometimes losing money makes you wiser..."

> Consolation isn't information. It's not about determining exact reasons for the pain. It's about sharing the awareness that there is purpose even when we don't have access to the information.

Those are easy things to *say*, but it's very hard to transmit them in a real and healing way. But if you become the kind of person who lives with that awareness through *your own* pain, you will be able to get it across, and you won't even need to say all that much. Your way of being, your eyes, your entire self, will radiate that you've made peace with your pain and that it's not necessary to suffer.

This is how you share meaning. *Consolation* isn't *information* ("Why is this happening?" "Why did that have to happen?"). It's not about determining exact reasons for the pain. It's about *sharing the awareness that there is purpose even when we don't have access to the information.*

That's called *faith.*

It's the highest of all wisdom.

Because the ultimate knowledge is knowing that you don't really know.

ASK FOR MERCY

THE INFINITE ONE CREATED THE universe so as to reveal the fullest extent of Divine compassion and, as we've learned, we are an integral part of this process. We can give "material assistance" — money, time, energy, compassion, a listening ear, advice. We can share an expansive and faith-empowered perspective, we can offer consolation, and we can also give something straight from the soul.

When we learned about Noah, and about Moses and the Thirteen Attributes of Mercy, we saw what a difference there was in their responses to danger and loss.

When Noah emerged with his family from the ark and saw only how the world had been laid waste, he cried out, "God of mercy, where is Your mercy?" You are supposed to be a loving God! How could You have destroyed Your world? *Where was Your so-called mercy?*

The Infinite One answered, "Noah...where was *your* mercy?" Noah, when I told you that the world was in danger, you only saw to your own safety. Even if you couldn't change your society, *why didn't you pray for their forgiveness and their survival?*

Even when all of our resources are expended and we've done all we can in the world of action, when it seems like there's nothing left to do, we can still make a difference with prayer.

Noah, why didn't you activate *your* quality of mercy and use it to pray that I should have mercy on the world? You had a part to play, and you stepped away from it.

And then we contrast this with Moses. When faced with the imminent destruction of the Jewish people after the Sin of the Golden Calf, he jumped into the breach to plead for their forgiveness. Moses saw a hole, he saw the apparent vacuum of Divine compassion, *and realized that it was meant to awaken his own capacity for mercy and prayer.* It was a Divine opportunity.

Even when all of our resources are expended and we've done all we can in the world of action, when it seems like there's nothing left to do, we can still make a difference with prayer. When we ask for mercy, our own power of mercy is strengthened. We become partners with God. We become givers even in the place where we have no ability to give.

I can't heal my friend who is suffering from cancer, but I can help him by giving of my time, my resources, my energy, and my attention. I can give him my love. And when I have no resources, energy, or attention to spare, I continue to give my compassion by doing that which remains to me — I can pray for him. I activate my Divine nature and become a *master of mercy.*

The world was created for me, for you, for every single one of us, and that means it's ours to look after, to seek its repair, to seek out and discover its empty spaces and work to fill them and pray they be made whole.

People like to talk about *tikkun olam;* Jews are always looking to fix the world. But the Hebrew gives us a clue of what it's about: it's the fixing [*tikkun*] of the concealment [*he'elem*], through drawing Divine mercy into the space. And, as far as I'm concerned, I'm the only one who can do it. I can't leave it for someone else to do. It's my Divine opportunity.

> The world was created for me, for you, for every single one of us, and that means it's ours to look after, to seek its repair, to seek out and discover its empty spaces and work to fill them and pray they be made whole.

I want to look out at the rest of the world and focus on becoming a conduit of blessing, because there are so many pockets of dark concealment where mercy is hard to find. This is how I align with the Divine Will and actualize my Divine potential — by realizing that I am meant to convey blessing outward, to share it with the entire world.

How will I be able to do it?

With actions — and with prayer.

THE NOBLE
NOBODY

AFTER TALKING ABOUT HOW IMPORTANT our actions are no matter how insignificant they seem, why am I calling this chapter, "The Noble Nobody?" I mean, didn't we just learn that no one's really a *nobody*? That everyone has their part to play, and every part is important?

The ideas in this section really get to the heart of the entire *Living Aligned* concept, and right here at the outset I want to ask you to open your mind because these are ideas that challenge some of our strongest-held assumptions.

Earlier in the book, I spoke about concepts that are like dragons — they inhabit territory we tend to avoid, no-go zones because they're "big and bad," difficult to understand, or politically incorrect. The concepts I'm sharing with you are grounded in the Kabbalistic tradition. Even when they appear dragon-like, it's important to remember that they're ancient...and they fly. These ideas are cosmic truths that serve as pathways to connect with our Source. My goal is to help you see how it's possible to incorporate them into your own life, and in this way change yourself...and change the world.

So let's get back to our nobodies — who are they? As we saw in the parable of "The Wall," compared with the spiritual giants and warriors of earlier generations, *we're all nobodies*. Yet the wall comes down because of our seemingly small efforts. Can we really be nobodies, then? We are people who are, objectively, less gifted but who manage, *through the force of our desire and goodness*, to accomplish great things.

There's an idea beneath the surface of this model, and it's one of our elusive dragons. Why *does* God give some people greater gifts — spiritually, mentally, physically — than others? And when it comes to material gifts, why do we live in a world of such gross inequality? Why is there such an imbalance between the 1% and the other 99%?

Why would a just God seem to show such favoritism? Doesn't it lead to hatred and exploitation?

Does a loving father make gross distinctions among his children? Does he give gifts to one that he doesn't give to the others? If he does, we'd probably agree that he's not being a loving and compassionate father.

Our hard questions surface because we *do* believe certain fundamental truths:

> *The Infinite One is goodness itself.*
> *The Infinite One is compassionate and loving.*
> *That which God does is for the absolute best.*

If we didn't believe this — consciously or unconsciously — we wouldn't have any question about inequality. But we do believe in Divine justice, and that's why the very obvious imbalances that fill our world disturb us.

All human beings are created in the Divine image; everyone is equally valuable in the eyes of God. This means we need to safeguard each other's right not to be beheaded for our religious beliefs, guarantee equal access to education, and ensure basic human freedoms and protections.

But that essential equality doesn't mean we're all the same.

We are, most certainly, *not* equal in the distribution of our gifts, whether they're innate (like intelligence), or inherited (like a supportive and loving family with adequate resources), or acquired (by living in a land of opportunity). We can say that we ought to all have equal access to opportunities because of our essential human equality, but at the same time we still see that the Creator hasn't arranged for equal distribution of gifts.

There are fantastically intelligent and talented people in the world... and inept ones too. There are wonderfully beautiful people in the world...and plenty of unsightly ones. There are some amazingly athletic people here...and people whose handicaps make it difficult for them to function every single day. There are fabulously wealthy people in the world...and utterly destitute ones. Some of the "haves" were born to wealth, while others were gifted with *mazal* — good fortune.

But let's be honest...The "stars" are in the barest minority, and the other 99% run the range of "managing" all the way down to genuine suffering.

Is this just? Is this fair?

In many ways, the story of the unequal gift is reflected in the Torah's account of the conflict between Joseph and his brothers. Jacob recognized Joseph's great potential, and he gifted that son with something he didn't give the others — a special coat that represented that special relationship and Joseph's unique mission.

The sages taught that a parent should never show favoritism; didn't Jacob know that singling out one son would cause a rift among the brothers? How could he do it?

Joseph had a prophetic vision of kingship, to the dismay and disapproval of his brothers. Joseph was forced down into Egyptian slavery and eventually did come into his own, but the experience of opposition was a necessary part of his refining process. To be truly worthy of those gifts, Joseph was sent lessons — hard ones — through the agency of his brothers' jealousy. In the end, Joseph acknowledged that it was his brothers' catalyzing his exile to Egypt and all of his trials there that forced him into bloom.

Let's imagine a scenario to help us understand a little more about how this really works in everyday life.

Picture yourself in a little village in Ukraine of two hundred years ago. No cellphones, no electricity, no vehicles...*no money.* Everyone lives on potatoes, and it's a meager and difficult life for everyone. There are maybe fifty families in the whole village living a life of bare subsistence.

One day, Boris gets a message by the postal coach from Kiev. His uncle, a member of the government far away in the big city, has died and left him one hundred thousand rubles.

The whole village is overjoyed that one of their own has inherited a fortune, right? Of course not! Soon enough, Boris is the most despised man around for miles. And this baffles him. These are his relatives, his neighbors, his friends — they've been through good times and bad together. But now he's suddenly been set apart.

Wealth isn't really the final answer, because when you're given a gift and you don't know how to fit the gift into your relationship with others, it's a burden.

At first Boris says to himself, "This money is mine. He was my uncle, it's my mazal, and I even put in some effort by writing him letters every so often. And I don't owe any of the people in this village a thing." And he becomes more out of touch with everyone around him — he's afraid they all want his money, and they resent him for having what they don't.

Boris's old friend Misha goes over to visit one day. Misha is known throughout the village for his honesty and goodness, and he's been paying attention to the changes Boris is going through. And he's decided to try and help if he can.

Misha says, "Boris, we've always been friends, but now you're different. You don't mean to be, but you are. Why? Because God gave you something that none of us have. I don't know why He did it, and neither do you, but He must have had a reason. But you're really not any different from us, except that you were given something we weren't.

"We've been friends a long time, and I can see you're suffering. No one really likes you anymore, and you're afraid everyone's only out to get your money. Do you really want to live like that?"

Boris is struck by Misha's words. He's happy he's wealthy, but what he really wants is to live his old life, with his old friends in the village...just without poverty. But just because he's no longer poor, doesn't mean the village isn't. How can he really enjoy this blessing completely?

Boris says, "Misha, you've always been an honest and true friend, and I feel that you, at least, really want to help me. You're right; I'm not really happy even though I have the money, or maybe because I have the money. What do you think I can do?"

Misha answers, "Boris, maybe your gift wasn't sent from heaven only for you? Maybe it was also meant to help us, who weren't left a fortune? I'm not here because I want anything from you, but I think that if you don't change the way you're thinking about your wealth, you're never going to feel at home again in our village. You need to become a part of us again."

Misha is what we call a *noble nobody.*

With intelligence, grace, and compassion, he nobly enlightens Boris so that Boris can see that his gifts are actually responsibilities. Misha might be a "have-not" when it comes to wealth — and this could also be the case with any of the many gifts one can possess — but when it comes to wisdom he has a noble role. Boris might resist at first, but eventually he'll be pressured by his circumstance to change his attitude. In a noble and dignified way, Misha helps Boris to understand his role.

Newly aware, Boris will be able to say, "This is from God; it's a gift. And the fact that the rest of the village is looking over my shoulder all the time now, pressuring me for help, is also part of the gift — it comes along with it. I'm suddenly uncomfortable here, in the place my ancestors have lived for five hundred years, and why? *Because I took the gift for myself, but I didn't accept that I'm in a new relationship with the world at the same time.* The gift will force me to become a giver.

Anyone who's been singled out by a Divine gift has been chosen to carry out a mission.

Sharing a Divine gift demands a lot of wisdom. One must give to people in a way that empowers them, that doesn't make them feel less than. Giving needs to bring them to greater independence, and not further dependence.

The inheritance will make Boris into a partner with the Creator to fill the world's "empty pockets," both the literal ones and the spiritual ones, the pockets of darkness and concealment of the Divine Presence in the world in which suffering thrives.

This doesn't mean that Boris has to give all of his inheritance away. But he wasn't given the resource just for himself. He'll have to figure out exactly what his role is.

The "noble nobodies" help the alleged privileged few to remember that we're all recipients, we're all takers. They approach the "chosen one" and say, "Don't you realize you're no different from us? If God hadn't placed you in that big house on the hill, you'd be down here in the trenches with us. You didn't create yourself, your advantages, or your circumstances."

> Anyone who's been singled out by a Divine gift has been chosen to carry out a mission.

And when the "gifted one" takes that message to heart, he turns to the Infinite One and says, "Your mercy is needed by all of Your creations — even me. I might have all of the money — or talent, education, or resources — that I'll ever need, but I don't have anything unless You provide it for me. And if I need Your mercy, *how much more does the rest of Your creation!*"

When the one who has already been gifted also acknowledges his dependence on the Source, it's possible to draw down a much greater flow of Divine mercy and abundance for everyone.

The "noble nobody" wakes the privileged into a new state of awareness, and this new awareness is like a key that unlocks the door behind which lies boundless compassion and mercy.

Of all abundance, there is nothing like the abundance that belongs to God. And of all Divine attributes, there is nothing like compassion. Those people who act to unlock this most essential and most high Divine quality serve the noblest purpose. Their actions have ramifications that affect all of us, in ways we can barely imagine...

And now we can welcome in the biggest dragon of them all...the very complex and persistent problem of anti-Semitism. Based on the fundamental ideas we've learned in *Living Aligned*, concepts that are rooted in Kabbalah and the Chassidic tradition, we have a new set of tools to help us examine the question.

Why are the Jewish people called "chosen?" Is that fair?

Did the Infinite One set the Jewish people up for being hated by the rest of mankind?

The name of the mountain upon which the Torah was revealed was Mount Sinai. *Sinah* in Hebrew means hatred, and the tradition teaches that the singling out of the Jewish people for this gift — this responsibility and mission — is the root of anti-Semitism, of Jew-hatred.

Today, the world is reminding the Jewish people of the responsibilities of privilege. Sometimes it's with love — I've had many profound discussions with non-Jews who look admiringly toward the Jewish people for inspiration.

And sometimes the reminders have assumed a harsher form.

Until the Jewish people focus on acting as channels of Divine compassion with the rest of the world, the reminders will keep on coming. Because the chosen — of whatever form they take — need to wake up and arouse the mercy of the Infinite One...for the sake of everyone else. They have a mission to carry out that will not be denied.

THE HIGHEST
MERCY

WE'VE SEEN THAT THE "NOBLE nobody" has the mission of awakening the "chosen and blessed" into a new state of awareness, and that this higher consciousness has a powerful effect on everyone, everywhere. We're not only talking about the micro-environment of Boris and Misha, their village, and the "newly gifted" waking up to his destiny as a conduit of Divine mercy and abundance for others. We're talking about the way in which sharing a more encompassing, broader, endless, and unfettered understanding of God's love and compassion allows just that kind of unlimited mercy to reach us.

This isn't about Jews and non-Jews, because in our relationship with the Creator we're all on the same page — all of us are "noble nobodies" trying to unlock the treasury of Divine mercy of the ultimate Blessed One — the Creator Himself.

If you have awareness of the greatness of Divine compassion, you share it with those who don't. You uplift other people's consciousness as yours evolves, and change the world, mind by mind. This is the key to unlocking Divine mercy so the world can reach its potential.

Reaching out to touch minds and unlock hearts is our way of opening the Divine heart so that *the highest level of mercy* can really flow. That force is so powerful, it transforms everyone and everything it touches.

What do I mean by "the highest level of mercy?" Is there more than one degree of mercy?

Yes, there is!

The ancient text of Jewish mysticism, the *Zohar*, teaches us, "There is simple mercy, and then there is the *higher mercy* of the Hidden Ancient One." There are different degrees of Divine kindness, and sometimes "simple mercy" is just not going to be enough. If we want to really change the world and usher in a new age of peace, reconciliation, and abundance, we need to get that highest level of Divine compassion to flow. As the prophet Isaiah said so powerfully, "And I will redeem you in *great mercy*" (Isaiah 54:7).

The Kabbalists and the spiritual masters taught us how to access it.

The lesser degree of Divine mercy limits itself because of the limitations of the receiver. There's a trace of judgment there; if you're worthy, you receive. And if you aren't, you don't. If you're only worthy to a certain degree, you receive only that much and not an iota more. The lower level of mercy is a place of giving and abundance, *but always to a limited extent.*

What's more, simple mercy can also involve pain and suffering, because sometimes you have to be strict to be kind. In that realm, there are times when rebuke is necessary to bring the recipient to a better place. But, at this late date, we're finding ourselves less and less capable of handling harsh rebuke both as individuals and as a society. What we need is to tap into and unlock the highest, unlimited mercy of the Hidden Ancient One — the ultimate level. It is the primordial impulse of Creation — to share and give and act with love and compassion.

That higher degree is so powerful that it completely transcends the place of judgments; in fact, it's the *origin* of all mercy, and preexisted all limits and judgments. It's unlocked by having *transcendent consciousness* of the Infinite nature of Divine compassion. This is the secret of the Thirteen Attributes of Divine Mercy revealed to Moses after the Sin of the Golden Calf.

God always wants to share His infinite loving-kindness with us, but our limitations block the flow. The only person who can tap into this higher degree is one who really *knows* just how boundless is the Creator's kindness. That person helps it to descend so it can shower upon all of us, deserving and undeserving alike.

Jacob blessed his sons, "May God grant *you* mercy..." We can understand this to mean, "May the Infinite One *share with you the power to awaken the highest degree of mercy.*" May He give the quality of mercy *into your hands* so that you can work with it as required. Because God really wants to share the attribute of mercy with us so we can become partners with Him in the work of compassionate transformation.

But how easy is it for us to *really know and grasp* the infinite nature of Divine generosity? Anything infinite is, by definition, impossible for us to really grasp in our minds. So how can we get to this ultimate level and unlock its power?

The answer is that we use our access to that lower degree of mercy to help us reach the higher degree of mercy. We aim for the highest and most expansive awareness of Divine compassion we can get to, and then stretch one bit higher. We do it by knowing *that what we've known until now of God's mercy is nothing compared to its real extent, because the Infinite One's kindness is* **absolutely infinite.**

The mercy of the Ancient Hidden One has no limits, no judgments, no side effect of pain or suffering, and no end. And that's exactly what the world needs so badly right now. Because we're done, we've had enough, we're exhausted and desperate for healing and change *right now.*

We can reflect on this dynamic by way of a parable:

> *A loving father is in a desperate situation; his child suffers from a severe heart condition, and his medical insurance doesn't come close to covering the costs of surgery and therapy.*
>
> *In his city, there are two philanthropists — one of them is a millionaire, while the other is a billionaire. The father knows the millionaire personally, but he also knows that his friend's resources are limited. The billionaire, on the other hand, has vast resources at his disposal, but it's not easy to get to him. You need an "in."*
>
> *The desperate father sizes up the situation and acts with wisdom. Instead of appealing to the millionaire for the full sum (which his friend can't supply in any case), he appeals to his friend's mercy and asks him for a favor.*
>
> *"I'm really in need right now, and I know you want to help me but you can't really give me what I need. I ask instead that you go to the billionaire here in our city to ask him for help on my*

behalf. He can give me everything I need without any trouble,
but I have no access to him. You, though...you can get to him!"

Even my broadest grasp of Divine compassion and kindness is limit-ed, because I'm limited. In terms of my mind and heart, the furthest I can go is to that millionaire — the merciful man of limited means. But my access to that person (who is also really wealthy, but, even better, is *well-connected*) will get my need across to the one who can *really* help me.

However much I know of Divine mercy, it doesn't come close to what is really there — how powerful and pervasive it is, how transformative it can be. But when I'm aware of that gap, I open up the gateway to that highest degree of mercy. I tap into the vast — really infinite — resource of the Divine mercy that will change the world. I can appeal to God's simple mercy (because I can reach that far) and appeal to it to do me the kindness of reaching up toward the limitless mercy of the Infinite One on behalf of all of us.

As we learned earlier, Moses was given the gift of a vision of the Holy One "wrapped in a prayer shawl" while calling out the Thirteen Attributes of Divine Mercy. The purpose of the vision was to teach Moses the pathway of reaching up to access the redemptive power of the highest degree of mercy. This upward-reaching is called "God's Prayer."

The Holy One said through the prophet Isaiah: "And I will bring them up to My holy mountain, and cause them to rejoice in the House of *My Prayer*...

For *My house* shall be called a house of prayer for *all of the peoples of the world*" (ibid. 56:7).

This verse teaches us that the Holy One, Himself, also prays!

When we activate God's prayer, we're able to unlock the infinite mercy of the Hidden Ancient One that will transform the world. It will correct all damage, uplift all people, and bring us into a state of harmony and spiritual unity.

Dear reader, I'd like to crystalize these ideas by sharing with you a prayer authored by one of the great spiritual masters. And maybe a request, too...

If these ideas resonate with you, consider incorporating them within your own personal prayers, for every positive thought, word, and action has the power to tip the balance and illuminate the world. May we be blessed to see the earth filled with consciousness, compassion, and peace.

> *Merciful One, please send Divine consciousness down to Your world,*
>
> *so that anger and cruelty will cease to be.*
>
> *Please pray for us and awaken Your great mercy,*
>
> *for at this point in time there is no one but You who can fully do this.*
>
> *Your great mercy is powerful enough and limitless enough*
>
> *to help every single one of us align with You fully.*
>
> *In Your highest mercy, please bring us up to Your holy mountain,*
>
> *so that we can all rejoice in the House of Your Prayer...*
>
> *For Your house shall be called, "a house of prayer*
>
> *for all of the peoples of the world."*

WORKING
FOR THE KING

FELLOW SEEKER, BEFORE I SET you on your way, I want to share one last story with you.

We've learned that one of the missions of the great spiritual masters is to help us steer clear of baseless fears and fantasy dragons, and instead empower us with images that strengthen us in our relationship with the Divine. This story is a gift to you. It's an image that can impress itself into your consciousness and that you can take with you wherever you go on your path of alignment with the Infinite One.

When Reb Zusha of Anipoli first started on the Chassidic path, his holy older brother Elimelech of Lizhensk was still skeptical about the new teachings that had begun to take hold among the Jews of Eastern Europe.

Reb Zusha was a traveler, and like other tzaddikim, he often took to the road in his yearning to identify with God's exiled Presence. On one of his journeys he wound up in Mezritch, and it was there that he became a devoted follower of the Maggid. After Reb Zusha's return from his time with the Maggid, he ran into his brother, Reb Elimelech, who immediately noticed that something had changed within his brother, and this worried him.

Reb Elimelech saw Reb Zusha head out to the forest alone one day, and he decided to follow him and observe his behavior. From a distance, Reb Elimelech saw Reb Zusha bend over and stand on his head. And then he dropped over, recovered himself, and did a headstand all over again. And Reb Elimelech was convinced his poor brother had lost his mind. He decided to confront him straightaway.

Reb Elimelech said, "My brother, I'm sorry, I can't help but notice...?"

Reb Zusha grinned and said, "I'm sure you're thinking I've lost my mind, but I can explain. Let me tell you a story..."

A long time ago, a simple man and his virtuous wife lived in a small hamlet where they raised vegetables, had a modest orchard, and a little yard of livestock. Slowly, over the course of many years, they built up their homestead until it was quite prosperous. They hired hands, expanded their property, grew an increasing variety of produce, and made a very nice living. One day, the farmer — now a prominent figure in the little village — turned to his faithful wife and said, "You know, we have such a lovely operation going on here, but tell me...what's it all really for? I mean, what's the point of it all?" His poor wife seemed confused.

He went on, "Our wise and kind king lives in the capital. All of his subjects adore him, and you know what I think? I think we're really missing out on life."

His wife asked, "What do you mean?"

The farmer answered, "We really need to get closer to the king. We never get to see him, we never even hear news of him! We're just too far away here in our little village."

His wife wondered aloud, "What do you want to do, then?"

At that, the farmer brightened. "We could sell everything — all our livestock and property and land — and take the cash and move to the capital! It's true, we wouldn't be able to live in the city at the same standard as we live here, but we could get a little place, a little room close to the palace, and then we'll be close to the king. I mean, what's life worth if we can't be near the king?"

And the farmer's wife was a very good — even a righteous — woman, so she agreed. They sold everything, packed up the bare minimum into a horse-drawn wagon, and set off for the capital. With the money from the sale of their property, they managed to purchase a little place there, but it didn't take long for them to realize that being neighbors to the palace doesn't necessarily mean you're close to the king. A monarch very rarely shows himself in public.

After some time, the farmer approached his wife again. "I've got to get into the castle, my dear." He sounded a little desperate.

Naturally, she wondered how he planned to do it. He said, "We still have a little money left over from the sale of our home. I think I should bribe some official there so I can get a job on the inside," and she agreed. Anything to be close to the king!

Well, as they say, money talks. Our farmer found his connection and got himself a job within the palace. His new position? Assistant to the royal fire-arranger. Meaning, he got the entry-level job of stoking the furnace. But he did his job with so much enthusiam that the stewards started to give him more and more responsibility, until he was soon upgraded to official fire-setter within the royal chambers. What a dream!

One day, the king was toasting his royal feet at the fender when he noticed that the fire was really arranged very skillfully. It was perfectly balanced, always fed just right, always burned down perfectly...somebody was clearly putting a lot of thought into making sure the royal fire was done properly. The king summoned the head steward and remarked that the fire in his chamber was just perfect.

The steward responded, "Actually, we have a new attendant taking care of it."

The king said with feeling, "This fire is something special. Whoever is setting it is really putting a lot of love and attention into it. I want to meet the man."

So the next thing you know, the former farmer who gave up his comfortable life just to be in the king's vicinity was standing face to face with his royal majesty.

The king looked right at him and said, "You know, I really love your fires; I can see that you put so much into making them just right. They burn so evenly, and the wood is set up perfectly."

And the fire attendant was just melting as he stood there — he couldn't believe he was hearing the king say such words to him, that he loves his fires. He blushed, overcome, and stammered, "It's all for the king. It's my pleasure."

After a pause, the king said, "I've noticed your devotion and I want to give you a gift."

And now the former farmer/fire attendant was ready to just faint. He interjected, "His Majesty doesn't understand; the biggest gift I could receive is to be able to continue to make the royal fire. To be in the king's service is the greatest gift there is."

Now it was the king's turn to blush; he was so moved by the response of a simple man. But he pressed the attendant, "Maybe you're in need of money? Do you have children?"

The attendant answered, "No, Your Majesty. I have everything."

But the king insisted, "Please, think of something I can do for you."

And this is what the former farmer/fire attendant, came up with:

"The thing I want most of all is to see the king whenever I want."

And the king blushed again; he could not believe the simple devotion of this attendant. The thing he wanted more than anything else in the world was to see his king!

Recovering his royal composure, the king answered patiently, "You know, that's very flattering but it's impossible to see me whenever you want because sometimes I'm not willing to be on view — I also have my private moments. Nevertheless, because you've proven to be so loyal and dedicated, I'll do something else for you. I'll have a special hole drilled into the chimney in my throne room, aligned exactly with my throne. From your side of the chimney wall, you'll be able to look through the hole whenever you want. Whenever I'm sitting on my throne, you'll be able to see me."

Imagine the joy of this attendant! Every morning, before

setting up the fire, he checked to see if the king was upon his throne. The day came when he caught a view of the entire royal family sitting down to a feast. As he watched, a drama unfolded. Evidently, the king had a little too much to drink, and when the prince said something flippant, his father got angry with him and banished him.

"Leave the palace, and don't come back for a year! Away with you!"

After only a few days of exile, the poor prince was half out of his mind. He was used to seeing the king all the time, and in an instant he became an outcast. Feeling like a caged animal, he took to roaming the grounds, regretting his impulsive behavior.

While pacing around the castle one morning, the prince spied a pair of feet sticking out of one of the chimneys of the palace. Who could it be? It was our attendant, of course, maneuvering himself into the space behind the chimney wall where his peephole was located. Curious, the prince approached the attendant and tapped the foot nearest to him. The fire attendant wriggled out of the chimney and found himself facing the banished prince. The royal personage asked him, half-joking, "What are you up to? Are you a chimney sweep or a spy?"

The fire attendant, covered with soot, said to the prince, "I know your whole story, and I'm going to show you something that will make you really happy." He pushed the prince into his little space — headfirst! — so that he could lay his yearning eyes upon his father, the king.

After a few minutes, the prince emerged — all sooty — and said with feeling, "Thank you so much! It's like balm to my wounded heart, just seeing my father's face. Will you let me come back tomorrow? Please?!"

The fire attendant looked regretful and said, "Dear prince, you don't understand. You're part of the royal family, and this isn't the way you should see your father. I'm just a lowly servant

— this is my peephole, this is my way. This is how I can align with the king. But it's not the right way for you to align with him."

And then Reb Zusha turned to his brother Elimelech — whose name means, "My God is King." His nickname was just plain Melech, or "King," though. Reb Zusha said, "Melech, we're not cut from the same cloth. You have your own way of seeing the King. I went to my master, the Maggid, and he taught me that this is *my path* of connection. Holy brother, travel to the Maggid and he'll help you find *your own path*, one that suits your unique soul. He'll show you *your own way* to align with the Divine."

This story was a mind-changer for Reb Elimelech, and it eventually changed the world of Chassidism. Reb Elimelech listened to his brother Zusha, traveled to the Maggid, and became his disciple — and eventually became his successor. And it was all through the subtle work of the upside-down image of that simple fire setter that Reb Zusha shared — *I'm taking my way, and you need to go and discover your own.*

FIND
YOUR WAY

ONCE YOU BEGIN TO ALIGN yourself with the Divine Will — you just take that next right move, the next focused thought, one small step at a time — you're on the way to develop a sense of your unique mission in the world. And while it's true that the broad road of *justice* and *mercy* — of appropriate self-restraint and selfless giving — is the same for everyone, the way you travel on that road, the way you walk that path, will be the unique expression of your irreplaceable, unique soul.

There are infinite paths within the wide road, and each of us shines upon it an entirely new light, one the world has never seen before, and will never see again. It's the light of redemption — it can, and will, change you and change the world.

What are you waiting for, then?

Go on. Step on your path.

Get aligned.

ABOUT THE
AUTHOR

RABBI BARUCH GARTNER GREW UP in Baltimore, Maryland, and laid down roots in Israel close to forty years ago. He lives in Jerusalem, surrounded by his children and many grandchildren. For many years, he was known as a master scribe and devoted his energy to intensive Torah study. In response to popular demand, he founded Yeshivas Derech HaMelech, a place of higher learning geared toward spirituality. Rabbi Gartner currently helps numerous students and clients to strengthen their relationships, transcend self-defeating behaviors, succeed in the pursuit of their life goals, and deepen their spiritual life.